Defying Maliseet Language Death

# Defying Maliseet Language Death

*Emergent Vitalities of Language,
Culture, and Identity in Eastern Canada*

Bernard C. Perley

University of Nebraska Press | Lincoln and London

© 2011 by the Board of Regents
of the University of Nebraska
All rights reserved
Manufactured in the
United States of America
∞

A book in the Recovering
Languages and Literacies
of the Americas initiative.
Recovering Languages and
Literacies is supported by the
Andrew W. Mellon Foundation.

Library of Congress
Cataloging-in-Publication Data

Perley, Bernard C.
Defying Maliseet language death:
emergent vitalities of language, culture, and
identity in Eastern Canada / Bernard C. Perley.
p. cm.
Includes bibliographical references and index.
ISBN 978-0-8032-2529-9 (cloth: alk. paper)
ISBN 978-0-8032-4363-7 (paper: alk. paper)
1. Passamaquoddy language—New Brunswick—
Tobique Indian Reserve—History. 2. Passamaquoddy
language—New Brunswick—Tobique Indian
Reserve—Revival. 3. Language obsolescence—
New Brunswick—Tobique Indian Reserve.
4. Language and culture—New Brunswick—
Tobique Indian Reserve. 5. Communication
and culture—New Brunswick—Tobique Indian
Reserve. 6. Tobique Indian Reserve (N.B.)—
History. 7. Tobique Indian Reserve (N.B.)—
Social life and customs. I. Title.
PM2135.Z9T637 2011
497'.34—dc23
2011018952

Set in Quadraat by Bob Reitz.
Designed by R. W. Boeche.

To my grandmother.
Your spirit lives on.

To my mother.
Wisoki-woliwon 'ciw psi-te keq.
Koselomol.

## Contents

| | |
|---|---|
| Acknowledgments | ix |
| Notes on Terminology and Orthography | xiii |
| 1. The Specter of Language Death | 1 |
| 2. "Tipping" toward Maliseet Language Death | 31 |
| 3. Programming Language Maintenance | 63 |
| 4. From Spoken Maliseet to Text | 85 |
| 5. Elementary Language Curriculum and Practice | 101 |
| 6. Death by Suicide | 121 |
| 7. Language and Being in Maliseet Worlds | 149 |
| 8. Emergent Vitalities of Language, Culture, and Identity | 184 |
| Notes | 201 |
| References | 213 |
| Index | 225 |

**Map**

| | |
|---|---|
| Tobique First Nation and the Maliseet homeland | 13 |

# Acknowledgments

This book would not have been possible without the generosity and the encouragement of many people. I have had the great fortune to have outstanding teachers, friends, and family throughout the duration of my research and the writing of this book. The strengths and gifts that come from this work I share with all of you. The weaknesses, errors, and omissions are mine alone.

I owe a great debt of gratitude to so many people at Tobique First Nation. This book would not have been as rich without the support and participation by all the wonderfully complex personalities who exchanged ideas and opinions with me. A special thank-you goes to Sandra and Timmy for accepting this nosey anthro into their lives. Many thanks go to the staff of Mah-Sos School for their kindness and teasing. I also thank David Perley and Andrea Bear Nicholas for their conversations about Maliseet language and culture. Thanks go to former chief Stewart Paul for his support of my research and his insights on Maliseet language, history, and culture. I had the best of fieldwork scenarios. I was able to enjoy the lively bantering and laughter among relatives and family while playing cards and attempting to speak Maliseet. Thank you to all my aunts, uncles, and cousins for putting up with my stupid questions and cross-linguistic puns. Thank you all for repatriating a native son (even if he is an anthropologist!).

Special acknowledgment goes to David Maybury-Lewis, who passed away in the fall of 2007. David had been an extremely supportive mentor for me while I found my voice in anthropology. His quiet and patient guidance helped me make the transition from graduate school to professional practice. His work and dedication to indigenous cultural survival continues in my work and the work of colleagues he has inspired through his teaching, mentoring, and advocacy.

Many colleagues have made critical contributions to this work. From my graduate days. Steve Caton was a sharp critic and enthusiastic supporter of my intellectual explorations. Ronald Niezen encouraged and supported my exploration of the possibilities of Native American sovereignty in international relations. Robert Preucel was and continues to be a great friend and colleague. We have grappled with issues of repatriation and Native American self-determination. We have also promoted collaborative projects between anthropologists and Native American communities. Ruby Watson has been consistently interested and supportive of my work. Kay B. Warren has been an untiring advocate and confidant for me. Michael Herzfeld was generous in his willingness to provide lively conversation, professional advice, and friendship. James Watson and James Lorand "Randy" Matory were important professional development mentors who helped make my transition from student to assistant professor much less awkward. Thank you all for your friendship and tutelage.

Mentorship does not end in graduate school. My colleagues at the University of Wisconsin–Milwaukee (UWM) continue to provide me with mentorship, friendship, and critical debate. Special thanks go to Cheryl Ajirotutu for her unwavering support for my projects, be they writing, painting, or graphic novels. Thanks go to the Center for 21st Century Studies for a much needed year of critical "thinking and conversation."

In addition to my UWM colleagues I have had the great fortune to meet some remarkable scholars and truly generous people. I owe a great debt to Regna Darnell for her engaged and critical discussions on Native American languages and identity politics. I am grateful for her friendship and generous professional advice. Paul V. Kroskrity has been and continues to be a generous colleague in mentoring a junior scholar through professional development but also in engaging in critical language and cultural issues in Native North America. Frederic Gleach has been and continues to be a great friend and colleague whose unfailing support of my work is greatly appreciated. Thank you Laura Graham for your enthusiastic support of my work and the energy you bring to sharing ideas and solutions. Through the years, so many individuals have helped me explore the complexities between language and culture in Native North America. But it all started when Joel Sherzer predicted many years ago that I would be doing this work for the rest of my life. Thank you all for your continued support and friendship. Sincere thanks go to the anonymous readers of the manuscript, whose critical as well as supportive comments made this a better ethnography.

Many of the strategies for thinking through anthropology and language and how they can benefit Native American communities today came from lengthy discussions I had with fellow Native American scholars at Harvard University. Angela Gonzales, Gabrielle Tayac, Valerie Lambert, Phyllis Fast, and Darren Ranco were co-conspirators in our many activities to promote Native American programs at Harvard. Thank you all for your friendship and inspiration. I also had the good fortune to have a true friend in Sharri Clark, who gave me moral support when things seemed to be unraveling. Thank you Sharri for helping me keep things in perspective. We Native American students were fortunate to have Inés Talamantez as our mentor. Many thanks go to Inés for providing us with courage and determination as we worked to champion Native American perspectives in academia.

Words cannot adequately express the depth of gratitude I feel toward the people closest to my heart. Although she is long departed, I owe so much to my grandmother. Mimi, *wisoki-woliwon*. Thank you for your guidance. Mom, *wisoki-woliwon 'ciw psi-te keq*. You are the inspiration behind all my gifts. I continue to learn from you about life and love. My brothers Gilbert, Wendell, Leon, James, and John have been more than brothers. Thank you guys for many years of great friendship. Thank you also for your unquestioning and unreserved support. My accomplishments are yours too. I thank my dear friend and trusted wife for her keen mind and generous heart. Tracey, thank you for all your tough questions and keen insights. Thank you for all the time you invested in finding errors in grammar, argument, and exposition. Thank you for your encouragement when this project seemed unmanageable and interminable. Most of all, thank you for making my life rich beyond what words can ever express. Thank you, beloved partner. *Koselomol.*

# Notes on Terminology and Orthography

### Terminology

This ethnography uses the terms *aboriginal* and its derivatives interchangeably with Native American and American Indian as the context of the discussion requires. The Canadian context favors *aboriginal* and *aboriginality* to refer to the indigenous peoples of Canada. American Indian and Native American are more commonly used in the United States when referring to the indigenous peoples within its borders. Canadian aboriginal peoples also prefer the political designation of First Nation when referring to the reserves or reservations. *Reserve* is the prevalent word used in Canada, while *reservation* is used in the United States. I use them interchangeably as the context of the discussion requires. "Indian" is sometimes used within quotes or where the context requires its use for consistency. I have used pseudonyms for all members of Tobique First Nation, the only exceptions being my immediate family members. There is no logic behind the pseudonyms assigned to Tobique community members. I apologize in advance for any perceived innuendo or insult, which I promise is unintended.

### Orthography

The orthographic representation in this book is inconsistent and contradictory, and it is necessarily so. In this ethnography my goal is to represent the ethnographic material faithfully despite apparent inconsistencies and contradictions. As an ethnographer, I find that "correct" language usage and spelling are context and moment dependent. My goal is to understand why some representations are used instead of others and why community members change their minds.

There is a standardized orthography that has been developed since the 1960s work of Teeter, the '70s work of LeSourd, and important collaborative work of the Micmac-Maliseet Institute (Francis and Leavitt 2008:40). Today the standardized orthography is gaining popular acceptance at Tobique First Nation, but during my fieldwork (mid-1990s) that was not the case. A number of orthographic representations were competing for general acceptance by the community. Most of the Maliseet texts used in this ethnography come from the Mah-Sos Elementary School language program, and therefore I use the orthography used in the classroom. The orthographic system in the school also changed, which contributes to inconsistencies in orthographic representation. Given the orthographic variety, I use the appropriate orthography when I use examples from other Maliseet language programs and their respective publications.

## 1. The Specter of Language Death

On the reservation they call it "Indian time," and this was the perfect example. I was on time, but then again I had spent years in the white world. The notice said 2:00 p.m. at the school so I was there at 2:00 p.m. One by one people began to trickle in. Everyone on the reservation knew the meeting would not start until two-thirty at the earliest. That is, everyone except me. I had been away too long. At half past the hour only the native language teacher and the woman who had organized the meeting had arrived. At last nine people gathered in the fourth grade classroom. We were trying to seem comfortable in the downsized desks. There was small talk about families, band politics, and who won at bingo the night before.

The organizer decided there were enough people to begin the meeting. Those in attendance included the Head Start teachers, the native language teacher, and several women who had children in preschool. The organizer assumed control of the meeting and called it to order. She began by stating that the purpose of the meeting was to solicit support for a Maliseet language immersion program on the reservation. All of the participants were presumably interested in the prospects of an immersion program, either to have their children attend the program or to become administrators of the proposed program. In any case, as the organizer talked she handed out photocopies of several articles stressing the importance of immersion classes in Hawaiian, Maori (New Zealand), and Mohawk communities. Other articles dealt with the politics of language attrition ("Linguistic Genocide," to be precise). The organizer gave us a synopsis of the articles while everyone casually nodded either in agreement or in understanding. Then she asked us to focus our attention on one set of copies in particular. On the back pages of the collection was a chart that listed all the native languages spoken in Canada together with statistics recording number of members of each group, number of speakers, and most tellingly, the "viability" of the language listed. Everyone sought the Maliseet listing. In cold block letters the Maliseet language was listed as "On the verge of extinction." There was silence in the room as each of us assessed the gravity of the word *extinction* in personal terms. The organizer skillfully allowed the reflective silence to drag on for several moments. Finally she broke the silence by reiterating her reasons why an immersion program in Maliseet is desperately needed on the reservation.

The meeting I have described took place on a warm summer afternoon in 1993 at Mah-Sos Elementary School on Tobique First Nation in New Brunswick, Canada.[1] It is always difficult to understand the significance of an event from within the event itself. As a member of Tobique First Nation, I remember the meeting as being important to both the community and me. But I had no idea how important it would become. While the organizer intended to gain community support for a Maliseet language immersion program, the meeting successfully introduced to the community the specter of Maliseet language death. The meeting introduced the prospect that the approximately fifteen hundred residents of Tobique First Nation will witness the extinction of the Maliseet language within their lifetimes. In addition, the literature presented as evidence of imminent Maliseet language death diagnosed language death and language viability as a direct relationship between the number of speakers in the linguistic community and the survivability of the language in question. Furthermore, the literature represented respected knowledge from language experts and scholars from outside the community. The meeting organizer made the important contribution of transforming the abstraction of language death into an immediate and emotional community problem. Finally, the meeting made the specter of Maliseet language death a personal and professional matter.

Recalling that meeting at various times over the last decade and a half as I worked through my professional training in anthropology (continued research, articles for professional journals, book chapters, and this book) and continued to work on Maliseet language–related issues in my personal work (drawings, paintings, graphic novels, and exhibits), I realize that the most indelible message from that meeting is the specter of Maliseet language death and that is what has haunted (and continues to haunt) my personal and professional life. This book is an ethnographic account of how the specter of Maliseet language death has contributed to my critical appraisal of the literature on language endangerment, the methodology of anthropology, and current strategies of Native American self-determination. In short, Maliseet language death is not merely the cessation of Maliseet language use in everyday conversations. It has important implications for Maliseet culture, Maliseet identity, and Maliseet self-determination as well.

The chosen topic of this book, Maliseet language death, is depressing and disheartening, but this is not a doomsday ethnography. From my critical perspective as a native anthropologist I recognize that professional knowledge of the problem of language death is not a solution. My ethnographic work is directed toward becoming part of the solution to the problem of language death. This book represents my commitment to an engaged anthropology practice where professional knowledge serves the communities from which that knowledge is derived. This strategy recognizes the partial perspectives of "anthropologist" and "native" not as mutually exclusive positions but as the convergence of experiences that have the potential to create emergent conceptions of language, identity, and Native American self-determination. Ultimately this book is a program for language revitalization as an important aspect of Native American self-determination. The specter of Maliseet language death haunts the text but only to serve as the catalyst for rethinking unquestioned positions and as an invitation to imagine possible futures for Maliseet language, culture, and identity.

## Maliseet Language Matters

The UNESCO online atlas of endangered languages lists Maliseet as "severely endangered" and also states that there are only five hundred speakers, four hundred of whom live in Canada.[2] The Living Tongues Institute for Endangered Languages and National Geographic provide their own map of endangered languages on their respective websites. The map locates small geographic regions where a number of languages are endangered and identifies them as "language hotspots." While the map is loading on the National Geographic webpage, text in white letters against a blue background states: "Every 14 minutes a language dies."[3] Unlike on the UNESCO map, here the Maliseet language is not listed as endangered, nor is the northeastern Atlantic seaboard indicated as a hotspot of language endangerment. The website provides a link to a page that explains a "five-star scale to rank endangerment." This in turn explains that the number of speakers is not necessarily the best indicator of the degree of endangerment for any particular language and that an equally important criterion is the age of the speakers using the language. Both online maps stress speakers as the most important criterion for assessing language endangerment. Ironically, despite the recognition that speakers determine the vitality of language, both websites focus on language as the primary object of interest. It is this focal tension between speakers and language that I critically explore in this book.

The book is not intended to be a descriptive linguistic text, nor is it intended to be a how-to manual for learning the Maliseet language. My goal is to shift the focus of interest from the language itself to the community members and their engagement with the Maliseet language. This shift in focus requires the faithful representation of the peculiarities and inconsistencies of Maliseet language usage and representation by and among community members. My decision to represent the messiness of ethnographic moments accurately does not mean that the formal work of language documentation, analysis, and diagnosis by linguists, sociolinguists, and other language scholars is perceived as less important. On the contrary, in chapter 2 I use formal analyses of language endangerment across comparative case studies. Furthermore, those analyses are vital to determining the combination of factors that contribute to specific cases of language endangerment. For example, in his popular account of language death the linguist David Crystal writes: "To say that a language is dead is like saying that a person is dead. It could be no other way—for languages have no existence without people" (2000:1). Crystal goes on to add: "A language dies when nobody speaks it anymore" (2000:1). The distinction being made is between the everyday communicative use of language and the absence of such communicative use. Such statements may define language death, but they do not indicate the processes that endanger languages, such as language change, shift, and orthographic conflicts. I agree with Crystal that a defining characteristic for determining the vitality or morbidity of a language must focus on communicative use among speakers. However, in chapter 2 I emphasize the connection between speakers and language not only to determine the complexity of Maliseet language death at Tobique First Nation but to provide a background for a comparative analysis of contributing factors to language endangerment. I integrate complicating variables such as school, culture, politics, and economics to determine what processes are present in the endangerment of the Maliseet language. By introducing complexity to language endangerment processes I am able to evaluate critically the possible factors contributing to language death. Those factors are often discussed under rubrics like language attrition, language shift, language obsolescence, and language change. The Maliseet case reflects many of the factors for language death, including those that are explained as outside pressures imposed upon the speakers of endangered languages and thereby forcing them to change their communicative habits. I examine those pressures and by the end of chapter 2 I argue that the sociopolitical climate today in Canada presents opportunities for aboriginal communities to revitalize their languages.

In chapter 3 the discussion shifts from a diagnostic evaluation of Maliseet language vitality to a comparative discussion of various strategies and ideologies for Maliseet language maintenance, a process I refer to as the "domestication" of the Maliseet language. The various strategies of language domestication also reflect the ideologies of the language advocates who endorse and support the programs that are sponsored by a variety of institutions. I use domestication as my own ideological framing to allow me to analyze Maliseet linguistic ideology whereby a Maliseet worldview is formed from the coalescence of social programs, norms, and propositions that justify a collective identification understood as Maliseet. Woolard and Schieffelin suggest: "Not only linguistic forms but social institutions such as the nation-state, schooling, gender, dispute settlement, and law hinge on the ideologization of language use" (1994:56). The Woolard and Schieffelin review of literature and framings of language ideology has highlighted a number of areas of study that reflect the complexity of Maliseet language maintenance politics, from First Nations identity to orthography; from colonialism to linguistic change; and more. Their review reinforces many points I have made earlier, but one particular passage, under the heading "Variation and Contestation in Ideology," is particularly pertinent to my research: "The new direction in research on linguistic ideology has also moved away from seeing ideology as a homogenous cultural template, now treating it as a process involving struggles among multiple conceptualizations and demanding the recognition of variation and contestation within a community as well as contradictions within individuals" (Woolard and Schieffelin 1994:71). That passage succinctly describes the issues that characterize the various agencies' interactions at micro and macro levels. The need for such a study in Maliseet linguistic contestation is supported again by Woolard and Schieffelin as they state: "The topic of language ideology is a much-needed bridge between linguistic and social theory, because it relates the microculture of communicative action to political economic considerations of power and social inequality, confronting macrosocial constraints on language behavior. . . . It is also a potential means of deepening a sometimes superficial understanding of linguistic form and its cultural variability in political economic studies of discourse" (72). Language ideology is probably the best broad theoretical heading for my research on Maliseet language programs; however, the practice of language contestation and the ensuing identity politics require a closer examination of the particular politics involved between contesting Maliseet language maintenance agents, programs, and institutions. More recently, Kroskrity and Field's edited volume (2009) identifies three important categories of ideological engagement in Native American communities: language and language ideological change, language revitalization, and language activism/reflexivity. My own essay in that volume explores how the contingent aspect of Maliseet language maintenance strategies has the added benefit of offering the Maliseet communities a choice between language life and language death.

The theme of domestication continues in chapter 4, where I discuss the various attempts to codify the Maliseet language at Tobique First Nation. There have been other orthographic representations, but my focus is on the varieties found on the reservation and the reactions by community members to those orthographies during the time I was doing field research. The chapter not only examines the various attempts to "write" Maliseet but examines the ideologies of the various advocates who disseminate their texts to the community. I begin the chapter with a brief discussion of "cognitive shifts" between orality and literacy and how these shifts were reflected in the Maliseet language teacher's decision to teach the language using text-based pedagogy. The community responses to various printed materials in the classroom as well as in the public spaces present intriguing differences of acceptance and readability across different generations. Key to this discussion and the subsequent discussion in chapter 5 is the receptiveness of the children who are learning the Maliseet language as a second language.

The challenges to produce an orthographic representation of Maliseet that the community can agree upon serve as the backdrop for the development of the Maliseet language curriculum at Mah-Sos School. In chapter 5 I discuss how my fieldwork experience in a native language classroom put me in a position where I was able to observe various programs of language instruction, language program planning, and language politics. The strategies used by the teacher to help the students learn the Maliseet language were developed, evaluated, and changed according to student performance. Language drills and vocabulary were taught along with cultural and arts activities. I present daily practices and provide discussions that summarize language maintenance practices and the importance of their cultural and community entanglements. These entanglements are key to understanding why the Maliseet language appears to be dying.

The community responses to the efforts of Maliseet language brokers are examined in chapter 6. My overall impression of the language situation in Tobique is one of tacit support on one hand but practical indifference on the other. The few language brokers I worked with, interviewed, and observed were greatly outnumbered by community members who were and are concerned about Maliseet language death but for one reason or another are either unable or unwilling to commit to working on language revitalization. These observations have prompted me to argue that the Tobique community is committing language suicide. Not only is the method of language death a case of language suicide; it is also a recognition that language death is a process of language disembodiment. It is in this chapter that I share my own experience of the trauma of Maliseet language disembodiment.

The argument is not intended to "blame the victim," as many language scholars would argue. Rather, the goal is to problematize the use of affective descriptors in discussing language death and to put community actions and decisions back into the discussion of language life and language death. I discuss the role disembodiment has for "suicide" and introduce the possibility of rethinking language ontologies. In doing so, I offer an analytical and practical approach that advocates alternative vitalities for the Maliseet language.

With alternative vitalities I return the discussion to varieties of embodiments. Chapter 7 expands the discussion of Maliseet identity from language to include blood and aboriginality. This book is an extended argument that the simple definition of language death as restricted to spoken language precludes any possible alternatives that may contribute to language revitalization (either in the present or as deferred to a future generation). This becomes clearer in chapter 8. But first, I examine the shifting boundaries of aboriginal identity politics and how those politics reflect a variety of deployments for aboriginal languages. The Maliseet community is engaged in a number of sociocultural and political processes that are entangled in various scales of experiences. Those processes range from formal (the Indian Act, the 1969 White Paper, and Bill C-31) to informal institutions (language programs, translation work, curriculum planning) that can directly affect language politics, ideologies, and identities (Perley 2006, 2009). These entanglements create linguistic opportunities that lead to emergent Maliseet language ontologies. Most important, those emergent ontologies are also entangled with identity and cultural politics. The ability to recognize opportunities of linguistic and cultural emergence is the critical aspect or process of "aboriginality." In the Canadian context, aboriginality has particular relevance because of the acceptance of *aboriginal* as a valid descriptor for First Nations peoples. In the international (global) context, *indigeneity* has become the currently favored descriptor. At the time of field research *indigeneity* was not the preferred term for self-identity among indigenous peoples.

Throughout this book I promote alternative language vitalities to draw a distinction between a political economy of language and a domestic economy of language. One of the language revitalization ideologies commonly circulated is based on teaching language in the home. However, my observations of the language situation in Tobique suggest that the language is predominantly political, and only in few cases is the language domestic. This observation brings me back to Crystal's definition for language death and prompts me to consider whether the Maliseet community of Tobique is committing language suicide. This is a key distinction to make because if we accept the premise that language life is based on a community of speakers using the language for everyday communication, then based on my observations during field research, I would conclude that the community is committing language suicide. However, in chapter 8 I argue that alternative vitalities are valid criteria for language life and that the language continues to live in forms other than the spoken word. The importance of reframing the criteria for determining "language life" lies in the acknowledgment and acceptance of the social or cultural pragmatics of changing identity politics in aboriginal Canada. That is why chapter 8 is the most hopeful segment in an otherwise disheartening ethnography. This is where I discuss the creative ways in which members of Tobique First Nation have defied the odds of imminent language death and worked toward creating alternative vitalities for the Maliseet language. But these creative projects are not limited to language. They are also experiences and embodiments of Maliseet identity. I fully implicate my own partial practices through my cosmogenesis project, a program for language, cultural, and personal revitalization (see chapter 8). In short, this ethnography is about how Maliseet identify themselves as Maliseet and what markers—or "diacritics," as Appadurai (1996) calls them—are used to define Maliseetness. This book is a celebration of the role of the Maliseet language in Maliseet identity deliberations and self-making. Such deliberations and self-making have a long history in a landscape the Maliseet have called home for millennia.

One of the seldom discussed tragedies of language death is the erasure of aboriginal languages from aboriginal landscapes (Perley 2002b). The effect of erasure is to render problematic or threatening elements in the landscape invisible (Irvine and Gal 2000:38). The following brief account of "going home" reveals the ideologies of erasure and restores visibility to the invisible.

There are a number of ways to reach Tobique First Nation. The most likely approach is from the Trans-Canada Highway. From the "T-Can," you are informed by a bilingual highway sign in French and English which exit to use in order to reach the reservation. By following the information provided by the sign you pass through the villages of Perth and Andover. The St. John River separates Andover from Perth. After you cross the St. John River and enter Perth you need to make a left turn. As you reach the village terminus the road makes a Y-shaped split into two directions. The main road curves to the right and up the hill toward the village of Arthurette. The auxiliary road continues straight along the river. At this point you need to take the scenic river road along the St. John River. That road takes you right through the reservation. As you continue toward the reservation you wind your way up a hill, and as you crest the hill you come upon the Tobique Narrows Dam. You cross the dam (and the Tobique River) and you drive up "the dam hill" (often considered as "the damn hill" during the winter), where you encounter yet another official highway sign stating that you have arrived at "Tobique First Nation/Premièr Nation." To the right of the road as you continue up the hill the Tobique Fisheries Office and outbuildings are nestled among the trees. As the road curves to the right a sign on the left side of the road marks the entrance to the part of the reservation where the main village and residential areas are. This sign is special. It is not an official highway sign. It was designed and fabricated by one of the local Maliseet artists. The sign boasts two eagles with their wings fully spread as if soaring, the birds positioned on opposite ends of the plywood painted sign. The eagles are tilted away from one another at a slight angle. The eagles frame the text in large block letters—"NeGoot-Gook First Nation." The entire sign is mounted on spindly pipes loosely anchored into the ground. The sign looks proud but anemic.[4]

The main road continues to the woods and curves to the right. The road to the reservation village forces you to turn to the left off the main road and down the hill past the Bingo Hall/Lucky's Casino. As you follow the road into the reservation you continue to wind your way past copious trees interspersed with occasional fields. You also pass a mix of residences ranging from grand to modest, well maintained, and an occasional unkempt home. Eventually, after some driving, the road curves to the right and your diligence is rewarded as you find yourself cruising on Main Street—the heart of the reservation. As you continue driving you see the Catholic Church on the left. The cemetery is on both the left and the right sides of the road.[5] The band office is on the right.[6] The Tiger's Den is on the left.[7] Farther along Main Street is Mah-Sos Elementary School to the right and the attached sports complex.[8] Next door to the school is the Wellness Center, and next to the Wellness Center is an empty lot where the Training Center was before it burned down. The adjacent Fire Hall survived the fire that obliterated the Training Center.[9] The fire took place at night. It was a spectacular blaze! The rest of the buildings on Main Street are residences. Welcome to the place where I was born, the place where I did my fieldwork, the place I call home.[10]

The name Tobique is the term used by non-Maliseet to refer to the reservation.[11] As I have indicated, the name on the locally crafted sign was NeGoot-Gook.[12] That name is not on the official signs erected by the Province of New Brunswick. At least the official highway sign on the reservation uses the designation "First Nation." Because the signage does not use the ethnonym NeGoot-Gook, I argue that we are seeing evidence of a Euro-Canadian cultural hegemony in identity, language, and national politics that often goes unnoticed or unquestioned. As Irvine and Gal (2000) argue, the problematic elements in the landscape were erased. Those elements are Maliseet place names. This

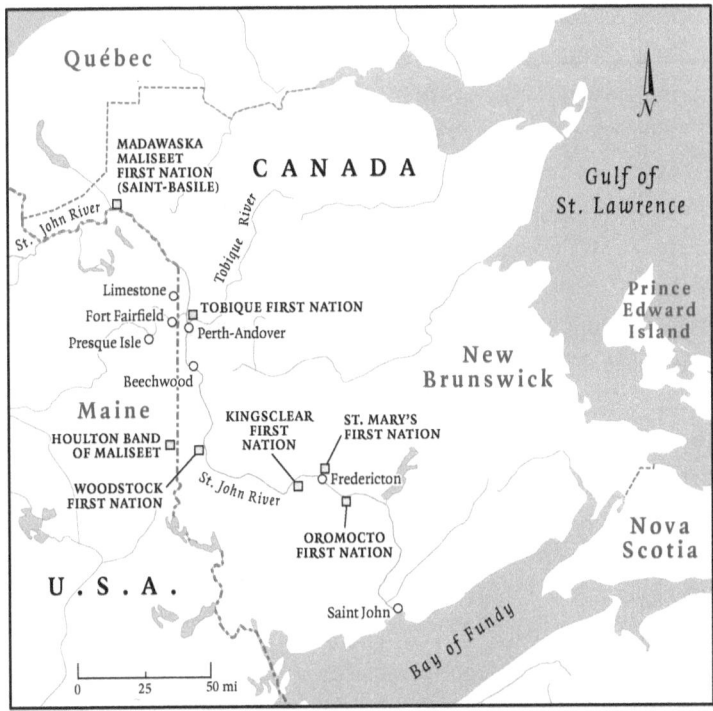

Tobique First Nation and the Maliseet homeland

book explores the coercive effect of these hegemonies and erasures and how they contribute to the endangerment of Maliseet language, identity, and politics.

The reservation is located at the confluence of two rivers, the Tobique and St. John rivers. It is only a twenty-minute drive from the United States border. There is a great deal of shopping on the United States side of the border. The largest Canadian city is the capitol city of Fredericton, just over two hundred kilometers away. The largest U.S. city is Presque Isle, Maine, about thirty-five miles away.

The area is a river valley with gently rolling hills covered in a mix of coniferous and deciduous forests. Autumn is breathtaking. The winters are cold and snowy and can be harsh. Summers are temperate, and spring is as striking as autumn, the difference being that in spring the colors are close to the ground.

When the new grass is growing and the violets are blooming, the violets create a purple sheen over the grass. The strawberry blossoms dot the grass and violet field like earthbound constellations. The rivers flow past the community with a serene steady meandering that is disguised in the winter when the river freezes over and is dramatized in the early spring when the ice flow breaks and tumbles in huge sheets of jagged ice. Unfortunately, development along the river in the form of dams has undermined aspects of Maliseet traditions and memories; this is discussed in chapter 2. Not only does the dominant culture have detrimental coercive force vis-à-vis Maliseet language, identity, and politics; Canadian national economic and technological hegemonies exacerbate the already precarious conditions of aboriginal traditions. Recognizing the dangers and coercive forces is only one goal for this book. My other goal is to present my understanding of the responses of members of the Tobique community to the various coercive forces undermining Maliseet language, culture, and identity.

During my field research the reservation was home to approximately fifteen hundred people. Most of the residents live in three residential developments that community members refer to as the Flatland, the Highland, and Laguna Beach. The Flatland is the oldest residential area and the residents are called Flatlanders. One street earned the nickname "Rodeo Drive" because the chief and a couple of council members lived on that street.[13] Another contributing factor for the nickname was the fact that their driveways were paved with asphalt, whereas most driveways on the reservation were gravel. The second oldest residential development, the Highland, is situated on the ridge above the Flatland. Its residents are referred to as Highlanders. A horseshoe curve in that residential development has earned the nickname "the horny horseshoe." The name comes from the coincidence of a large number of newborns in the families living along the horseshoe curve of the street. The third residential area is the newest and has been labeled Laguna Beach because it was built in close proximity to the sewage lagoon. These three neighborhoods account for most of the population, but a significant number of community members live away from the village and are dispersed along back roads that cut through the reservation. They live "out in the woods." Sometimes their homes are referred to as "camps." One cluster of houses along the Tobique River was named "Little Tobique." Some of the families who built their homes in the woods wanted to be close to the "Nation House," a building that was designed to serve as a traditionalist meeting place. One family "holds the keys" to the house. I was assured by one member of the family holding the keys that anyone on the reservation can use the house and that the functions that take place there are "traditional" in nature. How traditional is characterized is unclear to me, but the point is that there is a traditionalist sensibility exercised on the reservation. Such sensibilities are explored later in the book; I mention this here to highlight another facet of identity practices and self-making in community life.

The community is like many other First Nations communities. There are clusters of families with children (the horny horseshoe), traditionalist enclaves (in the woods), old neighborhoods (Flatlanders), and most important, changing fortunes and politics. This brief sketch illustrates the social, political, and economic complexity and diversity of the Tobique community. This complexity and diversity play an important role in analyzing the nature of language endangerment and the concomitant issues of Maliseet cultural identity.

The following discussion is not intended to be a brief history of the Maliseet. Rather, it is a selective assemblage of historical, linguistic, and ethnographic details that collectively highlight the complexity of Maliseet identity. To begin with, the complexity of Maliseet identity is echoed in synonymy and intertribal intersections. The synonymy of terms used to designate the peoples known today as Maliseet goes as far back in the written record as Samuel de Champlain, who in 1603 referred to the people he encountered at Tadoussac as Etchemin (see Ganong 1899; Morrison 1975; Erickson 1978; AFSC 1989).[14] Other terms that have been used to refer to the Maliseet peoples are Abenakis, Meductics, Eastern Indians, Madawaska Indians, and St. John River Indians. Some spelling variations are Amalecites, Marisheets, Melicites, Malecites, Marisiz, and Milicites.[15] However, the most glaring omission from many sources is the term today's more politically active members of the Tobique reservation recognize as the name they use to refer to themselves: Wolastoqiyik, "people of the good river." The insistence by some members of the Tobique community on using Wolastoqiyik and the refusal to adopt the term used by the dominant Canadian society is indicative of some of the asymmetrical power relations contributing to Maliseet language death.[16]

Champlain's liberal use of Etchemin to name the native inhabitants from Tadoussac to the St. John and St. Croix rivers further complicated identifying the forebears of the present-day Maliseet (Erickson 1978). Adding to the complexity, historians divide the Etchemin into Eastern and Western Etchemin groups. The groups would then divide into the Micmac Alliance and the Wabanaki Confederacy. The Wabanaki Confederacy would later include the Micmac (Morrison 1975). The classification of the Maliseet under the umbrella of Wabanaki—which consist of Micmac, Passamaquoddy, Abenakis, Penobscot, and Maliseet—obscures the ethnographic distinctions raised by the members of each nation. The Maliseet and the Passamaquoddy are excellent examples. Some local accounts by community members suggest that the Passamaquoddy are Maliseet on the United States side of the border, and some others suggest that the Maliseet are a splinter group of the Micmac. While not scholarly accounts, these local views are important for recognizing self-essentializing identity differences between communities. On the other hand, scholars often hyphenate the two as Maliseet-Passamaquoddy because they "speak mutually intelligible dialects of the same language" (Erickson 1978:123). Philip LeSourd adds, "Since no one name designates the two groups together, their common language is usually termed Maliseet-Passamaquoddy" (2007:viii).

Despite the seeming equivalence of the terms Maliseet and Passamaquoddy it should be noted that a clear distinction is often voiced by members of both the Maliseet and the Passamaquoddy communities concerning identity politics and sovereignty. At this point some distinctions are worthy of note. The geographical locale for the Maliseet is along the St. John River in New Brunswick, Canada. The Passamaquoddy are located in Washington County, Maine (Erickson 1978; LeSourd 2007). The Passamaquoddy must engage the United States government and the state of Maine to address their grievances, whereas the Maliseet must engage the Canadian government and the provincial government of New Brunswick (Erickson 1978). The problem of sovereignty issues is complicated by the multiplicity of sovereignties. Furthermore, in addition to the Maliseet communities located along the St. John River, there are communities located in Viger, Québec, and in Houlton, Maine (Erickson 1978). Consequently, any amalgamation of the various Maliseet reservations toward a single sovereign Maliseet nation must recognize and reconcile a variety of spheres of sovereignties as well as claims to autonomous authority. Similarly, a Maliseet language standard must accommodate not only the various Maliseet dialects but also the various idiolects (see chapter 4).

These complications are compounded by others arising from previous research in the Maliseet language. Early documentation includes compilations of vocabulary terms, a grammatical sketch, collections of stories, and a prayer book with a few prayers in Maliseet.[17] The only substantial ethnographic work specifically addressing the Maliseet at Tobique was compiled in 1957 by Wallis and Wallis, offering a general ethnographic account of interviews and observations recorded over a ten-day period in 1953.

Since 1970 there has been an explosion in the production of materials related to the Maliseet-Passamaquoddy language. Much of the work was designed for language teaching and training. One of the key agencies initiating the production of much of the material is the Micmac-Maliseet Institute (MMI) at the University of New Brunswick, Fredericton. Some representative work consists of dictionaries, grammars, and a Micmac-Maliseet resource book.[18] In addition, and antedating MMI efforts, the Wabanaki Bilingual Education Program (WBEP) of Indian Township, Maine, produced storybooks.[19] The WBEP work is without question important and valuable, but in the context of Mah-Sos School and the Tobique community their products have proven to be controversial. Sometimes the work was dismissed or rejected with the comment, "Ah, that's Passamaquoddy!" The principal reason behind such disregard is that it was produced by Passamaquoddies, not Maliseet, despite the fact that both communities speak a mutually intelligible language with the exception of some differences in vocabulary and dialect.[20] The significant work done by Passamaquoddy language advocates and linguists since the 1970s has provided many valuable materials for Maliseet communities, and the establishment of the Micmac-Maliseet Institute has offered materials and curriculum for Maliseet language that could provide a kind of unifying standard for language revitalization work, but a long history of identity politics between communities makes such unification difficult. More recent work includes linguistic analyses (LeSourd 2003, 2004), a new dictionary (Francis and Leavitt 2008), a new compilation of Maliseet stories (LeSourd 2007), and a museum collection catalogue (Augustine 2005).

One additional reference work that figured prominently at Mah-Sos Elementary School during the last two years of my field research is Lászlo Szabó's *Indianisches Wörterbuch: Malecite-Deutsch-English* (1981). Szabó states in the preface to his dictionary that much of the work he completed was "deposited" in the archives in the Museum of Man, Ottawa. It was never published because (in his words) it "needed improvement." During my fieldwork Szabó had taken a much more active role in the preservation of the Maliseet language as an instructor through courses offered by St. Thomas University at Fredericton, New Brunswick. Despite his active role in teaching Maliseet phonology, his own work has yet to be popularly circulated within the community.

Given access to the language maintenance practices and literature, scholarly assessments of best practices, and community language advocates to motivate and guide community members in language maintenance and revitalization efforts, it would seem that the Maliseet language would step back from the precipice of extinction. However, from many informal conversations, through participant observations, and by simply asking about Maliseet language use on the reservation at Tobique, I have inferred the following general impression: the language is used most often by the elders, whom I delimit by the ages sixty and older. Members of the adult population, the forty to sixty age group, use the language often but with mixed proficiency and comprehension. Young adults, ages twenty to forty, vary in their Maliseet language use from some to little or none. I distinguish between language "use" and "speaking" because some young adults may understand the language but cannot speak it. For most of these young adults, the comprehension of the language begins to drop off from rudimentary to none at all from the ages thirty down to twenty; I fall into this category except for the age qualifier. Finally, people in the age group from one to twenty do not speak the language to any degree of proficiency and consequently do not understand the language, the exception being the children taking the Maliseet language class in the school—the subject of chapter 5. Broadly speaking, the number of proficient speakers is relatively small when compared to the numbers who cannot or do not speak the Maliseet language. These factors create for many community members at Tobique a general concern that there are ever decreasing chances for the survivability of the Maliseet language. Underscoring such concern is the recognition that English is the primary language (because it is the lingua franca for everyday activities and is the first language acquired by children), while French serves as the secondary language (because New Brunswick is officially English-French bilingual and French is a compulsory course in the provincial schools). This places the Maliseet language in a precarious tertiary position in both political and domestic domains. This sketch of Maliseet language use is my personal assessment of Maliseet language endangerment. It corresponds well with the criteria stated in the two online maps discussed at the beginning of this section. Both maps emphasized the number of speakers within a language community, while the Living Tongues Institute criteria included the ages of the speakers. I include myself within the discussion to indicate my partial perspective as a native anthropologist with a commitment to practice engaged anthropology. As noted earlier, this ethnography is more than a record of Maliseet language death. It is also a program for language revitalization and Maliseet self-determination. This work can be done only through critical reflexivity and a commitment to creative intersubjectivity.

## Reflexivity, Intersubjectivity, and the Stakes for Native Anthropology

The opening ethnographic vignette is intended to introduce the seriousness of the state of the Maliseet language, but it also serves to introduce the affective aspects of language attrition. Further, it introduces some of the principal players in the language attrition drama and the complex roles of this ethnographer, who is both native and anthropologist.

I claim no special status as a native anthropologist, nor do I claim that my negotiations of outsider/insider, analyst/actor, or observer/advocate statuses are unique. There are a number of precedents for what have variously been labeled "autoethnographies" (Reed-Danahay 1997; Kideckel 1997), "halfie anthropology" (Abu-Luhod 1991), or "native anthropology" (Limón 1991; Reed-Danahay 1997; Motzafi-Haller 1997). The authors and ethnographers credited with those works have explored and discussed the complexities and dilemmas they have had to negotiate while straddling the multiple borders in which they found themselves entangled. However, their reflexive accounts of their ethnographic experiences did not present any solutions for the complexities and dilemmas I have had to reconcile. Rather, they illuminated parallel universes of ethnographic experience. Echoing Herzfeld (1997), there seem to be "overlapping cosmologies" of similar "symbolic universes."[21] My position is not new and I do not presume to claim special authority on autoethnography, nor do I challenge the discourse on its theoretical or practical grounds. As a native, however, I do assert a willingness to "imagine alternative futures" for Maliseet language, as Kay Warren (1997:22) so aptly describes the goal of Pan-Mayan intellectuals.[22]

This reflexive explanation situates me as both native and anthropologist for the purpose of alerting the reader that this book oscillates between "objective" diagnostic analytical discourses and affective "embodied" discourses of language death as witnessed, experienced, and observed in the Tobique community.[23] On one hand, this study is about "going anthropologist."[24] On the other hand, it is about "going native."[25] More important, I do not see the two as mutually exclusive. I enjoy the mutually inclusive aspect of the research experience. By comfortably situating myself as outsider and insider, analyst and actor, and observer and advocate I draw inspiration from the work of Mayan intellectual activist and anthropologist Victor Montejo. His example illustrates how the dual identity of "native anthropologist" can produce a richness of work that serves both anthropology and indigenous communities. Though I draw inspiration from Victor Montejo, I do not suggest that this study is a "testimonial," nor do I wish to emulate the testimonial genre. Indigenous language and cultural revitalization are the topics Montejo and I have in common. Anthropology as a tool for critical and comparative analysis is another. Most important, my practice of native anthropology reflects an engaged anthropology where the stakes for the native anthropologist could very well determine whether the native can return home or not.

My explanation of reflexivity is important because it clarifies my position in this research. This ethnography is a critical study of the phenomenon of language death as presented by the Maliseet case at

Tobique First Nation. It cannot help but be an "ethnography of the particular" (Abu-Luhod 1991) because of the particular case study and the partiality of my position (Perley 2009). But it is also a critical contribution to the literature on the global phenomenon on language death because the Maliseet case presents a form of language death I describe as language death by suicide. In the following chapters I present ethnographic evidence as well as my critical literature reviews that compel me to characterization Maliseet language death at Tobique First Nation as language suicide. Equally important, my focus on speakers rather than the language identifies the emergent aspects of Maliseet cultural identity. Together, language suicide and emergent identities have serious implications for Maliseet language life or death. Finally, reflexively, I share through personal accounts and analyses the complexities and dilemmas I have had to resolve and continue to encounter while practicing the duality of dispositions that native anthropology presents.

All too often ethnographers present a polite reflexivity wherein authors give a perfunctory nod toward situating themselves in a foreign site—"Woe is me, a stranger in a strange place"—commonly as a confession limited to a single paragraph in the introduction.[26] Sometimes reflexive statements assert self-satisfied voices that proclaim: "I'm not one of them but I let them speak." On the other hand, the native ethnographer may assert: "I'm an insider, so I have a unique perspective" and thereby claim a privileged situated perspective. My personal and professional position is best framed by recalling a comment a professor once quipped in a class regarding ethnography, "Well, it's complicated." I regard reflexivity as never simple and something that should never be perfunctory, self-satisfied, or privileged. It is complicated, but I do not worry about simplifying complexity. Rather, I celebrate the complexity by recognizing "alternative futures" in the interstices of complex epistemic positions. It is not about maintaining or delineating borders. Nor is it about blurring or obliterating borders or boundaries. It is about looking at the phenomenon of language death as experienced by the Maliseet community of Tobique First Nation, of which I am a member with similar experiences, and using all the tools I have at my disposal to assess the nature of the threat to the language and to articulate how I conceptualize my role as outsider/insider, analyst/actor, and observer/advocate.

In the opening vignette I mentioned that I had been away far too long because I was operating on "white man's time." The vignette introduces, albeit by allusion rather than by example, all the complexities and ironies my native anthropologist position forced (and continues to force) me to negotiate as my research and analysis continue. This ethnography has personal interjections throughout to highlight affective engagement (or lack thereof) with language, culture, and social analysis. Thus the discussion and analysis are contextualized in personal as well as professional terms.

I saw the precedents of autoethnography and reflexivity not as solutions to the dilemmas and complexities I have negotiated but as parallel experiences that confirm my doubts about clearly delineated epistemological and phenomenological perspectives.[27] I suggested that my engagements in both native and anthropologist worlds were not mutually exclusive; rather they were overlapping and intersubjectively inclusive.[28] It is this aspect that I feel makes this ethnography an important exercise not only for the topic on language death but also for the quandaries faced by this native anthropologist. How do I articulate my negotiations of the epistemologies of my complex situatedness? There is much literature suggesting that the separation of analyst and subject versus subject among subjects is a potentially rich field for mutual interpretation, mutual deep readings, and mutual subjectivities.[29] One notable contribution is Donna Haraway's essay on "situated knowledge," wherein she describes the "objectivity" of science as a "god-trick of seeing everything from nowhere" way of knowing that is put into "ordinary practice" (1991:189). Her position seeks to subvert, destabilize, and challenge the disembodied all-seeing eye by replacing it with a feminist "objectivity as positioned rationality," with the attendant "partial views and halting voices into a collective subject position that promises a vision of the means of ongoing finite embodiment, of living within limits and contradictions, i.e., of views from somewhere" (196). My fieldwork experience resonates with Haraway's critical perspective as the "coding trickster" that enables "sources in many kinds of heterogeneous accounts of the world" (199). After all, "objectivity is not about dis-engagement, but about mutual and usually unequal structuring, about taking risks in a world where 'we' are permanently mortal, that is, not in 'final' control" (201). As Haraway suggests of feminist epistemology, the embodiment of observation from somewhere is partial, indeterminate, and it acknowledges "living within limits and contradictions." I as the participant observer was one subject among others, and the knowledge I acquired was from the engaged and intersubjective embodiments of living in worlds of limits and contradictions.

Haraway's critique of scientific objectivity has parallel and cleverly expressed popular cultural portrayals of anthropology. The traditional interpretation of anthropologists as adventurers going into the wilds to record the lifeways of wild and primitive peoples enjoys a rich circulation in popular imagination.[30] Cartoons from Gary Larson's "The Far Side" are excellent and humorous examples that portray the ironies and absurdities in the popular imagination regarding anthropologists. The image of the "primitives" in the grass huts dashing about hiding their televisions, radios, and other modern conveniences while shouting, "Anthropologists are coming!" illustrates a perceptive critique of the what was once the vision and method of anthropology. I mention this cartoon in particular to emphasize the "contaminated" aspect of the subjects under the anthropological gaze and to assert that the subject also has an awareness of the relationship, thus allowing the subject a degree of manipulation in how the anthropologist conducts fieldwork (Tedlock and Mannheim 1995:18). That is a lesson I learned early in my fieldwork experience.

I had been observing Maliseet language instruction at the elementary school for a couple of weeks. Things seemed to settle to a routine. Part of the routine was to leave at lunch and return before the next class began. One day the routine changed. Everything seemed as usual until I entered the classroom. As I walked into the room I had that "they've been talking about you" feeling, "they" being the Maliseet language teacher and her assistant. When I entered the room their conversation abruptly ended. As they watched me cross the room toward them they both had a hint of a malicious smile ("smirk" is perhaps a better description) on their faces and a telltale glint in their eyes. Their postures suggested a conspiratorial "fait accompli" and I immediately thought, "Uh-oh. I'm toast."

The teacher spoke first. She pointed to a chair facing her desk and commanded, "Sit there." I did. She was sitting back in her high-backed swivel chair and her assistant sat in a chair alongside of her desk, his back straight and his arms crossed.

"We want to know," the teacher continued. "We want to know the real reason why you're here."

I started to explain that I was there to learn and help in any capacity I could, but they did not wait for me to finish. Both of them, on some cue I missed, began to sing.

> Here come the Anthros, better hide your dead away.
> Here come the Anthros, on another holiday.

Just as they finished singing they laughed and laughed loudly. The kind of laugh that makes a person feel small. Still laughing, the assistant got up and sauntered out of the room. The teacher, also laughing, turned her attention to the class schedule in front of her. Nothing more was said. I got up out of the chair and went to sit in my usual spot against one of the walls and out of the teacher's way. I had just been told that I was an intruder and I was not welcome.

I have learned from this event as well as numerous other research experiences that the initial subject-to-object relationship is better characterized as reciprocally highly reflexive and as highly intersubjective as it was highly interobjective (reciprocal objectification).[31] As an ethnographer I experienced an ethnographic relationship that changed through time, that was first based on mistrust and antagonism, second on conditional trust and acceptance, and finally trust and cooperation.[32] Negotiations were bilateral and necessarily so. Observation was not enough, nor could it be. Participation was a major factor in gaining trust. During the first couple of months I was very much the subject as the community was observing and evaluating my actions. Through dialogue and interaction I discerned the reciprocal exchange of objectivities as well as subjectivities.[33] Having recognized the inevitability of these exchanges I also recognized that maintaining the simplicity of the observer/observed dichotomy became increasingly complex and untenable. The critical aspect of such intersubjective cooperation was that I became a contaminated agent, who in turn contaminated the practice of documenting the phenomenon I had intended to study. The experience could no longer be analyzed from some empirical detached "eye of god" or "god-trick" epistemology. It required reflection and recognition of complicity in what Tedlock and Mannheim have called *The Dialogic Emergence of Culture* (1995). Tedlock and Mannheim also caution that a dialogical ethnography is deficient:

> But a dialogical ethnography cannot content itself with the celebration of a multiplicity of voices, no matter how diverse their social origins. One of the key challenges is to reformulate the problem of the location of culture within a social ontology in which neither individuals nor collectivities are basic units. Thus reformulated, the task becomes one of identifying the social conditions of the emergence of linguistic and cultural forms, of their distribution among speakers, and of subjectivity itself as an embodied constellation of voices. (Tedlock and Mannheim 1995:8)

In this ethnography I identify the social conditions that promote, on one hand, the emergence of linguistic and cultural forms as distributed among speakers as well as nonspeakers. But on the other hand, I also identify the social conditions that promote the disappearance of linguistic and cultural forms and how such conditions are distributed among those who refuse to be speakers and those who are apathetic about speaking the Maliseet linguistic forms and practicing Maliseet cultural forms. Of course it is not that simple either. That is why intersubjectivity plays an important role. Discerning the linguistic and cultural forms that the community apprehends as Maliseet and who determines Maliseetness requires an analysis of "embodied constellations of voices," an analysis that includes not only my contributions to the emergence of linguistic and cultural forms but also outside hegemonic contributions to formative constellations of Maliseetness.

Those questions have no easy answers, as Teresa O'Nell had discovered while working among the Flatheads of Montana. To portray her understanding from an ethnopsychological perspective, O'Nell describes the kinds of cultural impressions that are distributed among the Flatheads in Montana in her work on depression. Despite her work focusing on the varieties of depression expressed by the members of the Flathead community, she presents a case of embodiments of linguistic and cultural forms that are articulated by members of the Flathead community who purport to feel depressed. Her finding suggests that the distribution of perceptions of Indianness can be drawn out from their personal stories. The stories are subjective accounts of embodiments of linguistic and cultural forms, but their reference to "really Indians" (O'Nell 1996:56–68) suggests an intersubjective dialogue that exercises coercive force upon identity politics among the Flatheads. The importance of recognizing the intersubjective and dialogic nature of conceptions of identity and their concomitant politics is also the recognition of the depth of intertextual embodiments.[34] "Indianness" is not limited to the circulation of personal narratives but they are also circulated in a variety of "texts." Furthermore, narratives as "texts" may invoke other texts in a variety of forms, such as books, articles, speeches, and textbooks. The notions of "real Indianness" have long narrative and textual histories and convey coercive forces that are distributed among subjectivities. For O'Nell, the key to understanding Flathead notions of depression is not to look at the clinical definition as diagnoses of the medical textbooks but to examine the linguistic indeterminacies of translations and the larger social hermeneutics of identity politics. O'Nell argues that the reason 90 percent of the Flatheads say they are depressed is because no term in the Flathead language captures the particular pathological state described by English textbooks. For the Flathead, the English word *depression* serves to describe states akin to English depression but that may not be pathological in nature. O'Nell attempts to understand the embodiment of emotional states through personal accounts and matching the emotional state with cultural expectations of behavior. She concludes that textbook diagnoses might in fact misdiagnose pathologies that are present in the patient but not identify pathologies that do not fit the textbook categories. The same may be said for linguistic diagnoses and language pathologies.

The power of the categories in the textbooks reveals the hegemony of clinical medical practice on the Flathead community, but so does the rhetoric on "real Indians." O'Nell notes that during many of her interviews the subject would often mention some concern over the degree of Indianness he or she embodies. I emphasize this aspect of her work to illustrate the coercive force of a disembodied discourse on subjects. O'Nell posits a phenomenon she labels "the empty center." In effect, all Flatheads are measured against the "really Indian." Vine Deloria Jr. (1988) anticipated O'Nell's observation by stating that the "Indian problem" is popular expectations of performing to the "mythical super-Indian" of Hollywood stereotype. Alcida Ramos (1994) describes the "hyperreal Indians" and the popular imagination in Brazil. Complicating the identities of empty-center Indians, mythical super-Indians, and hyperreal Indians is the recent proliferation and dissemination of discourses on "indigeneity." All these expectations need not undermine identity self-making. While acknowledging the limitations, I also explore in greater detail in chapter 7 the creative potential these expectations can promote.[35]

Professional transformations of experiences into disembodied textbook analyses recall the god-trick of seeing everything from nowhere that ignores the lived experiences of those who share their experiences. Kleinman and Kleinman (1995) warn:

*The anthropologists' interpretive dilemma is that they participate in the same process of professional transformation. The interpretation of some person's or group's suffering as the reproduction of oppressive relationships of production, the symbolization of dynamic conflicts in the interior of the self, or as resistance to authority, is a transformation of everyday experience of the same order as those pathologizing reconstructions within biomedicine. Nor is it morally superior to anthropologizing distress, rather than to medicalize it. What is lost in biomedical renditions—the complexity, uncertainty, and ordinariness of some man or woman's world of experience—is also missing when illness is reinterpreted as social role, social strategy, or social symbol . . . as anything but human experience.* (Kleinman and Kleinman 1995:96; italics in the original)

The Kleinmans continue their critique of anthropological interpretations of experience by cautioning: "Ethnography does participate in this professional transformation of an experience-rich and near human subject into a dehumanizing object, a caricature of experience" (1995:96–97). Is there a way out of the dilemma of transforming subjective everyday experiences into dehumanized objects? Does the same dilemma affect the native anthropologist? Yes, it does. My presentation of material in this ethnography in chapters 2 through 5 reflects a distanced, dehumanized analysis of Maliseet language death. It serves as a diagnostic tool to suggest that comparative analyses with similar case studies of endangered languages can approach a better understanding of the uniqueness of the Maliseet case despite similarities. The uniqueness of the Maliseet case then allows the discussion to move toward an analysis in chapters 6 through 8 examining what form of death the Maliseet language is undergoing and the consequences of language loss. In these later chapters the lived experience of language loss is an important factor in assessing the importance of language death for the community of Tobique First Nation. To quote Kleinman and Kleinman once again, "It is our opinion that a contextual focus on experience-near categories for ethnography should begin with the defining characteristics of *overbearing practical relevance* in the processes and forms of experience. That is to say, *something is at stake* for all of us in the daily round of happenings and transactions" (1995:97; italics in the original).

That is precisely where the importance of this ethnography lies—what is at stake for the community if the language eventually dies, as predicted, in the next twenty years? By extension, what is at stake for the native anthropologist who also faces the same existential crisis regarding Maliseet language and cultural identity? Finally, how does anthropology either clarify or confuse the dilemma this native anthropologist faces while experiencing both worlds as native and anthropologist? When this research was first committed to text, the answers to these questions seemed at times elusive, open-ended, and contradictory. Today I can only suggest that the answers continue to be elusive, open-ended, and contradictory. But as stated earlier, the project is not my attempt to simplify the complex but to see what becomes of the complex. What is at stake is partially about the past, and partially about the present, but is it also about the future. This ethnography is an examination of the past and the present in order to anticipate alternative futures.

## 2. "Tipping" toward Maliseet Language Death

In the late nineteenth century the United States expansion had stretched out to the West Coast and the dream of transcontinental "manifest destiny" was finally fulfilled. In the taming of the West there was still some work to be done in pacifying hostile Indians. The military machine that was used to win the "war between the states" was turned to winning the West. Delaying the winning of the West were Native Americans who stood in the way of "progress." It was this sense of progress that allowed politicians and military leaders to "remove" Native Americans from their tribal lands. If that strategy did not work, then eradicating them would (this was the nineteenth-century iteration of a long process of colonizing the New World that started in 1492). Concurrent with forced progress at the hands of U.S. politicians and the U.S. military was the development of scientific paradigms of progress. These paradigms are reflected in the preoccupations of evolutionists and social Darwinists (Albert Gallatin, Samuel Morton, Ephraim Squier, and Lewis Henry Morgan being the most notable). Even though the pacification and removal of Indians in the West were traumatic events for Native Americans, the lasting social and scientific legacy of race and progressive hierarchies continues to have detrimental consequences today (Wilson and Yellow Bird 2005; Cobb and Fowler 2007). When the two progressive programs came together (Hinsley 1981) it produced a popular imagining of American Indians, namely, the vanishing race.

The irony of the vanishing race imaginary is that it seems the race is still vanishing![1] The popularity of Edward S. Curtis photographs today continues to promote that myth of vanishing while freezing Native Americans in sepia tones of still photographs as though Indians were trapped in amber for all time.[2] At the time Curtis was taking his photographs ethnologists and ethnographers were also rushing West to preserve what was left of the vanishing race before it was lost forever. Pioneering figures such as Frank Hamilton Cushing ventured out to salvage the remnants of Indian cultures. However, Cushing provided the authorities of the new science of ethnology with some methodological challenges (Hinsley 1981) that continue to be debated today. The challenges include grappling with the danger of going native, developing an objective/scientific method for salvaging vanishing peoples while preserving their pristine state, and keeping a professional distance to avoid the contamination of the ethnographer or ethnologist.

Franz Boas was determined to provide such an objective scientific approach to preserving the vanishing peoples and their languages and cultures (Boas 1940). From his "everything is important" method of collecting ethnographic material he advocated a four-field approach to cultural anthropology. A significant component of this approach consisted of linguistic recording and analyses. The project resulted in the recording of American Indian languages before they were lost forever. It was via that attention to vanishing American Indian languages that American anthropology began to address what is today called language death. Nineteenth-century scholars were witnessing the detrimental effects of linguistic colonialism (Greenblatt 1992; Pagden 1993) on Native American languages beginning in the sixteenth century. Colonial ideologies (Errington 2008) would lay the foundation for subsequent Native American language extinctions. In the late nineteenth century these colonial ideologies would perpetuate linguistic chauvinism (Harris 1993:20) favoring European linguistic heritage as superior to the "primitive" or "barbarous" native languages. Furthermore, the early studies on non-European languages had two primary "motives: conquest and conversion" (Harris 1993:20). Fortunately, assumptions about language based on European languages were challenged by research in American Indian languages, most notably by Franz Boas (Boas 1940; Harris 1993), Edward Sapir (Mandelbaum 1985), and Benjamin Lee Whorf (Whorf 1970). Boas in particular, in 1917, set the agenda for research in Native American linguistics in his introduction to the "International Journal of American Linguistics" (Boas 1940). In the introduction Boas acknowledges the difficult task of documenting language change through extended contact with European languages (1940:201). Not only were vocabularies lost, but the languages were undergoing morphological and syntactic changes as well.

The anthropological identification of language death and the processes contributing to death took major steps with comparative analyses done in the 1970s and since. Nancy Dorian's work on East Sutherland Gaelic (1981) was an important study that detailed the social factors contributing to language death. Her effort to bring together scholars who were working on similar language cases reflected a professional move toward a broad-based understanding of language attrition and the many forms it may take. Not only did she attempt to identify the factors in language death, but she also began cataloguing languages that were in danger of extinction. The examples brought together in her edited volume (1989) were gathered from all areas of the globe. It brought to the attention of language scholars the important fact that language endangerment was a global phenomenon. Joshua Fishman's 1991 text on language shift is another key comparative analysis that attempted to coordinate disparate case studies into a coherent program for reversing language shift. Similarly, Matthias Brenzinger's edited volume (1992) brought language scholars together to focus on the issue of language death for East African languages. In the most recent works published on language death the tone has changed from a hesitant theoretical delineation of the phenomenon to an urgent appeal to advocate the recording of the remnants of the endangered languages before they disappear. One of the recent books went as far as displaying on the front cover the image of a half-naked Ishi, "the last Yahi" of Kroeber fame (Nettle and Romaine 2000).

Linking Ishi's image and the word *vanishing* in the title recalls the romantic nineteenth-century preoccupation of the vanishing race. I am struck by the irony that the salvage anthropology of the nineteenth century has been echoed in the late twentieth and early twenty-first centuries. I note one additional irony—in many cases the people involved in contemporary salvage operations are themselves native speakers of the endangered languages. In my particular case, as noted in the previous chapter, the fear is not will I "go native"? Rather, it is will I "go anthropologist"? I have gone anthropologist, and doing so has given me the tools to be able to assess the state of the Maliseet language. While engaged in fieldwork at Mah-Sos Elementary School on Tobique First Nation I was able to observe the dissemination of articles that purport the imminent extinction of the Maliseet language. These language advocates—the organizer of the meeting, I, and the authors of the articles and books being disseminated—are collectively sounding the alarm to alert community members to the prospect of language death.

### Language Death: Sounding the Alarm

I began this book with an account of a language immersion organizational meeting that took place at the school. I spoke of the shocked silence as the participants assessed the severity of the projected Maliseet language morbidity. Not only was the organizer disseminating the dire prediction of Maliseet language death, but she was also sharing information on languages that have died (that became extinct), those that are in the same category as Maliseet (on the verge of extinction), and those languages that are endangered. She distributed a short article that predicted the demise of all but three aboriginal languages in Canada. The organizer disseminated information gathered by other researchers and academics who are concerned with the disappearance of languages worldwide and who are mobilizing people to actively document and to revitalize endangered languages.

These scholars identify the seriousness of language endangerment and describe a variety of reasons promoting language death. Recent publications addressing the topic of language death, disappearance, or endangerment have given broad surveys of the range of languages that are perceived to be moribund while also suggesting many reasons why the moribund languages reached such a state. At the turn of the twenty-first century three studies in particular—Grenoble and Whaley (1998), David Crystal (2000), and Nettle and Romaine (2000)—offer reasons why the moribund languages should be preserved, maintained, or revitalized. In response to scholarly attempts to understand the nature and the extent of language endangerment, other language scholars and language advocates, such as Fishman (1991, 2001), Hinton and Hale (2001), Hinton (2002), and more recently Grenoble and Whaley (2006), Baldwin and Olds (2007), Harrison (2007), and Kroskrity and Field (2009), have shared strategies and best practices for language maintenance and revitalization. It must be noted, however, that many of these studies and reports were published long after the 1993 meeting where the organizer shocked Tobique community members with the prediction of imminent Maliseet language death. With the benefit of hindsight and over a decade of professional research on language endangerment, an assessment of the accuracy of the 1993 diagnosis for the state of the Maliseet language can determine whether the Maliseet case as represented by Tobique First Nation is a case of language death, language obsolescence, or language shift.

### Language Death

We must now determine how to understand language death as distinct from shifts, attrition, endangerment, or obsolescence. "By language death, then, we do not simply mean this gradual alteration over time. We are referring to a more dramatic and less normal event, the total disappearance of a language" (Aitcheson 1991:197).

When photocopies of aboriginal language assessments in Canada were passed around to the Maliseet community members attending the language immersion meeting in the summer of 1993, as mentioned in the opening paragraphs of chapter 1, there was a morbid silence in the room. The word *extinction* made a profound impression on everyone in that room. Most had not considered the state of the Maliseet language in such ominous terms. Yet Robert Leavitt published a paper (1985) about language death and ambivalence in which he sketched a scenario describing the state of the Maliseet language almost three decades ago.

*The skeptical observer of Native language instruction at a federal or provincial school in the maritimes might—were he not afraid of the outrage he would encounter—be tempted to ask the teacher, "Why are you doing this? These kids aren't speaking Maliseet at home. Their parents don't teach it to them, so why should you? Where will they use it anyway, and what good will it do them?"*

*You get the picture, I'm sure. In fact, you probably have gotten it—or else have been in it in one role or another. "Anyway," this brash observer might conclude, with the satisfaction of having the last word, "they don't need to speak Maliseet to be Indian."*

*Some teachers, confronted in this way, have their own discouragement about the Native language confirmed. Others react angrily, particularly to the last point: "When the language is gone," they say, "then our culture goes with it." So they continue to teach, against the odds. (Leavitt 1985:262)*

In the same report Leavitt states: "We must confront language death—and openly acknowledge that language is a non-renewable resource. We should be stockpiling and identifying new sources of energy. We must confront language ambivalence and learn what both languages contribute to personal success. For young people, speaking the Native language remains a source of great pleasure. Understanding what it holds is a crucial factor in building cohesive and stable communities" (266). In the years since the publication there have been efforts to avert the erosion of the Maliseet language. Robert Leavitt's continuing work, in conjunction with the Micmac-Maliseet Institute, has included publication of studies, reports, and language teaching and reference materials; the establishment of native language classes in the schools; government-sponsored efforts to develop curriculum for teaching native languages and culture; and public meetings informing the Maliseet communities. All these efforts have helped in drawing attention to the severity of the problem. But as Leavitt points out, "The disappearance of a language is not uniform: there are pockets of resistance and strongholds of tradition. It is not precipitous either: for years to come people will continue to speak Micmac and Maliseet-Passamaquoddy. Yet life will never be the same" (264).

Despite the warning Leavitt voiced in 1985, participants in the meeting were still affected by the specter of language death. Yet Leavitt's warning was preceded by an even earlier warning. In their ethnography of 1957, Wallis and Wallis state: "People of all ages know and use the native tongue, but in many young households it is seldom heard. All small children understand English, and most of them speak it easily. Old women, the most conservative group, deplore the decline in the use of Malecite and pay their highest compliment to an English war bride who, they say, addresses her red-headed brood in the language of their father's people" (Wallis and Wallis 1957:16). The Wallis and Wallis observation that the children understood and spoke English easily may be the point at which the Maliseet language was "tipping" toward obsolescence (Dorian 1981).

It has been more than fifty years since that report, and the situation has become much more precarious for the Maliseet language. Today the "small children" of that generation have their own children who do not speak the Maliseet language. Compounding the problem, they have grandchildren who do not speak the language. There are at least two generations in which there was little if any Maliseet language transmission to Maliseet children. The Wallises' statement that "people of all ages know and use the native tongue" is certainly inaccurate today.

The specter of language death and the finality of language and culture loss are issues facing aboriginal and minority communities worldwide.

The pressures contributing to the precarious position of aboriginal languages and cultures are sometimes attributed to colonialism and imperialism. Johannes Fabian's (1986) provocative study of the politics behind colonial domination, linguistic control, and linguistic appropriation offers a number of observations that parallel the Maliseet case and may be used in a comparative analysis. One area where the cases coincide is the process of "domestication" by "codification" through grammars, vocabularies, and prayer books in the indigenous languages. Also, Fabian addresses the politics of orthography (26), which has a similar process in Maliseet and which continues to be contested today. There is, however, an additional similarity between the two cases that has bearing on Maliseet language death. Fabian states:

*Pagan religions did not consist of superficial, ill-assembled superstitions and barbarous ceremonial, or of timeless myth and ritual (admittedly, descriptions oscillated between the two); nor did native languages exist in hopeless dispersion and confusion (dispersed in space and mixed-up logically). The work of evangelization and that of linguistic appropriation—let us call it "grammaticalization"—were therefore not, and could not have been, to elevate what was low, to develop what only existed in traces or to illuminate what was in the dark. On the contrary, the real, practical task soon became, if not to eradicate and replace, then to take control of, direct and regulate what was there. (Fabian 1986:83)*

In the Swahili and Bantu cases, the establishment of Swahili as a vehicular language (the language of administration and education; Fabian 1986:71) where the Bantu languages are indigenous is presented as a colonial strategy to control labor and production in the Belgian Congo. Fabian's argument is convincing for that particular scenario and perhaps similar colonial cases. But the Maliseet case differs in that the colonial powers were not importing a different indigenous language (for example, Micmac) as a vehicular language; rather, the strategy was the outright conversion and assimilation of the Maliseet. The objective was to eradicate the Maliseet worldview in favor of the civilized worldview of the colonials. While convincingly presenting colonial strategies of linguistic control, Fabian's study does not address death or imperilment of Bantu languages and cultures. The impact such imperilment has on aboriginal communities is suggested by the following testimonies:

*Life is changing everywhere, all the time. It has changed completely since my childhood and in the future it will not be at all the same as it is today. Some of the young people don't even know the language any more. Some of them no longer know how to write in syllabics or, if they do, they write in English the words they don't know. The young people will never be white and yet they are forgetting how to speak their own language.* (Issuqanqituq Inuit; Cowan 1976:89)

*If we do not retain our Native languages, we will lose one of the most direct links that we have to our cultures. If this knowledge of our culture is lost to us, it is lost to all mankind, for all time.* (Mohawk)[3]

Shkilnyk consultant to the Toronto office of the Department of Secretary of State reported that of the 53 distinct Native languages in Canada:
—only three (3) have a chance of surviving the next ten years.
—eight (8) are facing extinction.
—twenty-nine (29) are deteriorating very rapidly, and
—thirteen (13) are moderately endangered. (From United Native Nations Report, Vancouver)[4]

To emphasize the finality of language death, Nancy Dorian provides the following East Sutherland proverb in the front of her book on Scots Gaelic: "Tha leigheas air gach càs, Ach cha'n eil leigheas air a'bhàs" (There's a cure for every condition except death; Dorian 1981:vi). There is no cure for Maliseet language death. However, the Maliseet language is not dead yet. Perhaps language obsolescence is a better descriptor for the state of the Maliseet language.

### Language Obsolescence
Obsolescence is defined in *Merriam-Webster's Collegiate Dictionary* as "the process of becoming obsolete or the condition of being nearly obsolete" (1993:803). For language, David Crystal has cast it this way:

> *The formal characterization of what has been called language obsolescence is still in its early stages, as a research field, but its importance is evident. When is an emergence or loss of a form, or the advent of a greater degree of language mixing, an instance of a "change" introduced through the normal processes of language contact, and when is it an instance of "decline"? (Crystal 2000:23)*

A Maliseet social event provides an opportunity for consideration. The bingo hall was full of spectators. We were all gathered to hear the promises and acceptance speeches that our newly elected chief and council would deliver to their constituencies. The new government stood at the front of the hall just under the bingo boards and the native motifs painted on the wall. One by one the politicians gave their standard speeches expressing their concerns, goals, and promises. It was George's turn. George did his best to present his acceptance speech in Maliseet. His manner was hesitant, as was his speech. George is in his mid-forties. His wife speaks Maliseet. They are considered to be "traditionalists." They have two daughters and one son. The daughters are in the seventh and eighth grades and they do not speak Maliseet. The son is in the second grade and does well in Maliseet language class. George, in a low, barely audible voice, promised to work for the people. He would be the only council member to give his acceptance speech in Maliseet. There were older council members who had been reelected and who knew how to speak Maliseet with great fluency, but they chose to give their speeches in English. These older and experienced councilors knew that few people in the audience would know what was being said if the speeches were given in Maliseet. This public event was just one more social context where the language of effective communication was English. It was one more example of Maliseet language sociopolitical erasure. Does this qualify as a case of obsolescence?

As David Crystal notes, language obsolescence is still a field in its infancy (2000). In introducing the edited volume *Investigating Obsolescence*, Nancy Dorian states: "Few of the contributors to the first two parts of this book would identify themselves as specialists in some one particular area, which this volume could be said to be devoted to. There is even some difficulty in locating any such area: 'obsolescence,' 'contraction,' and 'death' all fall short of a precise (perhaps even an acceptable) rubric" (Dorian 1989:1).

In that same volume Allan Taylor offers a provisional sketch of Gros Ventre language obsolescence. In the article Taylor never defines obsolescence. He does characterize the phenomenon as "contraction," Observing that "in theory, if the group is of sufficient size at the start of the investigation and the contraction of the linguistic community is gradual, there may be time and evidence enough to identify some of the phenomena early on and to observe their development" (Taylor 1989:167).

Taylor, a descriptive linguist, examines the changes in phonological and syntactic structures to evaluate the change the Gros Ventre language is undergoing. In his conclusion he states: "Apart from the examples, which probably are the product of the dynamics of language death, much of what I have said may require further refinement" (177). As Dorian points out and as Taylor shows in their 1989 publications, the term *obsolescence* presented fieldworkers with an imprecise term for the phenomena they were observing. Eleven years later Crystal has difficulty in presenting a precise definition for the term *obsolescence*. Because of lack of precision in defining obsolescence one could argue that the political acceptance speech qualifies as an example of obsolescence.

If we return to Webster's dictionary for the definition of *obsolete* we may get a better idea of how to interpret language obsolescence phenomena.

*Obsolete—a: no longer in use or no longer useful; b: of a kind or style no longer current: old-fashioned.* (Webster's Collegiate Dictionary 1997:803)

Based on this definition I conclude that George's speech defies obsolescence only because he was the only one of the elected politicians to present his speech in Maliseet. Unfortunately, the other elected officials chose to use English as their preferred language to give their speeches to the community. I argue this indicates that the Maliseet language has lost much of its "usefulness" and is therefore becoming (if not already) obsolete in many public events.

### Language Shift

Sam, a senior attending the local provincial high school, was commenting on what a "waste of time" taking the Native Culture class was at the off-reserve high school. He was voicing his dismay at the seeming lack of authenticity in the language taught by the teacher. His example was: "We asked him what the Maliseet word for *counter* was and he said, 'counterok.' We then asked him what the Maliseet word for next week was and he said, 'nexta wok.'"

It is tempting to view this example as evidence that the Maliseet language is undergoing language shift. The use of English roots with Maliseet suffixes might suggest language shift. J. Joseph Errington describes language shift in the following way: "Typically, language shift occurs as a community's native language (usually minority or 'ethnic') is progressively displaced by or relinquished for another (usually majority or 'national'). These are cumulative, 'long-term' processes which occur among collectivities of speakers, and as such can sometimes be read as mediating effects of 'large-scale' forces—political, cultural, economic—which shape broader senses of collective identity" (Errington 1998:4). There is certainly a displacement of root words in this example, but does it reflect the "long-term" process that Errington suggests? Because Sam is learning the "Maliseetized" English words as Maliseet, and since he did not know the proper Maliseet words himself (nor does he speak Maliseet), I interpret Sam's example as an instance of language shift.

Don Kulick (1992) published a monograph on language shift in Papua New Guinea in which he raises a question then posits an answer, "Why and how do people come to interpret their lives in such a way that they abandon one of their languages? Viewed in this way, the study of language shift becomes the study of a people's conceptions of themselves in relation to one another and to their changing social world, and how those conceptions are encoded by and mediated through language" (Kulick 1992:9). In evaluating the high school example with Kulick's focus in mind, it illustrates language shift on two levels. Sam the student is evaluating the teacher's speech and recognizing the use of English words in Maliseet as one example of shift. The acceptance speech, as an example of shift, is in the actual everyday use of English rather than Maliseet by elected officials as the language for communication. In both these examples, shift is not occurring—it has been completed. This corresponds to Errington's characterization of a "long-term" process. At what stage is Maliseet in this long-term process? Kulick states: "This issue of transmission is at the very heart of language shift, since languages cannot be said to be shifting until it can be established that children are no longer learning them. By the time the first generation of non-vernacular-speaking children has been raised, the boundary between language shift and incipient language death has in most cases quite intractably been traversed" (Kulick 1992:12). Although he is referring to Papua New Guinean vernacular languages, Kulick could very well be describing Maliseet language death. These examples from fieldwork experiences suggest that the Maliseet language has shifted beyond the precarious state to the "intractably . . . traversed" state toward language obsolescence and eventual death.

**Varieties of Erasure**

A useful study for understanding the multiple factors in assessing the state of endangered languages was conducted by Annette Schmidt and colleagues in which they coordinated a three-year effort to catalogue endangered Australian Aboriginal languages and list the causes for such endangerment. Their findings identify the types of erasures I organized into three categories—social upheaval, assimilatory pressure, and changes in economy and values. Under social upheaval the factors are patterns of resettlement, breakdown in isolation, urbanization, and increased intermarriage. The factors that characterize assimilatory processes are media, education, and stigma and cultural hegemony. The last factor is changes in values. In this category are included the lack of aboriginal literature, reduced language use and loss, reduction in number of speakers, and most important, speaker attitudes. "Changes in values" becomes a significant factor in assessing the relative viability of the Maliseet language.

### Social Upheaval

As a category for language loss among Australian Aborigines, Schmidt discusses the dormitory program through which Aboriginal children were taken from their homes and put into girls' and boys' dormitories. The children often came from a number of language groups and were often unable to communicate with one another. She quotes one former dormitory resident as saying, "I couldn't understand them. I couldn't speak to anyone because they didn't know my language. The only one I had to talk to was the hospital cat. He was my friend. I talked language to him" (Schmidt 1990:12).[5] The real damage done to Aboriginal languages was the failure to transmit the languages to the children residing in the dormitories. This forced the subsequent generations to rely increasingly on "English as a primary code of communication" (Schmidt 1990:13).

There was a similar process of removal in Canada. The term used in Canada is *residential schooling*. There is a growing literature of testimonials from former residential school survivors. Often the residential school experience is characterized as traumatic. The residential school that served the Maritime Provinces was at Shubenacadie, Nova Scotia. A number of Maliseet children from Tobique were sent to Shubenacadie Residential School along with a large number of Micmac children. Today some of the survivors of Shubenacadie are participating in Canadian government–sponsored healing seminars and programs in recognition of the kinds of traumas caused by such social upheaval programs initiated by the government decades ago.

One survivor, Isabelle Knockwood, a Micmac woman, wrote of her experiences in her 1992 book Out of the Depths, also providing testimonials from other former students of the school. One testimonial parallels the Australian language trauma example:

Peter Julian and his sister Teresa were sent to the school from Antigonish County in 1938 when he was about seven. Like so many other students, his most vivid memories are of isolation and of being punished for speaking the Mi'kmaw language:
Neither me nor Teresa could speak a word of English because at home we had spoken all Indian—our native tongue. So they started off with an interpreter who was one of the older kids who told me if I was caught talking Indian again I was to be beaten and that sort of put a fright into me. I had to put out with as much English as I could and keep from talking Indian. So inside of four or five years, I forgot all my Indian. When I got out in '47, I knew very little of my native tongue. I felt sort of ashamed in talking Indian. Well, just think, it was pounded out of me with a few strappings from the nuns. Also, I had missed a few meals every time I got caught talking Indian. (Knockwood 1992:34)

This is just one example of the growing body of testimonials recounting residential school abuses. The Canadian government issued a formal "Statement of Reconciliation" in January of 1998:

Against the backdrop of these historical legacies, it is a remarkable tribute to the strength and endurance of Aboriginal people that they have maintained their historic diversity and identity. The Government of Canada today formally expresses to all Aboriginal people our profound regret for past actions of the federal government which have contributed to these difficult pages in the history of our relationship together.
　One aspect of our relationship with Aboriginal people over this period that requires particular attention is the Residential School system. This system separated many children from their families and communities and prevented them from speaking their own languages and from learning about their heritage and cultures. In the worst cases, it left legacies of personal pain and distress that continue to reverberate in Aboriginal communities to this day. Tragically, some children were the victims of physical and sexual abuse.[6]

While the examples cited make a clear case for a variety of erasures—language, heritage, and culture—such upheavals account for only some of the pressures brought to bear on aboriginal communities in Canada. However, it is not clear that the residential school experience is the greatest contributing factor for the Maliseet language erasure at Tobique. I state this because there are a number of individuals who did attend Shubenacadie Residential School and who continue to speak Maliseet with great proficiency. This is not to say that the accounts I have quoted are in error; rather, that the members of Tobique First Nation who attended Shubenacadie did not lose the use of their language. One factor may be that they attended the school at a later date than those who provided the testimonials quoted. We must look to other reasons for the contraction of the Maliseet language.

PATTERNS OF RESETTLEMENT

Patterns of resettlement suggest the movement of aboriginal peoples, both by force and by their own volition. The most damaging is the forced relocation to distant reservations or territories. Often this would destroy the connections between the people, languages, and the land. Schmidt identifies the resettlement as contributing to language loss: "it destroyed the cohesive nature of many Aboriginal language communities by reducing and splitting speaker population; it also eradicated many sociolinguistic contexts for language use through the disintegration of kinship systems and social organization" (Schmidt 1990:13). In the Tobique case, it was not so much relocation and resettlement as a great contraction in the traditional land base that the Maliseet once occupied. Adding to Maliseet land/language contraction is the erasure of Maliseet place names in the landscape (Perley 2002b, 2009).

BREAKDOWN IN ISOLATION

Schmidt's discussion of breakdown in isolation is characterized as the transformation of aboriginal communities into "fluid, open-ended structures with State and nation-wide networks of social life and movement" (Schmidt 1990:14). Schmidt also suggests that such a breakdown was especially evident after World War II. Some similar factors contributing to the breakdown of Tobique Maliseet isolation may be attributed to post–World War II "social life and movement." Participation in the war effort by several men from the reservation, the building of the Tobique Narrows Dam, and increasing employment opportunities contribute to the perception of a breakdown in community isolation. However, there has been a long history of semi-migratory labor practice, be it to rake blueberries, pick potatoes, or to work in distant cities (Erickson 1978; LeSourd 2008). The argument of isolation is certainly an important factor, but it is not the only reason for Maliseet language attrition.

## URBANIZATION

The Australian Aboriginal example already described parallels the Maori experience as described by Augie Fleras:

*But following sustained settlement by Europeans after 1840, the status of Maoridom began to decline. Consistent with public perception of Maoris as a "social problem" in need of solution, Maori cultural values were dismissed as irrelevant to New Zealand requirements.... Maori youths were for the most part cut adrift from even tacit recognition of their language and cultural background.... The conclusion was obvious: apart from its symbolic and emotive properties (Biggs, 1972), the viability of Maori as a system of daily communication was imperiled by the pressures of rapid urbanization and assimilation. Only massive intervention could possibly avert the inevitable demise and disappearance. (Fleras 1991:19)*

How does the Maliseet case fit this form of erasure? In urban settings the opportunities arising to speak Maliseet are seldom to none at all. There is a great deal of pressure to speak English, and the result is a recognition that communication in urban settings away from the reservation is going to have to be done in English (French may be an option in Francophone Canada). As Schmidt stated, "The pressures to switch to English and to adopt associated Western identities, role models and aspirations are immense. Moreover, there are many fewer opportunities to speak an Aboriginal language, in terms of both availability of speakers and suitable contexts of use" (Schmidt 1990:14). Schmidt's example describes Aboriginal peoples living in urban settings. A number of families from the Tobique reservation have spent years off the reservation and have lived in urban settings. In practically every case I am aware of, the parents may speak Maliseet but the children invariably do not. I too am an example of such erasure due to "urbanization."

INCREASED INTERMARRIAGE

Increased intermarriage as a form of erasure is explained by the greater mobility factor and the breakdown of isolation. With these two factors the opportunities to find marriage partners out of the group are greatly increased. "With extended communication networks and patterns of mobility, intermarriage between Aboriginal groups increased. Individuals from radically different language backgrounds often shifted to the community of their spouses, thus adding to the linguistic heterogeneity of the population" Schmidt 1990:15). A similar pattern exists for Tobique First Nation. One big difference in the Maliseet case is the intermarriage between whites and aboriginals. Yes, there are numerous examples of intertribal marriages, such as marriages between Maliseet and Micmac, Maliseet and Cree, Maliseet and Hopi, but most often the marriages are Maliseet and Canadians of European descent (and U.S. citizens). In most cases the language spoken in these families is English. I asked one of our tribal councilors, who married a Cree woman, if his sons and daughter speak Maliseet. No, was the answer. "Do they speak Cree?" Again, no was his answer. "They speak English." I then asked him why they did not speak one of the aboriginal languages, and he responded by explaining that he did not want to privilege one aboriginal language over the other. The result was that English was privileged over both aboriginal languages.

*Assimilatory Pressure*
Beyond various forms of dislocation, active pressure toward assimilation has also occurred in several social spheres.

## EDUCATION

One key assimilatory pressure exerted on the Canadian aboriginal population was education. The most traumatic education experience has often been associated with the residential school system already discussed as a form of social upheaval. Yet the reservation schools exerted similar assimilatory pressures. The nuns and priests were responsible for teaching native children proper white values so that the aboriginals could become good citizens. The adults who talked about their school experience on the reservation would often describe how mean some nuns and priests were, how nice others were, and the kinds of tactics that students used to aggravate the nuns and priests. In addition to these conversations they would often talk about helping the nuns and priests prepare the church for the holidays and other special events. As in residential schools there was a prohibition on speaking Maliseet on school and church grounds.

In the 1970s the reservation residents decided to build their own school. At first, they staffed the school with the nuns and priests but later, as more Maliseet became trained as education professionals, the nuns and priests were replaced with Maliseet teachers. Despite the change of staff, English remained the language of instruction. Although there were no prohibitions for speaking the Maliseet language, the problem was, there was no established curriculum in Maliseet. Today, there is a Native Language Class but the rest of course instruction is done in English. In the "old days" (the thirties, forties, and fifties) I pointed out that the children were restricted from speaking Maliseet but that did not prevent them from speaking Maliseet at home. What can account for the loss of the language in the later generations?

## MEDIA

When I asked why one particular generation did not pass the language on to their children the elders would blame television. It was explained to me that the television became the entertainer and the babysitter. Today the reservation has cable, satellite dishes, Internet connections, newspaper and magazine subscriptions, video stores, and all the richness of modern media. All these forms of media communicate their messages predominantly in English. Again, in the past parents and grandparents used to tell their children stories about the old days or the legends of Koluscap. That does not happen any more. The children have their own televisions and computers. The children can entertain themselves. That entertainment is in English. This is not to say that English media were not previously present on the reservation. There were radios, newspapers, books, and magazines. The difference is the proliferation of English media and the distribution and availability at all times of the day in all aspects of social and cultural life. Drawing again on Schmidt's analysis, she says of media importance in the Australian context:

*A major instigator in the promotion of English as the most viable and prestigious code at the expense of Aboriginal languages was the powerful media of television, video, radio, newspaper and glossy magazines. Even in many remote Aboriginal communities, media forces (especially English video and television) have become a central aspect of contemporary life. While detailed research into the precise relationship between media and language loss has been very limited to date, it is widely accepted that media can play an important role in patterns of language use, language attitudes and language shift. (Schmidt 1990:16)*

As that statement suggests, understanding of the precise relationship between media and language loss or shift is limited, but in the Maliseet case the shift in language transmission is expressed by the impression that one particular generation did not pass the language on to their children. It was also that generation for whom television became the ubiquitous entertainer and babysitter. Today, with all the exposure to all the rich forms of media available to them, members of Tobique First Nation are facing a tremendous obstacle to overcome in maintaining the Maliseet language.

## STIGMA AND CULTURAL HEGEMONY

There is a long history of assimilatory pressures exerted on aboriginal communities worldwide. The history is varied and complex. Despite variation and complexity there are common denominators. The dominant sociocultural systems exert pressures on the dominated to assimilate the values, lifestyles, and languages of the dominant. In Canadian terms, the aboriginal peoples needed to be freed of the burden of "Indianness" by eliminating the category of Indian for all government programs and services as outlined in the White Paper of 1969 (McRoberts 1997:121–22). Similarly, Schmidt says of Australia's assimilation pressures on Aborigines,

> In the post-contact period, Aboriginal people across Australia were subject to intense pressure to assimilate to white Australian values, lifestyle and languages through a wide variety of devices. Aboriginal language, along with cultural values and identity, became stigmatized and unnecessary in a world in which the English language and lifestyle were viewed as the ultimate end in a unilineal progression of cultural and linguistic achievement by the church, school and other institutions. Due to the stigma attached to Aboriginal languages, many parents regarded their Aboriginal language as not useful and unworthy of passing down to future generations. (Schmidt 1990:19)

The idea that aboriginal people can be stigmatized for using their languages is also reflected in the Maliseet case. I asked one elder woman about her language experience in school. She told me that the nuns would reprimand students for speaking Maliseet and punish them in front of the other students to shame them into not speaking Maliseet again. She also told me the nuns told her "that's the devil's tongue." This elder woman did not pass the Maliseet language on to her children. Today her grandchildren do not speak Maliseet either. She is not the only example. Others told me that they were prohibited from speaking Maliseet in school but they did not lose the language because they spoke it outside of the school. They spoke Maliseet at home. For the most part, this generation did pass the language to their children, but their children broke the chain of transmission. Why? Again, the pressures to assimilate white values, lifestyles, and language were too much to resist. These pressures took the form of education, media, and changing values.

Related cases of stigmatization refer to the attempt by some members of the community to "pass for white." I do not have firsthand observations of these practices, but a number of people on the reservation have identified them on a consistent basis with comments such as, "Oh, she was ashamed of being Indian so she tried to pass for white." A comment that was most condemning was, "Now that there's money in being Indian she's the Super Indian." This stigmatization was not exclusive to the Tobique reservation. While I was visiting my uncle in Kingsclear Reserve, two hundred kilometers to the south, he commented, "Yeah, a lot of young people try to pass for white. They go to the mall and act like white people." This is possible because many of the children of mixed marriages between aboriginals and whites can appear to be phenotypically white. More important though, the examples suggest a stigma associated with being aboriginal.

*Changes in Economy and Values*
I am often confronted with the sentiment from various people on and off the reservation that it would be nice to go back to the old days before Columbus made his fateful voyage. This is an idyllic scene painted by people indulging in nostalgic reveries. They often evoke a simpler time when aboriginal lifestyles and values were still intact; when the economy consisted of subsistence and the values were communal. The pictures of a Maliseet past are similar to the generalized nostalgia of Indian pasts. The comment I often hear is, "Ah, times were simpler then." I usually respond by saying that I do not think times were so simple. "In the old days, if I was hungry I'd have to track down a moose, I'd have to kill it with only a bow and arrows, I'd have to skin the beast and cut up the carcass and bring the food and hide back home. Today, I just go to the store and hunt and gather my favorite foods and put them in my shopping cart. Go to the checkout counter and return home with my bounty. I don't know. Things seem simpler today." My example illustrates the reliance on the cash economy as the new means of subsistence. In the cash economy the primary language of exchange

is in dollars and cents, but the transactions are done in English. This is reflected in the households as well as in the band administration. As Schmidt stated of the Australian case, "English, rather than Aboriginal languages, is associated with the acquisition of technical skills, education, youth, modernity and material success" (Schmidt 1990:15). The lingua franca of economics is English. All negotiations with the Canadian government and financial institutions are done in English. All of the financial reports and audits are in English. In some cases there may be some French text provided for government forms and publications, and French may be included on bank brochures and forms too. However, the predominant language of economics is English. At the household scale, the predominant language is, yet again, English. All of the merchants in the neighboring villages and towns conduct their businesses in English. The town of Grand Falls, forty kilometers away, is the linguistic border for French and English. Businesses conduct their affairs in both English and French. Despite the bilingualism of businesses, English is the language of economy for the members of Tobique First Nation.

The change from a subsistence economy to a market (cash) economy also signaled a shift in values toward the "acquisition of technical skills, education, youth, modernity and material success" (Schmidt 1990:15). As the community became more dependent upon the commodities of the market economy there was a shift in values placed on material acquisition. This indicated a degree of success in obtaining the material goods of modernity. Traditional foods, clothing, transportation, and material production were replaced by store-bought clothing; processed, packaged, and marketed foods; vehicles; and manufactured items such as furniture, entertainment systems, appliances, etc. By becoming consumers in the market economy, community members were also buying Western values and lifestyles. "The move into a Western economy has been accompanied by a shift towards Western values, lifestyle and the English language. In particular, many of the younger generation focus on Western images, desires and expectations that form social identities incongruous with the use of Aboriginal language" (15). Even though Schmidt is referring to the Australian Aborigine context, the comment applies to the shift in values on Tobique First Nation. The value placed on purchasing the latest technologies (computers, satellite dishes, big screen televisions, cell phones), the latest fashions (Nike Swoosh, Tommy Hilfiger, Starter), and equipment for the latest kinds of recreation (golf, MUDDing, snowmobiling) are all primarily preoccupations of the middle (forties and thirties) to younger generations (twenties and teens). These are also the generations who do not speak the language. I should point out that some of the forty-somethings do speak the language, but that is the generation where the drop-off is precipitous. Nevertheless, the currency of all the new economies, lifestyles, and values is primarily expressed in English. Maliseet is ill equipped to deal in the market economy. The endangerment of Maliseet is the unfortunate side effect of changes in economy and values.

## LACK OF ABORIGINAL LITERATURE

In her discussion of Aboriginal literature in Australia, Schmidt suggests that the lack of literature is coupled with the poor quality of the literature that does exist, with the two combining to create the situation in which "English emerges well ahead of Aboriginal languages as the prestigious viable code" (Schmidt 1990:17). The problem for Maliseet can be viewed as quite similar. In later chapters I present some of the attempts to codify the language, but for the moment I argue the lack of literature is one of the key problems. As mentioned in chapter 1, at the time of my fieldwork, publications in the Maliseet-Passamaquoddy language existed in the forms of dictionaries, lexicons, booklets for Maliseet reading instruction, and an occasional linguistic sketch. These documents are not widely circulated. When they are circulated they are tossed aside because they are Passamaquoddy or they are too difficult to read. The fact the materials are Passamaquoddy and therefore tossed aside is suggestive of the identity politics between neighboring aboriginal communities. This example may serve as to illustrate boundary maintenance. The difficulty of reading the texts also indicates the "oral language" ideology that I have heard from a number of speakers. The language was always transmitted orally and was never taught in the schools while administered by the church. Hence the speakers were not literate in their own language. Compounding the lack of literacy is the absence of transcriptions of oral "texts" and their subsequent distribution among the Maliseet speakers. In this particular case it is not erasure we are discussing; rather, it is best described as omission. In such an omission, the absence of literature is indicative of the devaluation of Maliseet oral "texts." This not to say there is not a "literature" available. There have been collections of Maliseet stories (and related Algonquin stories) in publication for over a hundred years, but those works are largely in English and reflect the translation ideologies of non-Indian collectors (Perley 2012b). What is lacking are Maliseet stories told by Maliseet in the Maliseet language.

### REDUCED LANGUAGE USE AND LOSS

As indicated in the preceding sections there are a number of public contexts in which the everyday communication is conducted in English rather than Maliseet. From economics to politics, from religion to education, there are fewer and fewer contexts were the Maliseet language can be heard. The only place I have been able to hear the language used as the primary mode of communication is when I am among the elders of the reservation. The social settings vary from the chit-chat of impromptu visits to organized gatherings for card games. One notable observation in these gatherings is the absence of young people. There may be a number of factors associated with their absence. As already discussed, the younger generations have their own forms of entertainment and social gatherings. The elders' gatherings are of little interest to them. The other factor may be directly associated with language. Much of the conversation at gatherings of older people is in Maliseet, a language with which the younger generation is unfamiliar. In effect, they would be excluded from the conversations.

This is similar to the "downward spiral" model explicated by Schmidt for explaining the loss of Australian Aboriginal languages. In effect, the process starts with:

- Limited Aboriginal language usage
- Limited exposure to the language
- Reduced language knowledge and fluency
- Lack of confidence in using that Aboriginal language
- Increasing reliance on English
- Limited Aboriginal language use
- CYCLE REPEATS. (Schmidt 1990:21)

The cycle does capture the general shift toward English as the preferred code for communication among younger generations. However, this points to another problem associated with constricted language use—with fewer opportunities to use the language, there are more chances for language loss. The loss can be expressed in terms of loss of language practice but also loss in number of speakers.

REDUCED NUMBER OF SPEAKERS

Perhaps the most tragic aspect of Maliseet language loss is evidenced in the loss of speakers. In the last few years there were a number of deaths of language speakers. For a number of analysts the common sentiment is that the loss of a speaker is the loss not only of a valuable lexicon but also the loss of language practice. What good are the words if you are not aware of how the words are used? As each speaker dies, so too does another possible link in the transmission of the language to a younger generation. I qualify the previous statement with "possible" because I have not witnessed any transmission of the language from the older generations to the younger generations in today's community life. Part of the irony of this research is that the tragedy of language loss is not seen as a tragedy for a large majority of the Tobique population. However, if the younger generations and the older ones establish some common goal to preserve the language and begin the transmission process again, they would have to coordinate their efforts very soon. As each year passes, the community's elder population decreases. The passing of every elder is also the passing of language models and lexicons.

SPEAKER ATTITUDES

The loss of elders is a tragedy, but equally tragic is the fact that the elders do not transmit the language to the younger generations because the younger generations are doing just fine without the Maliseet language. As described, all the economic and social interactions are conducted in English. Maliseet has not served as a vital tool for communication since perhaps the 1950s and '60s. This time period is critical because that generation is the generation of people (who are today in their seventies and eighties) who have not transmitted the Maliseet language to their children. When I asked a number of them why their children do not speak the language, they often cite some of the reasons presented in the preceding discussion. The most damaging comment I have heard, which practically condemns the Maliseet language to extinction, is the perception that "you don't have to speak Maliseet to be Maliseet." That sentiment is the topic of discussion in chapter 7.

## Tipping toward Death

From the criteria described, I have presented the various forms of erasure that contribute to language death. Taken in isolation, none of the factors could imperil the Maliseet language toward extinction. The last few indicators suggest a change of economy and values that in turn suggest a social/cultural change. Again, change is a part of social/cultural life. Change is an aspect of language life. For language scholars and advocates working in and on endangered languages the ability to discern when "language change" turns to "language shift" and then toward "language obsolescence" is important for determining what next steps should be taken regarding the perceived vitality of the language in question. Significantly, Nancy Dorian explains in her seminal text on East Sutherland Gaelic that the processes leading to language death may seem to occur suddenly. While this is a crucial observation, she points out:

> English seemed to come suddenly to eastern Sutherland, but the climate which led to its rapid adoption had been centuries in the making. In terms of possible routes toward language death, it would seem that a language which has been demographically highly stable for several centuries may experience a sudden "tip," after which the demographic tide flows strongly in favor of some other language. In eastern Sutherland the end of a protective isolation precipitated this tip locally, exposing Gaelic speakers to the forces which had greatly favored English nationally for several hundred years. (Dorian 1981:51)

The Maliseet case at Tobique First Nation echoes Dorian's Sutherland Gaelic case quite closely. There are a number of similar factors in the two cases (education, economics, and communications in particular), but I would add one more factor to the assessment of Maliseet language tip toward obsolescence—the erasure of language and cultural continuity.

### Continuity Submerged

Sharing a story provides a way to illustrate another form of erasure. Koluscap, or Kluskap, is a name of a medeulin, a name

> meaning "bewitched" or "in cahoots with the devil." This is the belief of the St. John River Indians, from St. John, New Brunswick to Edmunston. This man was considered to know more than anyone else and was more or less chief of the tribe. He had one enemy and he was called the "Beaver," whose name was Gwabid. One day they had a big battle at Grand Falls which is called Gupsquick. The Kluskap was trying to catch the beaver on the riverbank. Since the beaver lived on water he could travel faster than Kluskap. He gave up trying to keep up with him, and went to the riverbank and picked up a large rock and threw it at the beaver, thinking that if he hit him he would kill him on the spot. After he threw it he found out that the beaver was farther away than he had thrown

*the rock. The rock landed at the mouth of the Tobique River. When Kluskap saw that, he picked up another rock and threw it with more force, only this time the rock was much bigger. The rock is still at the mouth of the river. The Indians still believe that it is the very rock Kluskap had thrown at the Gwabid. Mrs. Black (Ives 1965:18)*

With the construction of Beechwood Dam the geological changes not only affected the landscape but affected the Maliseet cultural and mythical landscape as well.

One late summer afternoon I was standing on a hill while talking with my mother. We were looking over the Maliseet village and the river valley below. She pointed beyond the point where the two rivers met and told me that that was the location of the Tobique Rock. I looked and I could see a couple of ospreys engaged in playful arabesques; I could see the waters of the two rivers converge, but I could see no rock. My mother then fondly recalled her days as a young girl getting up before anyone else so that she could go out to the rock and meditate while the dawn's light brightened to early morning. Since her days of morning meditation there have been three generations of Maliseet children who have not had the pleasure of meditating on the rock. Sadder still, there may have been three generations of Maliseet children who have heard the story of Kluskap and Gwabid and how the rock happened to rest at the mouth of the Tobique River but who have not seen the physical evidence of the story. Most important, they have not heard the story in Maliseet.

The story is a transcription of one collected for a folklore class and published in 1965. The account is ascribed to Mrs. Black (my mother), the daughter of Viola Solomon (my grandmother), who in turn is the source of the stories presented in the said publication. Preceding the Kluskap and Gwabid story in that publication is the version Viola Solomon presented. However, rather than focusing on the variations of the story, I prefer to highlight a comment my grandmother made regarding the Tobique Rock.

[Kluskap] *picked up a rock and tried to hit him, but this beaver was too smart, too fast for him. He went up the St. John River, and the first hiding place he came to was going up the Pokiok Falls. That's where he struck the first rock landed. So this Beaver thought that was too much for him. So he went further up the St. John River, and right now you can see them rocks. I mean you can't now; since they built the dam* [i.e. at Beechwood] *they're all under water.* Mrs. Solomon (Ives 1965:17; asides and italics in the original)

As mentioned, three generations of children do not have the pleasure of seeing the rock, or hearing the stories of how it got there, but even more critical is the erasure of evidence confirming the stories told by the elders. Likewise, the erasure of evidence of a viable spoken Maliseet language is submerged under the waters of decades of gradual obsolescence and processes of assimilation. The Tobique Rock illustrates the symbolic complexity that ties language to landscape and community identity. It also illustrates how environmental change through state development projects can change social/cultural memories and awareness. The geological erasure of a mythic landmark is also an erasure of mythic origins that had once been told orally in the aboriginal language. I grew up with the story of the Tobique Rock, but I do not remember seeing it. Many children (indeed, adults too) have never seen the rock. More tragically, they have not heard the story in Maliseet. The Tobique Rock is just one example of an oral tradition that is no longer shared between community members in what was once a traditional practice of storytelling (Erickson 1978). Today the stories are recontextualized and repackaged by both native and nonnative story collectors to satisfy the expectations of new audiences (Perley 2012b). The irony in this tragic erasure is that the oral traditions seem to be more valued as entertainment than for recognizing the importance of the integration of language, landscape, stories, and what these connections mean for Maliseet worldviews. Not only are we seeing erasure of landmarks and language from the landscape, but we are also seeing a change in values.

Associated with these changes in values and an important factor in contributing to language death is loss of prestige for the heritage language. As indicated by the examples cited, the stigmatization of language is also stigmatization of person. The loss of prestige for heritage languages has deep colonial roots that cannot be separated from longstanding ideologies and practices of domination and subordination (Wilson and Yellow Bird 2005). While reminding the reader of the significance of a long history of domination Nancy Dorian emphasizes the importance of language "prestige" as a factor in determining the value of the language and the value of the person in eastern Sutherland. Dorian argues that Gaelic was associated with the lower classes, and when the elites switched to English the "masses were following" their lead (Dorian 1981:52). Similarly, despite being First Nations peoples in Canada, the reality of everyday life for many generations of aboriginal Canadians was that of second-class citizen status. The legacy of colonial domination and ideological entrenchment has created the conditions for language, cultural, and social stigma, thereby undermining the prestige of aboriginal identities. These many processes and factors in and of themselves cannot condemn the Maliseet language to a state of language death. It is the particular combination of factors discussed that created the conditions that impelled the Maliseet language to tip toward language death. However, despite the disheartening assessment of Maliseet language viability, the social and cultural climate in Canada has changed and aboriginal languages, cultures, and identities are regaining recognition, respect, and prestige.

The scholarly work of dedicated linguists, sociolinguists, and other language advocates is extremely valuable for alerting the public to the growing global tragedy of language death. The diagnostic and analytical studies to define the problem, diagnose the problem, and determine relative language vitality and morbidity are critical materials for assessing the kinds of interventions language advocates in endangered language communities may consider developing and implementing. The most crucial variables in "expert" assessments of language vitality are the people and their relationship with their languages. This ethnography is an exploration of the relationship between the members of Tobique First Nation and the Maliseet language. The life of the Maliseet language is dependent upon its integration into the lives of the Maliseet people of Tobique First Nation.

## 3. Programming Language Maintenance

The formal exercise of diagnosing the vitality of Maliseet language in terms such as those presented in the previous chapter conveys rational knowledge of the causes and factors that contribute to the phenomenon referred to as language death. The seeming objectivity and rationality of linguistic diagnostic analyses are not ideologically neutral. Experts trained in the language sciences focus on language itself as the primary pivot of scrutiny and intervention. The resultant strategies are to "document" dying languages through descriptive texts and audio or video recordings and to produce grammars and dictionaries that preserve what is left before the last speaker dies. These interventions are valuable, but they do not take into consideration the people who have a direct relationship with the subject language. Language maintenance practices are also ideological as they draw from formal and rational practices for language maintenance and revitalization. But the interventions and programs these language advocates promote are designed to consider the communities and speakers who have a stake in the life and death of their languages. Including people in their assessments of language programming complicates the ideological dimensions of language maintenance efforts. My own ideological stance regarding Maliseet language maintenance views the rationalization of language through orthographic representation, grammatical description, and language practice as a process of domestication (see chapters 4 and 5).

I do so for two reasons. First, I draw from the characterization that Jack Goody (1977) uses to describe the difference between the written and the oral as one of "domestication" and "savage"; and second, I draw attention to the irony that the "domestication of language" produces a practice of the political economy of language (practice in public) that in turn removes language from a domestic economy of language (practice at home). The second point is instrumental for assessing the efficacy of institutionalizing Maliseet language practice as symbolic capital and a shift away from embodied practice. But first, a brief introduction to the programs and the people behind them establishes the various domains of authority or ideology and influence over Maliseet language maintenance programming.

### Institutionalizing Maliseet Language Maintenance

There are two areas where Maliseet language domestication by institutionalization is taking place. The local area of domestication of language is on Tobique First Nation, where most of my research was completed. Many of the local domestication processes were observed in the native language classroom at Mah-Sos School. There were additional attempts to domesticate the language but they were not as systematic. At times Mah-Sos School, as well as other local language preservation and codification activities, created an overlap and confusion of constituencies.

Significant contributions to the domestication of the Maliseet language come from institutions of learning; Mah-Sos Elementary School on Tobique First Nation, St. Thomas University, and the University of New Brunswick. St. Thomas University has a Native Studies program that was being restructured at the time of my field research. The university had just appointed a member of Tobique First Nation as the chair of Native Studies. She would prove instrumental in generating a framework to promote aboriginal language immersion programs in the Maritime Provinces. The University of New Brunswick also offers several programs of interest to aboriginal students. Equally important, the Micmac-Maliseet Institute is located on the University of New Brunswick campus. In fact, the two universities share facilities as well as students. St. Thomas University has a few of its own buildings but the campuses are adjacent to each other. St. Thomas was the sponsor and was the location of the language symposium discussed later in this chapter, while the University of New Brunswick was the location of many of the language-related meetings I attended as a representative for Mah-Sos School. These three institutional programs were working toward the same goal of Maliseet language maintenance and revitalization, but they were not working in concert with one another. Their respective constituencies created expectations that the principal agents were compelled to accommodate.

It is important to note that this ethnography is focused on the Maliseet language case at Tobique First Nation and that there are many other institutions, agents, and programs that could have been included in this ethnography. I have no doubt the ethnography would be a much richer if I presented the efforts of language advocates from other Maliseet First Nations. Similarly, the extremely productive and valuable work of Passamaquoddy linguists, language teachers, and language advocates has made positive contributions to the Maliseet language programs both directly and indirectly over the years. However, the constraints of field research limited my opportunity to expand the scope of my ethnographic assessment. The omission of these other programs is not intended to denigrate or to be disrespectful of their work. It is merely a practical consideration for making manageable the complexities of the many overlapping domains of language maintenance programs.

*Overlapping Domains*

My participation in the events and my observations of the agents involved in the various institutions and programs described here occurred between 1993 and 1996. Much of the literature on language maintenance "best practices" was yet to be published. These agents and their respective constituent domains were engaged in face-to-face deliberations in an attempt to solve the complex problem that many language scholars were themselves trying to identify. Even though more than a decade has passed since the accounts that follow, I employ a narrative strategy describing the events in the present tense to maintain an ethnographic "present."

The native language teacher, whom I represent as Sue, is the principal agent in the Mah-Sos School native language class because of her role as the Maliseet language teacher. Her efforts and the activities in her classroom are significant contributions to this ethnography. However, the interconnections with extra-classroom events and activities are important conduits for the transmission of language teaching techniques and ideologies. By observing and participating in the activities associated with the classroom I was able to discern a number of substantive as well as tenuous extra-classroom connections to other Maliseet language maintenance agents and their activities. This chapter describes the entangling of the Mah-Sos School domain with two other Maliseet language agents and their respective contexts and constituencies.

My primary field site is in the Tobique community, which places me within Sue's domain. Therefore, Sue became a key agent for this ethnography. Her work within the community provides an excellent "grassroots" perspective to Maliseet language maintenance. Two other agents and their programs provide contrasting perspectives and approaches to language maintenance. One, Dan, is the aboriginal education consultant for the Province of New Brunswick. He provides a "provincial" perspective to language maintenance. The other, Barb, is the chair of Native Studies at St. Thomas University. She provides an academic context to both pedagogical and political perspectives for language maintenance. I selected these individuals as my key Maliseet language advocates because all three are members of the Tobique First Nation and their affiliations represent a trio of contexts—communal, governmental, and academic domains. In addition, the three agents share two critical common denominators. First, they are Tobique First

Nation "citizens," and second, they are actively involved in Maliseet language maintenance projects. However, despite those important commonalities, their ideas, programs, and constituencies at times diverge from one another and at other times converge with one another. Because of such dynamics they exhibit varying degrees of interaction. The interactions I was most interested in observing were those between the Mah-Sos School program and the other two programs sponsored by the Province of New Brunswick and St. Thomas University. Because my focus was directed toward the Mah-Sos School context my knowledge of the interactions between the other two is less extensive. Nevertheless, the kinds of interactions among the three agents revealed differences in their respective ideologies, constituencies, and programmatic practices. Those differences are explained as the agents are presented under their respective domains.

COMMUNITY

Stating that Sue is representative of the Tobique First Nation community does not imply that she is the sole representative. Rather, her residence, her work, and her constituency are located on the Tobique reservation. Sue lives on Rodeo Drive in the Flatland, the oldest of the three residential developments on the reservation. Her employer is Mah-Sos School—the community elementary school. The children attending Mah-Sos School represent her constituency. By association, her constituency extends to the children's parents. Hence these three factors firmly locate her language transmission efforts within the community. It is in this sense that I argue that Sue represents the community context.

GOVERNMENT

I identify Dan with the government context because his employer is the Province of New Brunswick. His office is in Fredericton, 250 kilometers away from the Tobique reservation, and he resides in Fredericton. His constituency is very broad. In a telephone interview he explained that he works to facilitate native education across the province for

Micmac and Maliseet children in the provincial schools. He defines his constituency as all native children attending provincial schools.

### ACADEMIA

As the chair of Native Studies, Barb represents the academic context. Her office is on the St. Thomas University campus in Fredericton. She also resides in the environs of Fredericton. Like Dan's, her constituency is broad. Being situated in the university, she has a constituency represented by all students attending it. However, her native language program efforts are the main reasons for her inclusion in this ethnography. Her immediate constituency consists of the students and participants of her domain-sponsored activities and who may become potential Micmac and Maliseet language teachers.

### *Contextual Constraints*

The aspect of context I choose to examine are the methods used by institutions such as the provincial government, the universities, and Mah-Sos School as they exercise control over the actions of the language agents under their employ. Such control influences constituency demarcation as well as ideological assertions. In effect, the respective institutions can terminate ideologies or practices that may not be deemed acceptable from their authoritative standpoint. Each subordinate director is subject to expectations, explicit or implied, of the directors and authority inherent in the super-ordinate domains; namely, the institutions. The employers of those super-ordinate domains can also exercise tolerance of the subordinate agents' activities in accordance with their particular ideologies. Those institutions exert some control or constraints on the kinds of programs and methods that each subordinate agent can employ. For example, Dan must direct his efforts to serve the provincial schools. Sue's primary responsibility is the children attending Maliseet language class. Barb's position is the most flexible in creating opportunities to address a variety of constituencies. From the academic setting her primary constituents are university students, but she can use the academic platform to conduct outreach programs. In doing so, Barb can amplify her constituent base. The contexts from which the agents work provide avenues for action but can also limit some other forms of action.

### Agents of Language Maintenance

Profiles of the three agents provide a fuller sense of their interconnecting roles and activities.

#### Sue

Sue accepted the job of teaching Maliseet language to the children attending Mah-Sos School in the summer of 1993; the same summer I began my fieldwork on the reservation. In many of our conversations she often told me that she had an intense summer of preparing materials for teaching the language. She had two assistants to help produce the teaching materials (discussed at length in chapter 5). She also explained that she did not receive formal training in language instruction or linguistics. The responsibility of developing a Maliseet language curriculum was hers, and she was learning by trial and error. After the classes began she was solely responsible for making adjustments and the continued development of the curriculum for all the grades taking Maliseet language class. Her domain of responsibility was the Mah-Sos School classroom. However, the continued development of the curriculum required inquiries beyond the classroom. Much of the cultural material of Maliseet and other Native American communities was obtained from the expanding Native Resource Center in the school's library. Additionally, Sue would ask members of the community for information, participation, and cooperation in creating and disseminating language materials.

In the most optimistic of scenarios the entire community would be the collective cultural resource for Sue. Her constituency consists of the students taking Maliseet language class as well as their parents. Not only the language classroom but the reservation community as a whole is the immediate domain. Other sources that need to be recognized are the parents of those students whose children do not attend Mah-Sos School and adults who can potentially contribute to the language effort, such as elders, off-reserve band members, and interested non-natives. The domains from which Sue can draw Maliseet language material are multiple, cross-cultural, and situated both locally and more distantly. These domains are only available, however, in the most optimistic scenarios.

The daily practice of language transmission to the children of the community is Sue's by virtue of her position as Maliseet language teacher at the school. In addition to the responsibility of transmitting the language, many community members assume that she is also responsible for promoting and disseminating cultural information on any Native American community or practice in North America. For example, one day the principal told us that an elder was going to talk to us about the oral traditions—both Sue and I were excited about the prospect of an elder coming into the classroom to tell the traditional stories to the children. When the elder came to the classroom she immediately asked us for information on Maliseet oral traditions. When Sue told her we had expected her to share her stories, the elder offered no comment. Instead, she continued to suggest we collect stories for her because she was getting paid to collect stories. Sue, in a rather terse manner, told her that the only way she could do that would be under the assurance that the elders would participate in the Maliseet language class. Again, there was no comment. The elder never came back to collect her stories. Thus instead of drawing from the resource of elder's knowledge, Sue was expected to provide the elder cultural knowledge. Sue provided another example during a break between classes. She was telling me that "Mel" had recently shot and killed a black bear. Mel offered the carcass to Sue so that she could skin the bear and save the hide. If she could do so she could have the hide. Sue's remark to me was, "Hell! I don't know how to skin a bear! Just because I'm the native language teacher they expect me to know how to skin a bear?" The two examples illustrate the tacit expectations some community members have, not only of Sue but also of the Maliseet language class. I conclude that the optimistic scenario of "community as resource" is just that—optimistic.

Such surprises notwithstanding, Sue has made concerted efforts to draw members of the community into classroom activities. She would ask a number of community members to make various arts and crafts objects to decorate the classroom. From these objects she would explain to the children who made it and what significance the object had for Maliseet cultural awareness. For example, Sue has a number of baskets on one of the bookshelves. There are plain baskets as well as fancy baskets. She also has the raw materials for making baskets. From these items she could explain the process of making baskets, describe who the best basket makers on the reservation are, and show the class examples of their work. Additional props in the classroom included a medicine wheel, birch bark roses, birch bark canoe models, and model snowshoes.

One of the activities that incorporated extra-classroom assistance and time was the collection of sweetgrass. Next to *mahsosiol* (fiddlehead ferns), sweetgrass is one of contemporary Maliseet's most important cultural icons on the reservation. Today it is often collected, braided, dried, and then used for smudging. The sweetgrass activity would begin with the principal coming into the classroom to introduce sweetgrass to the children briefly. The presentation would be followed by a field trip, the principal taking the class into the field where this grass grows and showing the children how to identify sweetgrass among all the other grasses. He would then show the students how to pick the grass. After the picking is done it is time to return to the school. The following week the children are shown how to braid the sweetgrass. There is often a discussion accompanied by displays of how sweetgrass can be used to weave and be woven into baskets. The adults would let the braids dry so that they could be used for smudging. The children are not introduced to the smudging aspect, but most of them have witnessed the practice at one time or another.

These examples show how Sue was able to expand her reach to draw cultural information from community members into her domain—the Maliseet language classroom. Even though the daily practice does not replicate the most optimistic scenario, there continues to be great potential for expansive domains. Sue has recognized some of the potential and has taken advantage of it. Her domain is mostly defined by community boundaries, and the examples described show the kinds of interactions within those domains, but she does have potential constituency domains beyond the reservation.

### Dan

The auditorium was just like most university auditoriums. The seating was arranged in an amphitheater fashion. Spectators were finding their desired vantage points. I entered and surveyed the room. I noticed Robert Leavitt to the right and about midway down the rows of seating. I went over to say hello and sat in the chair next to Robert and another of his colleagues from the University of New Brunswick. Robert has been working with the Maliseet-Passamaquoddy language for many years and had been director of the Micmac-Maliseet Institute at UNB. He was attending the symposium for much the same reasons I was attending. We were both interested in the kinds of discussions that would be generated by the audience and Barb, the organizer of the event. Barb was the chair of Native Studies at St. Thomas University, and she and her university sponsored the event.

As Robert and I exchanged pleasantries, the rest of the participants found their seats and the session was about to open. Barb welcomed everyone and introduced the medicine man who would perform the opening prayer for the event. The medicine man approached the center of the stage. He was of average height, perhaps on the short side, and quite stocky. He had a haircut that resembled a Mohawk. He wore casual clothing adorned with "native" markers such as ribbons and beaded necklaces. He lit his pipe and allowed the tobacco to smolder. When the tobacco began to emit clouds of smoke he ceremoniously held the pipe aloft and gestured offerings to the four cardinal directions in accordance with his chanting of the opening prayer. To finish the offering he "smudged" himself with the smoke in an act of purification. Once he was purified he told the audience, "I love to do this. It's the only time I can smoke in a public building." His comment was met with laughter from a largely aboriginal audience. The symposium was officially under way.

Attending the symposium were many people from both Micmac and Maliseet communities who were interested in language issues and maintaining the aboriginal languages on their respective reservations. As the morning wore on I was able to observe who were Micmac and who were Maliseet among the audience. I also observed that the attendees at this symposium were well acquainted with one another. I would often write a note to Robert Leavitt inquiring about the identities of the respondents and inquisitors. He would politely scribble their names and affiliations. The exchange among participants made it clear that they have worked with one another in various other events or programs. For example, one young man who was attending the University of New Brunswick asked a question about the moral obligations of researchers when they conduct their research on the reservations. A man of about fifty raised his hand to respond. The moderator acknowledge him and he began to explain how he had approached the various reservations to conduct a study on native learning styles in elementary schools, middle schools, and high schools. He went on to talk about how his team had asked permission before conducting the study. I penned a note to Robert—"Who is he?" He penned back, "That's Dan. He works for the province." As Dan was finishing his explanation of ethics, a woman in the audience shouted out, "Where's our copy! We never got one!" Dan retorted, "That's because you guys quit the project." The woman responded, "We quit because you lied to us." At this point the whole room was buzzing with excited whispering. I asked Robert, "Where is she from?" Robert said, "St. Mary's Reserve."

That was my introduction to Dan. I wondered what could have caused such acrimony. Was St. Mary's Reserve part of his constituency? Dan defined his domain and constituency as the native children attending New Brunswick provincial schools. Unlike Tobique reserve, St. Mary's did not operate a reservation school. Their children went to provincial schools and therefore fell under Dan's authority. The particulars of the dispute at the symposium were never revealed to me so the enmity remains unexplained. Setting aside the altercation, the constituency parameters for Dan seem clearly defined, but a number of incidents prompt me to regard his self-described responsibilities as selectively restrictive. I do not mean to imply that these are not his responsibilities. Rather, if he chooses, he can expand his responsibilities, but he can also fall back to more restrictive parameters when the situation dictates a retreat. The evidence for my suspicions is detailed later.

Dan works and lives in Fredericton. He has an office in the suite of offices allocated to the Micmac-Maliseet Institute on the University of New Brunswick campus. I was puzzled by the location of his office and wondered if the institute was his employer. I was told that was not the case but that Dan was contracted to teach some classes for the university. If so, does he work for the province or the university when he teaches? When I am on the reservation and I ask for Dan's office phone number I always get the office number at the Micmac-Maliseet Institute. Whenever Dan calls a meeting it is usually held at the Micmac-Maliseet Institute. The meetings that Dan convenes vary among language issues. For example, I attended one meeting on language curriculum design and another that was geared toward oral traditions. I inquired about the difference between meetings and was informed that they were two separate projects. Thus I am left with the impression that Dan can expand his constituency if he so desires. When asked directly, however, he responded by stating that his responsibility was to provincial schools.[1]

The reason I characterize his duties as provincial is based on his response to the question I asked him: "How come you don't help the Maliseet language program on the reservation?" After I heard his reply about his constituency I asked a native studies teacher at the local high school if Dan had helped him with language teaching materials. His response was: "I don't get jack-shit from Dan. I gotta teach the language using my own resources." When I asked if he received anything he asked for from Dan, his response was: "I asked for a computer but I'm not going to get it. I did get an overhead projector from him and a couple of tapes." The key issue in the exchange was the Maliseet language curriculum materials. The curriculum project has been Dan's for several years, and the only production I have seen from more than seven years of effort was one alphabet book that nobody uses and a series of posters that speakers of Maliseet find difficult to read. The two projects were good ideas. The alphabet book incorporated local artists to illustrate basic Maliseet words for each letter. There was a parallel project in Micmac. The spelling of Maliseet words was often the source of some derision by other Maliseet speakers on the reservation. The unhappy result was the book is not used at all. The posters also employed a well-known Micmac artist. The illustrations were of good quality and quite striking. There was text at the top and bottom of each poster, one portion Micmac and the other Maliseet, both conveying the same message. As with the spelling in the alphabet books, the spelling of the Maliseet words used English phonetic equivalents. I observed Maliseet speakers at Mah-Sos School labor over reading the text, only to comment disdainfully that the writing was "too hard to read." I cannot comment on how the Micmac appreciated the parallel projects in Micmac because I was not in a position to observe their reactions. The examples illustrate how Dan's constituency is fluid but can be enlarged or constrained to suit his purpose.

### Barb

Barb was the catalyst behind organizing the symposium where I witnessed the challenge to Dan's pronouncement of ethical practice. She had lived on the Tobique reservation for a while but moved to Fredericton because of her new responsibilities to St. Thomas University. Over the course of my fieldwork, she proved to be generous with assistance and information. At the time I met her she had just taken on the responsibilities associated with being appointed the chair of Native Studies for St. Thomas University. In the subsequent years I have witnessed how her work practically consumed all her time. One of her first projects was the organization of the Symposium on Native Languages already mentioned.

The symposium, in retrospect, was very important for a number of reasons. The greatest benefit was the organizing of numerous presentations and committee meetings addressing the state of the Maliseet and Micmac languages, what should be done, and how to go about getting it done. The second important benefit was perhaps the key one for me. I was able to get a sense of the major players in language maintenance programs and projects. In attendance were representatives of many of the reservations, both Micmac and Maliseet. Also in attendance were non-native academics and officials concerned about the vitality of native languages in New Brunswick. Another important benefit, from my standpoint, was the opportunity to listen to the rhetoric from the various representative groups as they voiced their approval, disapproval, aspirations, and disappointments. During the two-day symposium I was able to ask Barb who certain individuals were and which communities they came from. As the symposium broke into groups according to interests and goals it was becoming clear that the collective audience was composed of smaller domains of interests. From her position as chair of Native Studies, Barb was able to bring together into a large room a dispersed aggregate of linguistic agencies so that they could see where their goals and programs overlap or diverge.

In contrast to those of the other two language maintenance agents, Barb's constituency is perhaps the most flexible and inclusive. Her immediate constituencies are the students attending the university. But as the preceding description indicates, the university sponsors outreach programs in an effort to highlight native issues in the Maritime Provinces. Through outreach programs the Native Studies chair can expand her constituent domains beyond the university campus and draw native communities into her domain. Programs that illustrate such expanded domains are the native language interest groups for Micmac and Maliseet, known as *Gig-na-moa-ne* and *Ga-kee-ma-neh*, respectively. These groups were established to promote native language programs in their respective communities. Another program that has proven to be influential in the Maliseet language classroom was providing Maliseet language immersion classes for "mature" students. This was an important gesture to invite elders from the reservation communities to participate in the classes. In effect, the hope was to draw the most fluent speakers of Micmac and Maliseet into the classes. After successfully completing the classes the participants could return to the reservations and start, participate, or plan language maintenance programs. Through these kinds of inclusive outreach programs Barb is able to access a larger constituency and by doing so has been able to contribute to the various language programs in New Brunswick.

One other area in which Barb has demonstrated the ability to expand her domains is through political outspokenness. She is often quoted or interviewed in the regional newspapers. Her areas of involvement are wide ranging but anchored in aboriginal political and cultural rights. Her academic training as a historian has not limited her work to history. Rather, it helped illuminate the areas history has chosen either to ignore or to engage reluctantly. Her other activities have larger political implications, but the most important activities for the purpose of this chapter are her work in native language maintenance.

### Constituent-Directed Ideology

I suggested earlier that context exerts some constraints on the kinds of activities the Maliseet language agents can engage by delimiting constituencies and the locale of the agents in relation to their constituencies. I have also observed that context plays a role in determining the ideologies that each agent can deploy in each of their domains. For example, Sue is teaching elementary school children and the goal is to have them learn to speak the Maliseet language. Politics has to wait. The elementary school classroom is not the setting for placing politics as one of the top items on the agenda. As for Dan's position, it is difficult to assess the political nature of his activities since I was able to observe the discourse of only a few meetings, some casual conversations, one interview, and his actions during the symposium. In all the instances when I observed Dan's actions and discourse I could not detect any politically suggestive rhetoric. Can it be that his position as a government employee precludes him from political action? Even his discussions of language loss were devoid of political implications. On the other hand, Barb has not been shy about asserting her views. Maliseet language loss is expressed in terms that implicate colonialist programs such as assimilation, boarding schools, and neo-colonialist agendas as the primary cause of native language death or, in her favored term, "linguicide." It seems her position at the university is amenable to political discourse and action. The position of chair of Native Studies may also elicit expectations of political action from native communities.

I have identified these three agents as the primary agents representing three different domains—community, government, and academia. I have also demonstrated that their context contributes to the kinds of activities possible to each agent. Operating within contextual constraints, the agents engage in varieties of language maintenance activities, but for the present discussion the activities that are of primary importance for Maliseet language survival are language maintenance strategies. I identify three separate strategies corresponding to the three agents and their domains. In addition, the strategies coincide with three different linguistic ideologies. One of the most interesting aspects of strategy, ideology, and context was the kinds of interactions that took place between the various agents and their respective domains. I found it ironic that the closest geographically situated domains are the government and academic domains, yet there is little interaction between the agents. Where I found the greatest overlap was between the community and academic domains. Upon consideration of that observation I recognized that ideological interaction between domains has greater value than geographic proximity. Ideologically shared domains are an important foundation for larger issues of language vitality and political self-determination.

### Institutional Ideologies

What do I mean by "institutional ideology?" To use the definition of ideology from chapter 1, I would tailor it to accommodate the ensuing discussion as follows: a system or cluster of norms or propositions that function to justify the actions or programs of the various Maliseet language maintenance agents. Practice, or action, is guided by norms or propositions, which in turn are contextually inflected. In the following paragraphs I present social/political values of language and transmission as reflected through the three different language maintenance programs, practices, and ideologies.

#### *Community: Mah-Sos School*

I present a more extensive discussion of the community ideology by discussing the Mah-Sos School program in chapter 5. For now, I highlight the pertinent points.

*Program*—Mah-Sos Elementary School native language class. Teaching the students to speak the Maliseet language is the first priority.

*Practice*—Chapter 5 describes in detail the means and methods to accomplish the task. However, as noted throughout this book, issues beyond language transmission have often crept into the classroom.

*Ideology*—Sue's ideology evolves as new methods are introduced, old methods fail, and new circumstances directly affecting the classroom arise. In the beginning, Sue used trial and error improvisation, but she became more directed in the next two years.

#### *Government: New Brunswick Department of Education*

*Program*—Provincial consultant on aboriginal education in New Brunswick. Promote successful aboriginal education policies and the advocacy of native language instruction in provincial schools.

*Practice*—Aside from the glimpse of Dan's practice at the symposium and various meetings, I did not have access to information concerning policies for educating native youth. But I have more information on his practice in language maintenance. It can best be described as very broad in its consideration of language maintenance paradigms but extremely limited in its programmatic applications. The intention was to disseminate Maliseet language-teaching materials to the provincial schools, but that had not happened by the time I left the field.

*Ideology*—My knowledge of the ideology behind Dan's practice is limited to Maliseet language transmission and consequently gives only a partial interpretation. If there was one dominating ideological paradigm that I can point to and say that it serves as a cohesive model for Dan's program, it would have to be what many native people refer to as the medicine wheel. At this point it should be noted that I am uncertain as to the direct connection between Dan's program and the medicine wheel, but it may be directly influenced by the recently introduced pan-Indian medicine wheel spiritualism and accompanying vision quests. The medicine wheel is one aspect of pan-Indian spiritualism that promotes what is assumed to be a "traditional" native worldview. The circle is the paradigm of choice and is a pervasive explanatory model. When I saw one of the drafts of the proposed Maliseet language curriculum that Dan and his team were working on I was impressed with the ingenuity with which the designers of the diagrams confined the universe into their model. The basic problem with the circular worldview is that it is actively celebrated only in the limited circles of Dan's cohort and some "traditionalists."[2] I was assured that the first draft of the curriculum was nearly complete and that I would receive a copy for review. I never received the copy and have yet to hear any more about it.

Another language ideology of which Dan was a proponent was the "language nest" practice made popular through successful implementation by the Maori (Fleras 1993). The "nests" on the Tobique reserve were held at Dan's own residence and circulated to others relatives' homes. It seems that the nests did not expand beyond the close family connection. One member reported to me that the family members could not agree on the way Maliseet should be spoken. Consensus seems elusive even in such closed collectives.

Finally, just as Sue adjusts her language ideology to suit pedagogical adjustments, Dan adjusted his ideas as he collected more methods and techniques from various programs and workshops he has visited. His language curriculum may codify an amalgamation of ideologies for language instruction in provincial schools.

### Academia: St. Thomas University Chair of Native Studies

*Program*—Chair of Native Studies, St. Thomas University. Barb's position as chair of Native Studies suggests that her position has a wide range of responsibilities, such as native student issues, course programming, administrative duties, and many others of which I may not be aware. Due to my limited contact with and observation of Barb's domain, I have to focus on the Maliseet language maintenance activities that I have been able to observe.

*Practice*—In the academic setting, coursework is one of the most time-consuming practices. Research is an aspect for which Barb has often lamented that she wishes she had more time. The administrative duties involved in managing native studies in the Maritime Provinces are also a time-consuming task. One of the areas in which Barb allocates much of her time is in native language maintenance. The promotion and establishment of language immersion training programs at St. Thomas University has proven to be a significant contributor to the activities at Mah-Sos School. It may be that the broad constituency addressed via the position of chair of Native Studies is influential in the expansive nature of Barb's domain.

*Ideology*—There is great consistency in the ideological orientation of Barb's approach toward native language maintenance. The dominating ideology is total immersion. The models Barb draws from are successful and they are also indigenous. The Mohawk language immersion model is the most emulated for practice and teacher training. The Maori model is used to bolster sociopolitical arguments. The most recent model to emulate has been the Hawaiian immersion program. All three emphasize immersion training as the primary means to linguistic maintenance. The dominant paradigm for Barb's program is language immersion.

As mentioned, Barb becomes politically involved with all current issues in aboriginal affairs. The benefit of her position as chair of Native Studies is based on the wide range of interests that this person must address. The drawback is the time-consuming aspect of the work.

Despite the workload, Barb has been able to organize an important series of language immersion training classes. It must be noted, however, that her ideology fluctuates, as do Dan's and Sue's. In particular, I mention the introduction of Hawaiian models and the incorporation of László Szabó's linguistic work on Maliseet.

**Agents (Subjects) and Interactivity (Intersubjectivity)**
Having established the three primary agents, their domains, and their ideologies, I focus now on the interactivity between agents and the implications such interactivity has. Briefly put, the interactivity between domains has the effect of multiplying not only the potential for action but also the potential action the agents can take. This is important for the prospects of language vitality.

While presenting a sketch of the agents and their domains I suggested that there was little interaction between the government and academic domains. This is not to suggest that these domains do not interact. Rather, when Dan and Barb are representing their specific domains they show little evidence of interaction. On the other hand, the interface between the community and academic domains shows great interaction. I would point out that through such interaction one domain does not subsume the other. It is more a case of distributing knowledge, ideology, and practice. The distribution of knowledge is not limited to "teacher teaching and student learning" unilaterality. Instead, I observed in the classrooms, meeting rooms, and auditoriums a feedback loop that helps the language agents learn what practice is effective and what adjustments should be made. Similarly, the interaction between the community and academic domains is based on feedback. One obvious example is ideology. If the community does not share the academic ideological propositions, then the nature of the interaction will either be less cooperative or will not occur at all. Dan's proposition that the provincial schools are the primary recipients of his services and support clearly shuts Mah-Sos School out of his constituent domain. This explains why there is little interaction between Dan and Sue in terms of Maliseet language maintenance. Yes, the posters and the alphabet book were present in the classroom, but those were exceptions. I did represent Mah-Sos School at a few meetings Dan held in Fredericton, but after those few meetings I was not informed of subsequent meetings. Mah-Sos School was left entirely out of Dan's program. Further, Dan's connection with the University of New Brunswick does put him in the academic domain but not in Barb's domain. At Dan's meetings I noticed that Barb was not present. Even though she was a five-minute walk away from where the meetings were held, she was not present. I do not know whether she was invited, but it was clear that Dan's domain and Barb's domain did not intersect on those occasions.

Why focus on interactions, or lack thereof, between domains? To reiterate the point made earlier, the interactions between domains distribute knowledge, practice, and ideology. In this way Barb's domain has had a direct influence on Maliseet language transmission in the community, whereas Dan's domain has had none. As a result, Barb's efforts can be seen as having benefited the community as well as the Maliseet language, whereas Dan's program has had little effect. The interactivity of domains at the local level has broader implications for interactivity at the macro level. The agents' willingness to interact with other domains is the means by which top-down practice is potentially fed back to the top. The linkages between domains provide opportunities for individual as well as collective action, which may have implications for language vitality and aboriginal identity politics.

In summary, the ideological differences I noted were linked directly to context and constituencies. Similarly, the practical orientation of the various programs also corresponded to the various program constituencies. The targeted constituencies of the various language maintenance agencies are the catalysts that shape the ideologies and practical applications of language maintenance. The constituencies may be the catalyst for action but it is the agents who deploy their respective language ideologies. The various language ideologies crosscut constituencies as well as authoritative domains. Agents' intentions oscillate between language and politics. On one hand, discussions about language can be devoid of political implications, and on the other hand, discussions of politics need not address language issues. Even so, Maliseet language agents reflect similar processes that many Native American communities engage when Native American language endangerment is conjoined with politics. However, conflicting language ideologies among language advocates on the reservation reveals the tensions between Maliseet language, Maliseet culture, and Maliseet identity as expressed by members of Tobique First Nation.

## 4. From Spoken Maliseet to Text

One day I watched students at Mah-Sos School come into their Maliseet language class carrying pencils because they had just come out of the French class. Sue asked why they had pencils, and they responded by saying that they were told they would need pencils "because they needed them for French. Sue replied that they did not need them for her class" (Perley fieldnotes, September 16, 1994).

Needing pencils for French class and their uselessness in Maliseet suggests more than just a literacy-orality dichotomy. French has been standardized, institutionalized, codified, and propagated through text for centuries. Maliseet, on the other hand, has occasionally been recorded but has not been standardized, institutionalized, codified or propagated to the degree French has. Of course there are major differences between the circumstances of the two languages, but their juxtaposition in the Maliseet classroom, in the community, as well as in Canadian national politics, is a source for continued reflections on empowerment and the disenfranchised, on colonists and the indigenous peoples, on language vitality and morbidity. I argue that those number two pencils symbolize all this and more. They also symbolize the gulf between Lévi-Strauss's (1966) "science of the abstract" and "science of the concrete" as well as Goody's (1977) differentiation between "domesticated minds" and "savage minds." The assumption that the students do not need pencils for Maliseet language is acquiescence to colonial hegemony and its concomitant depreciation of indigenous languages, cultures, and peoples. The unsettling consequence of such acquiescence is that it supports unquestioned cognitive essentializing from without as well as within. The perceived uselessness of pencils for Maliseet language instruction changes as oral-based Maliseet language instruction moves toward text-based instruction. Concurrent with classroom deliberations regarding Maliseet orthography was the variety of orthographic representations of the Maliseet language used by a variety of language advocates within the community. These orthographies reflected a variety of ideologies regarding language, literacy, and identity that would prove to be problematic for the Mah-Sos School language program.

**Problems with Orality Pedagogy**
Maliseet language instruction at Mah-Sos School was based on the teacher's philosophy that "Maliseet is an oral language and should be taught orally." The practice of teaching the language orally consisted of holding up a flashcard with an illustration of the anticipated vocabulary word. Sue and her assistants had created numerous sets of flashcards over the summer. The general headings for the cards can be described as animals, activities, plants, and numbers. Augmenting the flashcard teaching approach was a series of posters providing images and vocabulary for food and clothing. In addition to the cards and posters, they developed charts listing terms and illustrations for colors and weather conditions. These were the basic teaching materials when the Maliseet language class began. In each class period the teacher would flip from one card to the next, one poster to the next, and one chart to the next. The process produced a rhythm and cadence that gave the class instruction routine and expectation. The children knew what to expect and dutifully repeated each word or phrase after the teacher. After several weeks of the same routine it was apparent that teaching Maliseet could be deadly boring if flipping cards was all

there was to it. The students began to lose interest and their attentions waned. The novelty was wearing off for the teacher and the students. One attempt to change the tempo and routine was to ask the students to identify what words the illustrations were supposed to depict. It was through this kind of inquiry that the teacher realized that flipping cards and oral repetition were not enough of a practice to inscribe the vocabulary in the long-term memories of the students.

### Sounds Unfamiliar

When it became apparent that the students were not remembering the vocabulary and their attentiveness was waning, it was time to evaluate what causes might contribute to the students' lack of retention. One of the reasons considered was the suspicion that Maliseet sounds were foreign to the students. Most of the students' parents spoke only English, and the older students had already taken some classes in French. The students whose parents spoke Maliseet at home retained more of the vocabulary and often did a much better job of pronunciation than those whose parents did not speak Maliseet at home. During one exercise one frustrated student exclaimed that she could not "say that word." It was during this period of evaluation that Sue fully realized the extent of Maliseet's third language status. English is the first language on the reservation because it is the language children learn at home, while French is the second language on the reservation because of New Brunswick's official bilingual status, thereby making Maliseet the third language.

### Not Enough Time!

Unfamiliar sounds were one of two good reasons for the decreasing interest and performance by the students. The second reason is that the Maliseet class meets only twice a week; French classes are held three times a week for the lower grades and four times a week for the upper grades. To make matters worse, the second class-day in the Maliseet language class is dedicated to arts and crafts or native interest activities. The problem becomes clearer when the total time allotted for teaching and learning Maliseet is only forty to forty-five minutes a week. This is in contrast to meeting three to four times a week for French language instruction, further illustrating the tertiary status of the Maliseet language in the school as well as the community.

Twice-a-week meetings were clearly not enough to promote any kind of retention on the part of the students. In that first year of Maliseet language instruction, we were well into the fall semester, so it was too late to change the schedules to accommodate more Maliseet language class time. The other option that was implemented was to use the second class per week for language exercises instead of arts and crafts. It was not a popular decision from the perspective of the students. The compromise was to have an occasional arts and crafts project.

The second year began with a Mah-Sos School staff meeting the week before the classes started. At that meeting Sue made a forceful argument to increase the meeting times for Maliseet language to three times a week. Her argument included the fact that Mah-Sos was a native school and not a French school. Why should the students take more French than Maliseet language? One teacher quickly voiced her support for Sue's argument and promised to send her students to Maliseet language class three times a week. The teacher was one of the native teachers on staff. The other native teachers followed her lead. The non-native teachers did not raise any objections. Consequently, in the second year of native language classes at Mah-Sos School the meeting times were increased to three times a week.

Why should the students take more French than Maliseet? The principal answered the question by stating that the school had to keep up with the provincial guidelines so that once the students finished their coursework at Mah-Sos School they would not be at any disadvantage when transferring to off-reservation schools for middle school or high school. This programmatic consideration is sound and reasonable, but the problem it creates for Maliseet language class is that most of the hours in the week have been allocated to meet the provincial guidelines. To accommodate increased hours for Maliseet language instruction the school would either have to add hours to the day or compromise other subjects. The result was the squeezing in of one more class meeting per week per grade for Maliseet language. In the third year of Maliseet language instruction there was no increase in hours or meeting times.

### Orthographic Representations of Maliseet

The two reasons for the failure of passive language transmission—unfamiliar sounds and two forty-five-minute meetings a week—were key factors that prompted Sue to make a critical decision regarding not only Maliseet language pedagogy in Mah-Sos School but also the very nature of the language itself. This is where the symbolism of the number two pencil figures prominently. When she told the students that they would not need pencils for Maliseet language, she highlighted a glaring disparity between French and Maliseet. The Maliseet language had to gain linguistic respect as well as linguistic equality. My earlier observation that French required pencils while Maliseet did not was about to change. Sue decided to move to text-based teaching methods. I had witnessed that critical moment of linguistic domestication that Goody characterized as the domestication of the savage mind. But would domestication help bolster respect and equality for the Maliseet language and in turn enhance the prospects for language maintenance? Sue's move to text presented unanticipated challenges requiring flexible solutions over the following two years as the Maliseet language was objectified and codified by various members of the community.

### *Cognitive Shifts*

Moving from an orality-based method of teaching Maliseet to a text-based method presented a significant shift in perceiving the language. Although there were transcriptions of stories and descriptive linguistic analyses, they were largely the work of academics. These products would play an important role as the teacher made her pedagogical shift. As the shift took place there was also a shift in cognitive perception for both the teacher and the students.[1] The shift is best illustrated by what I term multiple objectifications. The language was being transformed into graphic representation. Words were no longer just a series of meaningful linkages of phonemes. Maliseet words were becoming meaningful graphic representations of concordant phonemes. The sounds were being objectified. The significance of this shift has great implications for developing a generation of literate Maliseet speakers. The following fieldnotes indicate that the shift was already taking place from the teacher's perspective and that the students would be responsive to the pedagogical change.

### It Starts with an M

*It's been a while since the last report. I'll begin with the story behind the title. Sue was reviewing the flashcards with the students and the image of a wolf was the next vocabulary word. There was silence in the room. Sue asked, "Doesn't anybody know this?" Still the room was silent. Finally Sue gave them a hint: "It starts with an m." One student replied emqansis! Sue finally had to tell them it was malsom. I have a couple of responses to this moment. First, I thought it was funny to hear the students mistake em for m. Sue was trying to get them to register the letter m as the hint, but the student registered the sound em as the hint. This points out the awkward position in which Sue finds herself as she tries to teach Maliseet as an oral/aural language while using the tools of text as aids in memory. This also goes back to the differences between English and Maliseet as literate versus oral traditions. In addition, it calls attention to some of the problems faced by Sue in teaching Maliseet. When and how will text be a beneficial aid in the effective teaching of Maliseet must be determined on a trial basis.*

*An additional observation, although not directly related to the story above, is related to the review sessions. When some of the cards were presented to the class there were some students who would raise their hands to volunteer to say the words. I take this as a very positive sign. The students are becoming more enthusiastic about learning the language and take pleasure at retention and participation. There was a comment that Sue made that suggested that the students* hesitated in speaking out in class for fear of standing out and become the object of teasing and/or ridicule. I have heard this argument before and I believe it to carry some weight but I also believe that some of the students are genuinely excited about learning the language. Today's fourth grade class seemed to have enjoyed the review and they were especially adept at reviewing the future-present-past exercises. When Sue introduced these exercises I heard one student ask, "Are we going to learn to make sentences?" I am encouraged by the degree to which some of them want to engage the language.

Another note from today's class: Sue had provided new color review cards. The difference was that the cards did not have any text. Sue had noticed that the students were trying to read the word rather than relying on their memories to remember the sound of the word. (Perley fieldnotes, October 26, 1994)

These notes were taken during the last few days of orality-based teaching. The final sentence regarding the students "trying to read" rather than relying on their memories indicates that the students were already thinking of the language learning in terms of text. The shift is probably more challenging for Sue because her experience with the Maliseet language had been primarily oral. The day she started producing teaching materials placed her face to face with objectification dilemmas. Because the students are freshly introduced to the Maliseet language and because they are learning to read and write French and English, learning to read and write Maliseet is less disorienting than it is for Sue.

How did classroom instruction change when Sue made the decision to use text as a teaching tool? Many of the exercises were the same but the text had become an important review exercise. The alphabet exercise was the same as before in the "repeat after me" practice. However, there was added weight given to the correct pronunciation of the graphic representations for Maliseet sounds. The graphic m was not equal to the phonetic em. The confusion described in my fieldnotes did not happen again.

The flashcards and the charts were now performing double duty.

The flashcards were now used to exercise vocabulary recall as well as providing reading exercises. For example, the flashcard with a drawing of a grasshopper has the word *cols* written on the obverse side of the card. When Sue holds up the card with the picture facing the class the students have to remember the word *cols*. If they cannot remember the word, Sue can flip the card and show them the word *cols*. At first there was confusion in the correct pronunciation of *c*. The children's experience with English and French prompted *c* as in *cat* or *c* as in *decision*. The correct phonetic expression is the English equivalent *j* (or *ch* if it occurs before a consonant). Thus the word *cols* should be pronounced "jols" rather than "chols," "kols," or "sols." This kind of confusion occurred most often with unfamiliar words. The familiar words did not produce such difficulties.

The vocabulary posters were also used for both exercises. When Sue pointed to the picture and the students could not remember the word, then she would point to the word underneath the picture. Usually, that was enough of a clue to help jog the student's memory. For difficult words Sue would wait for the student to "sound out" the word. For more difficult words she would remind the student, "Remember, in Maliseet the *c* sounds like a *j*."

The transition from oral to text was not a radical departure for the daily practice in the classroom, but there was a significant change in cognitive approach to teaching and learning the Maliseet language that was not obvious at first glance. Much of the foundation had been established for teaching Maliseet textually when Sue made her cards and charts by inscribing the Maliseet words on the obverse side. Initially the text was for her benefit as she held up the card to the students. She would know which card she was holding and could wait for the appropriate response. But the move to text allowed her to use both sides of the cards. The daily vocabulary exercises also became reading exercises. This cognitive shift would produce interesting results (discussed later) as the students became familiar with the Maliseet text.

## Orthographic Models

When I asked the principal about the previous attempts to teach the language at the school he said that there had been two previous attempts. One resulted in the teacher quitting because of the frustration of not having materials, coupled with the difficulties of producing materials. The other attempt did produce a number of booklets and materials, but that attempt also lapsed. From the first attempt there were no documents and from the second there were only a couple of vocabulary booklets. So when Sue began to produce her materials she did not have the benefit of the earlier attempts at creating a Maliseet language-teaching curriculum. Sue had to look elsewhere for her models for Maliseet orthography.

The reference used most often in the first and second year of the language program for spelling and lexical confirmation was the 1984 edition of *Kolusuwakonol: Philip LeSourd's Passamaquoddy-Maliseet and English Dictionary*. The 1984 edition of the dictionary was edited by Robert M. Leavitt of the Micmac-Maliseet Institute at the University of New Brunswick and David A. Francis of the Title IV-A Program of Pleasant Point, Perry, Maine. This edition was edited to be a "grammatical" dictionary in order to allow the user to construct Maliseet words from the entries and grammatical rules presented with each entry. The stated purpose for the expansion of the earlier dictionary was to serve as "a resource for elementary school teachers and children, and for speakers and students of the language" (Leavitt and Francis 1984:iii). In the summer of 1993 the dictionary fulfilled its stated purpose by being a valuable resource for Sue while she put the teaching materials together.

A second source of information was the MMI publication *Nihtawewest: I Know How to Speak*. The stated purpose for *Nihtawewest* was to bring "together ideas and approaches appropriate for teaching beginning speakers of Maliseet-Passamaquoddy" (Leavitt 1986:iv). The publication is celebrated as the cumulative effort of people representing diverse occupations such as curriculum developers, teachers, counselors, and directors of education programs. This diverse group collaborated on what is best described as "a curriculum of initial instruction in Maliseet-Passamaquoddy for children in elementary and secondary school programs" (v). Sue used some of the dialogues and exercises in the publication in the classroom. She did make modifications to the exercises where she felt changes needed to be made.

One reason for using *Nihtawewest* was the assertion that the guide "is an oral-language curriculum. All of the language lessons in this guide can be presented without the use of writing" (Leavitt 1986:xxv). As explained earlier, Sue followed the orality instruction paradigm but found that it did not adequately promote long-term retention of the material. She switched to text as a response to the lack of retention on the part of the students. The suggestions for text-based teaching in *Nihtawewest* state: "It is recommended that written Maliseet-Passamaquoddy be introduced only *after children already know how to say what they are expected to read or write* (Leavitt 1986:v, emphasis in original). The reason given for that strategy was to prevent the children from learning to speak Maliseet "haltingly" and to prevent them from "pronouncing the words poorly" (xxv). Sue decided that was a difficulty that can be overcome with practice and guidance. The most important point was that the children did retain the vocabulary and the phrases much better. One other point that was recommended by the guide was to start "actual literacy instruction . . . in grade 4 or later, by which time most children have a firm grasp of reading in English" (xxv). Sue decided she could not wait to use the children's English proficiency as the foundation for Maliseet literacy. She began introducing text and reading to them shortly after classes began.

Sue was always looking for opportunities to learn language teaching methods and she attended classes sponsored by St. Thomas University. She took a Maliseet phonology class from the linguist László Szabó. I remember Sue's comment about her first encounter with him. She had gone to Fredericton to participate in Maliseet language classes Szabó was conducting. Sue said that his accent when he spoke Maliseet was cute. "He couldn't pronounce the initial Ws so when he said *woliwon* it came out *voliwon*." Just the same, she was impressed with his knowledge of the language. Sue initially had reservations about his orthography but was later convinced that it reflected the language better than the system she had adopted during the previous two years.

### Problematic Orthographies

Several reactions led me to recognize that some orthographic models were deemed problematic. Where one model may be appropriate to one group, another may not accept it. The reasons given for such objections also reflect the linguistic ideologies of the agencies and their constituencies.

The first example comes from an incident that was prompted by the desire to have the children practice the alphabet at home. Sue had introduced the children to the alphabet and was trying to find a way to reinforce the correlation between signs and sounds. She had obtained a copy of the Passamaquoddy language package wherein was provided a set of cassette tapes and accompanying booklet. The booklet is not a workbook as much as it is a reference to be used as a guide to proper pronunciation of Passamaquoddy and Maliseet words. The booklet boasts the following:

*Because this writing system has been developed jointly by native speakers and linguists, it reflects with great accuracy not only the sounds of spoken Pass./Mal. but also the structure of words. It shows how sounds are related in different forms of the same word, and it shows historical and recent changes that have occurred in Pass./Mal.*

*This simple writing system has only a few rules for pronunciation of written words and for writing spoken words. There are 17 letters used in the writing system, five vowels and twelve consonants. Basically, each letter has only one sound. Seven of the letters may have their sounds modified in certain situations. Also, an apostrophe (') is used at the beginning of some words.*[2]

Following this the editors provide their Passamaquoddy and Maliseet alphabet.

ACEHIKLMNOPQSTUWY'

Their alphabet corresponds well with Sue's with two exceptions. Sue included the vowel/consonant pair *eh* with her alphabet (at first) but did not include the apostrophe. The similarities were close enough to use as a model for the children's pronunciation practice at home. Having accepted the model, Sue asked me to make copies of the pronunciation pages of the Passamaquoddy booklet for each of the students. The students took the copies home to ask their parents to help them with pronunciation exercises. A few days passed and one morning Sue came into the classroom and said, "I guess we won't use the Passamaquoddy stuff again." I asked her why and she responded that she had received negative feedback from parents, who threatened to pull their kids out of Maliseet language class if she did not quit teaching them Passamaquoddy. We were both surprised at the animosity toward the work and realized after the fact that we should have copied the text without the Passamaquoddy/Maliseet heading. It would probably have gone unnoticed.

A second example of objections toward models of orthography came from the orthographic transcription used by László Szabó. In 1981 Szabó published a Maliseet-German-English dictionary with a German publisher. He had also been recruited to teach the Maliseet phonology class as part of language immersion instruction at St. Thomas University. Sue had attended the first meeting and came from that meeting grumbling about the "apuckol *e*" (upside down *e*) or, in English, the schwa. Szabó was using the schwa where the Passamaquoddy used the *o*. Sue had to adjust to the use of the schwa and the graphic preference in Szabó's orthography. However, as she became familiar with Szabó's system her objections were ameliorated by her recognition of where the substitutions occur (and why they occur) as well as her mastery of the system. In this case, the objections eventually turned into advocacy of the system.

The disseminated products from the aboriginal education consultant,

Dan, illustrate a third example of problematic objectifications. Dan had given Mah-Sos School a series of three posters designed to encourage Maliseet and Micmac educators to promote aboriginal language and culture. One example of the text from the posters is:

*Skijinuwigisowewane knijanug.*
*Let's read to your children in our language.*

The orthographic example Dan used was explained as an attempt to use English equivalents with English letters since most people are used to those. Hence where Dan would spell the Maliseet word for "Indian" as *skijin*, Sue spells it *skicin*. The following is Sue's correction, from my notes:

*Let us read to our children in our own language.*
*Skicinowəkkiswehwahneh knicohnnuhwək.*

The reason for putting this example under the heading of problematic is largely based on the comments I heard when I witnessed a number of Maliseet-speaking teachers responding to the posters. While admiring the artwork on the posters, they were muttering that the Maliseet spelling was too hard to read. "That's not how I would spell it," was the common response. In time, Dan and his cohort would abandon that method of orthographic representation.

One last example of problematic orthographies comes from Bob, an elder member of the Tobique community. This example is intriguing because it represents a "vernacular" orthography. The preceding examples were developed with the assistance of trained professionals such as linguists or educators. On one hand it is not fair to characterize Bob's work as problematic because there may be some people on the reservation who are perfectly happy with his orthographic representations. On the other hand, however, characterizing his work as problematic comes from an incident requiring a public statement from Mah-Sos School to clarify the distinction between his orthography and that practiced by the Mah-Sos School language program.

Bob has worked on developing Maliseet language and cultural materials for many years. Through those years various versions of his word lists appear in equally various informal print venues (newsletters, photocopies, pamphlets). The incident that brings him into this discussion occurred in January of 1995 when the community health newsletter *Kikahan* printed his lists of words and phrases. Sue and I did not think this was a problem until some parents approached Sue to complain about the way she spelled some Maliseet words. The confusion was generated by the fact that Sue and I had prepared review materials for the children and their parents, which we had published in the newsletter earlier, in 1994. When we began to include our own exercises we made a note explaining the orthography we used:

*The following is a guide to the alphabet used in the Maliseet Language class at Mah-Sos School. There are many problems associated with transcribing a primarily oral language into written form and there is no consensus for transcribing Maliseet. However, most teachers and institutions teaching the Maliseet language have used the following method. We offer this guide to interested members of the community and especially to those parents who want to help their children with their Maliseet Language assignments.* (Kikahan, March 29, 1996)

When Bob's work was printed, it was confused with the Mah-Sos School language program. We found it necessary to print the following cautionary note: "Please Note: To avoid confusion in the future, any material published in *Kikahan* or any other publication related to Maliseet Language that comes from our program at Mah-Sos School will have either our school logo or the Maliseet Language Program title on it (as shown above)" (Kikahan, January 16, 1997).

The difficulties arose when the school program was confused with Bob's transcriptions. As an example, the school would spell the number one in Maliseet as *neqt*. Bob offered *nequet* as his orthographic method (Kikahan, January 9, 1997). Included in the newsletters were some word-search puzzles for the children. The words were Maliseet and their orthography coincided with ours. One of the puzzles also spelled the Maliseet word for one as *neqt* (Kikahan, March 19, 1996). One other instance of the difficulties that came from the simultaneous printing of Maliseet exercises involved standard greeting dialogues. The standard dialogue for greeting begins with "How are you?" The response would be "Fine. And how are you?" In the Maliseet language class the transcription is:

*Tan kahk?*
*Mec ote pesqon. Tan kahk na kil?*

Bob's orthography for the same dialogue is as follows:

*Don a gock alo gil*
*Medge ata, gil lo?* (Kikahan, January 16, 1997)

As this comparison indicates, the system used by Bob suggests an English word/sound equivalent spelling method, as exemplified by the word "medge"; it is supposed to sound like the English words *hedge* or *ledge*. "Gock" should sound like *lock* or *dock*. But why not use the English word *gawk*? The third example is the use of "Don," which could be substituted with *dawn*. As mentioned earlier, Dan also attempted this method.

Spelling is only half of the problem. The other half of the problem is the extra phonemes and phonemic misrepresentation. For example, the extra phoneme "a" between "Don" and "gock" does not appear in the Mah-Sos School version (nor the MMI version). The phonemic misrepresentation in the preceding example occurs in Bob's "ata." Sue and MMI transcribe the word as "ote," clearly indicating a difference between the first and second vowels. Bob made no distinction. This is not to suggest that Bob was wrong and may reflect Tobique-specific idiolects. Rather, it highlights the confusion that multiple orthographies posed for the parents who were sending their children to the Mah-Sos School program. Furthermore, it reveals not only dialectical differences between Passamaquoddy and Maliseet but also the complicating aspect of Maliseet idiolects within the Tobique community.

In summary, the examples of Bob's transcriptions have proven to be problematic because they conflict with the Maliseet language program at Mah-Sos School. However, Bob's work may be viewed by some members of the Tobique community as useful because of the lack of orthographic consensus. He has found this system to suit his purposes, and perhaps there are members of the community who find his orthography easier and more intuitive than the system used by Sue. Even though his orthography may seem problematic, there is another aspect of his work that may prove to be vital; namely, the simple fact that he has worked to preserve his knowledge of the language as well as the social and cultural history of Tobique First Nation.

The variety of orthographic representations is one of the key difficulties in establishing a communitywide language program. Not only are the orthographies in competition, but the orthographies themselves are inconsistent. Without a single authoritative institution (be it chief and council or a language curriculum committee) to designate a single orthographic system as the standard, the competition between systems will continue to undermine language immersion efforts. Agreement on a single system will require the community to see and hear beyond the differences in dialects and idiolects, and it will require a willingness to learn a standard system. In the recent Leavitt and Francis Passamaquoddy-Maliseet dictionary (2008) the editors proclaim that there is a standardized orthography and it is the result of collaborative work between linguists and Passamaquoddy and Maliseet speakers since Teeter's work in the 1960s. The Micmac-Maliseet Institute at the University of New Brunswick adopted the system as the standard, but it has yet to become the standard at Tobique. Today more students are learning the system through Maliseet language classes at the University of New Brunswick. Perhaps those pencils will be important for Maliseet language class after all.

## 5. Elementary Language Curriculum and Practice

Mah-Sos School was the elementary school on the reservation when I started my research. The school provided instruction to kindergarten students as well as students in grades one through six. During the years of field research, the school was located at the heart of the village next to the medical clinic and fire hall, adjacent to the ballpark, not far from the Catholic Church, and across the street from some small-scale commercial ventures such as grocery stores, craft shops, and sandwich businesses.

The name is symbolic in that *mahsos* (plural *mahsosiol*) is the Maliseet word for "young ferns." Before the ferns blossom into broad leafy plants their leaves are coiled into the shape of a fiddlehead, hence the English name fiddlehead. Mahsosiol is symbolically important because many members of the community regard them as one of the traditional foods that go back to "time immemorial."[1] Mahsosiol are seen as having sustained the Maliseet people for eons, and the school is seen as providing a similar sustenance for the present as well as future generations of Maliseet children attending the school.

In addition to this being the name for the school, the school's floor plan takes the shape of the mahsos. The entrance is at the stem of the mahsos. As you walk through the administrative area you can literally wind your way through to the classroom area. The core of the spiral, at the central space of the school, is the library. It serves as the center point for the surrounding classrooms. The library lost some of its space to accommodate a computer lab. At the opposite end of the school, at the base of the stem, the gymnasium/auditorium anchors the school. Just inside the entry, on the floor, is a terrazzo fiddlehead design welcoming all who enter the school. The mahsos and the architecture successfully merge to convey the importance of the school for recognizing the Maliseet cultural past while anchoring contemporary and future goals in traditional symbolism.[2]

**Language Practice**
The practice of teaching the Maliseet language to the students of Mah-Sos School is a process that changes as expertise, confidence, and new materials are introduced or obtained. The structure accommodating change is the daily routine of the classroom. A detailed description of the daily routine of language instruction in the Maliseet classroom, coupled with observations and remarks, will serve as the ground from which subsequent discussions on teaching adjustments, content variations, orthographic dilemmas, orality/literacy decisions, identity politics, and competitive agency are drawn.

Maliseet language instruction is offered from kindergarten through grade six. The classes meet three times a week for forty to forty-five minutes each session (kindergarten meets only once a week for fifteen minutes). This is a substantial increase from the first year of instruction, when Maliseet language was taught only twice a week. The difficulty in language instruction during the first year was exacerbated by the fact that one of the two days of class time was devoted to arts and crafts. The increased instruction in Maliseet was a direct result of the efforts of Sue, the Maliseet language teacher, when she pointed out that a reservation school allocates more time to teaching French than it does to teaching the native language. The increase in native language instruction class meetings did not address the disparity of time devoted to language instruction between French and Maliseet, especially in the upper grades (five, six). French language instruction occurs four times a week compared to Maliseet instruction at only three times a week. The reason given for such disparity is linked to issues of economic expedience and declining prestige for the Maliseet language.

### The Maliseet Language Classroom

Sue has the good fortune to have her own classroom. The students must come from their homerooms to attend the Maliseet language class. In contrast, the French teacher must cart her teaching materials to the students' classrooms. The classroom is trapezoidal in plan. The base of the trapezoid is the outside wall, which is punctuated with four large windows. The door and adjacent window are located on the opposite wall. The main walls contain the blackboard on one wall and open wall space on the other. The ceiling is vaulted from the low point at the outside wall upward to the skylights at the library located in the center of the teaching wing of the school.

The decor of the classroom consists of mostly native arts and crafts. Maliseet ash baskets, some Micmac ash flowers, handmade snowshoes, various small carved pieces such as masks, dioramas, pipes, and miniature birch bark canoes are distributed about the room. Additional items hanging on the walls or sitting on counters are a number of color copies of popular genre portraits of native children, a medicine wheel, native artwork salvaged from an old calendar, and, resting in various locations of prominence in the room at various times of the year, a painted ceramic bust of a warrior.

The desks are arranged in a large rectangle approximating a square as closely as possible. I suspect the ideal arrangement would have been a circle but rectangular desks exert a ninety-degree design constraint for arrangement. Sue's desk is off to the side in front of the file cabinet. Against the open wall are the file cabinet, a couple of bookshelves, storage bins, and my area, which consists of a chair and the surface of the bookshelf and storage bin. Some craft objects sit on the shelves against the window wall.

## Curriculum and Practice

The following is a recreation of the atmosphere in which the students are receiving language instruction. I provide a running commentary to indicate the amount of work involved in teaching language to the various grades. Occasionally an event or something said in class elicits some thoughts about "process" that I scribble down labeled as "observation" in my fieldnotes. Those observations are the primary sources for my commentary.

Typically, I arrive at the school just before the first class starts. I set my backpack down, take off my coat, and sit in my chair at the periphery of the classroom. I take my notebook out of my backpack and arrange my makeshift desk to anticipate the day's activities. Sometimes Sue and I exchange small talk before the students arrive. The students enter the room in single file from their homerooms. About ten feet into the classroom they break file and scramble to their favorite desks, always subject to change. After some noisy pushing and rattling of desks and chairs the room becomes quiet again as Sue goes to the front of the class.

### *Maliseet Language Practice*

In this section I present an account of daily language instruction at Mah-Sos school because it is critical for illustrating how language maintenance at this local level draws on resources from outside and how those resources were adapted for elementary classroom instruction. The following discussion also identifies how macro-level language policy and ideology are reproduced, rejected, or reformed as the classroom situation dictates. In the interest of full disclosure of my ideological perspectives and ethnographic accuracy, in the following discussion I use and thereby privilege the orthography and spelling practiced in the classroom despite inconsistencies and inaccuracies (as may be perceived by other Maliseet-Passamaquoddy specialists and advocates).

## GRADE THREE CLASS ROUTINE—NOVEMBER 4, 1996

There are six children in grade three, four boys and two girls. Sue writes the numbers from one to twenty in the upper left corner of the chalkboard.

"We'll do the numbers three times. *Neqt, nis, nihi, new, nan, kamacin.* Am I getting deaf? I don't hear anyone." To which the children repeat along with her but a little louder. "*Olowikonok, okomulcin, esqinatek, qotinsk. Qotankok, nisankok, sankok, newonkok, nanokok, kamacin kas onkok, olowikonok kas onkok, okomulcin kas onkok, eqonotek kas onkok, nisinsk. Opc* (again). *Neqt, nis . . ."*

Sometimes Sue would call on the children one at a time to recite the numbers for her until all had successfully recited them from one to twenty.

Following the numbers Sue moves to a flipchart and turns the pages to diagrammatic drawings of weather conditions. The top of the chart reads *Tan olokiskot?* (How's the weather?)

"Next we'll do the weather. Ready?" Sue points to the chart title. "Can anybody read this?"

Sometimes one of the more intrepid students would attempt to read the title and sometimes the child would "read" it correctly. Sue proceeds to point to each of the other Maliseet words and the children would identify the weather conditions in unison. There are only six to remember: *kamiwon* (rainy), *kisuhswiw* (sunny), *psan* (snowing), *alukot* (cloudy), *wocowson* (windy), and *tkeyu* (cold). The next part of the exercise is to cover either the illustration or the text and then ask individual students to identify the weather condition, again until all had responded correctly.

A turn of the page on the flipchart shows a similar chart. This chart has *Tan olocite?* (What color is it?) across the top in large bold letters. The color chart has the text to the left and a small swatch of color to the right. The colors are *pqeyu* (red), *wisaweyu* (yellow), *mokosoweyu* (black), *staqoncite* (green, or literally "the color of fir trees"), *musqoncite* (blue, or literally "the color of the sky"), *tupqoncite* (brown, or the color of dirt), and *wapeyu* (white). Sue points to the heading and then points to the words while the children dutifully repeat in unison the words presented before them. After going down the chart Sue then randomly selects one word and awaits a response before going on to another color. This part of the exercise is more difficult for some students than it is for others. As reinforcement Sue asks individual students to come up and point to the color she asks for in Maliseet. For example,

"Robert. Can you show me wisaweyu?"

Robert goes to the chart and points to the color he thinks is wisaweyu. For the most part the children do well until Sue asks,

"Can you show me mokosoweyu?"

The difficulty increases because there are two colors that begin with the letter m and they are about the same length. This requires the student to read the words carefully before selecting one. The key point here is that the students are reading the Maliseet text.

It is time to move on to *micuwakon* (food). On a large piece of poster board Sue or one of her assistants from the preparatory summer of 1993 had cut out some images of different foods from magazines like *Better Housekeeping*, *Ladies Home Journal*, and *Woman's Day*. The top of the poster is titled *Micuwakon*. The illustrations have the Maliseet words written under them. Sue points to the food illustration and the children respond. The items selected as a vocabulary exercise are not noteworthy until more advanced exercises are developed in the higher grades. For the third grade class building their vocabulary is a more important exercise.

Once the micuwakon exercise is completed Sue goes to the board, and if she has not done so she writes the following dialogue on the board (not including the English).

| | | | |
|---|---|---|---|
| 1 | | Tan kahk? | How are you? |
| 2 | | Mec ote pesqon. | Still the same. |
| 2 | | Tan kahk na kil? | And how are you? |
| 1 | | Nil na mec. | I'm fine, too. |

| | | | |
|---|---|---|---|
| 1 | Kekw toliwis? | What's your name? |
| 2 | Nil toliwis \_\_\_\_\_. | My name is \_\_\_\_\_. |
| 1 | Tama k'tuceow? | Where are you from? |
| 2 | Neqotkuk. | Tobique. |

The numbers correspond to speaker number one and speaker number two of the dialogue. Sue first asks everyone to read and repeat the dialogue in unison. When she feels the students are responsive enough she selects students to be speakers one and two. The two students must then engage in the dialogue as written on the board. The selected students then exchange speaking roles. Speaker one becomes speaker two and vice versa. This continues until the whole class has had practice with the dialogue.

When the dialogue exercise is finished, class instruction shifts to more interactive projects initiated in a previous class period. With the children's previous class work in hand, I distribute the next exercise along with their earlier work from the previous session. In this particular case the children are working on a book titled *Ehem* (the chicken). They are working on pages illustrating *etutluket ehem* (the chicken is working) and the *eksku ehem* (the chicken is sneezing). Sue writes the Maliseet text on the board, and the students copy the text onto the bottom of the photocopies illustrating the chicken working and sneezing. When the writing is done the children color the illustrations.

By now the class is running out of time and there is one last exercise to do. Sue gathers her animal flashcards and flips from one card to the next. The children identify the animals depicted on the flashcards. This exercise is repeated three times or as time permits. The animals selected are readily recognizable; bear, wolf, beaver, deer, porcupine, eagle, caribou, skunk, fox, and pig. At first the children could not remember the word for the illustration of the beaver, not because they did not know the word but because they did not recognize the beaver from the illustration provided. (In all honesty, I could see how the children could mistake the beaver for a pig—the drawing was that bad.

However, they have become accustomed to the ambiguous illustration and now the memory lapse does not occur much anymore.)

Children are lining up outside the door. It is time for the fourth grade to come in. Sue says, "Okay. Line up! *Apqoteh khakon* (open the door). *Opc oc* (see you again)." The third graders line up at the door and file out much as they filed in.

### GRADE FOUR CLASS ROUTINE—NOVEMBER 4, 1996

As soon as all the third graders have exited the room the fourth graders file in. Like the third graders, the students rush to their favorite desks; again like the third graders, the fourth graders' favorite desks often change). Sue approaches the front of the class and says: "We're going to do the alphabet three times." She points to the large block letters strung above the blackboard. "Ah, ah, ah."

All the students chant the alphabet chant along with her. "Juh, juh, juh. Eh, eh, eh . . . Yah, yah, yah. *Opc* (again). Ah, ah, ah . . ." Finally the class completes the repetition of the alphabet chant a third time. Every once in a while one of the students looks at his fellow students with wide eyes and intentionally exaggerates the vocalization of the letter t by saying "duh! duh! duh!"—causing the others to snicker. Today there was no such playing around.

Sue instructs the class: "Open up your scribblers to the last letter we did."

The fourth grade class has been working on a dictionary for several weeks and each letter has a minimum of four entries. It is hoped that the dictionaries will grow as new words are learned. The letters for today are t, u, w, and y. The words are collected from dialogues, stories, and exercises the students have done since the beginning of the school term. Part of the intent of the dictionary exercise is not only to have a reference but to give the children practice in writing Maliseet words and have them become used to seeing Maliseet in text. In addition, the exercise reinforces their reading ability by giving closer attention to spelling and phonetics. (One drawback I observed is the lack of

English translation. Most of the words were familiar to the children but there were some words with which the children were not familiar.)

"Okay, put your books away. We're going to do the prayer."

Sue distributes photocopies of a document titled "Nolosweltom." She finds a vacant desk, sits down, and begins reading:

Nolosweltom

*Numiqosiyin cuwitpt, nolosweltom eli pomawsi.*
*Woliwon skitkamik ci psi te kekw.*
*Woliwon samakwon psi tec wen kissossmu.*

This translates loosely as:

I Give Thanks

*I give thanks for my life.*
*Thank you earth for everything.*
*Thank you water for providing everyone water to drink.*

Rather than provide a linguistic analysis or grammatical breakdown, I draw attention to the importance of the receptivity of the children to such an extended Maliseet text. When they were first presented with the text their comments were: "Wow! We'll never learn all this!" However, when Sue pointed out that they knew most of the vocabulary words, the students were willing to try. In the course of a few weeks their reading of the text became quite competent. After Sue and the students had completed the entire text together, Sue asked one of the students to read the first line. Upon completion of the first line, the second line would go to the next student, and so on around the room.

One day one of the students counted ahead and realized that she could not read the anticipated line, so she traded places with her neighbor, thereby hoping to avoid the difficult line. Even though Sue was looking down at the text she saw the exchange at the periphery of her vision. When the exercise reached the two girls who had changed places, Sue skipped the first student and asked the second student to read the line she was originally supposed to read. The student had to read the line she had tried to avoid. She did indeed have difficulty reading that particular line of prayer. Despite the difficulty, the lesson learned was twofold: pay attention while reading the text and do not trade places with a neighbor to avoid the sentences that are not familiar. She never tried trading places again.

When the last line had been read Sue gathered the photocopies of the prayer and put them away. She went to the front of the room and pointed to the row of letters above the blackboard and began to review the alphabet for the students. The exercise was virtually the same as that given to the third grade class.

Next on the agenda was the reading of the "Toqaqwiw" story, a story the students had composed themselves. Sue would give them the subject Toqaqwiw and the students would have to answer the five Ws—who, what, when, where, and why. Then the students had to provide three details and finally a one-sentence conclusion. The fourth grade class came up with the following:

| Toqaqwiw | "in the fall" |
|---|---|
| who | native people |
| what | hunting and gathering food |
| where | the Tobique reservation |
| when | in the fall |
| why | to get ready for winter |

Next they had to provide details.

1. In the fall the leaves blow off the trees.
2. It gets cold and the days become shorter.
3. The animals prepare their places of hibernation.

Finally, the children provided the conclusion to the story. Everyone is ready for the winter. The completed story in Maliseet is as follows:

*Toqaqwiw*

Skicinuwok kotunkahtuwok naka maqenikahtuwok, Neqotkuk, toqaqwiw, ciw puniw.

*Toqaqwiw yaq monolamsonuwol mipiyil. Maceh tkeyu naka cilkokiskot.*
*Weyossissok na tolituniya toponuwol.*
*Psi tec wen kisahcu ciw puniw.*

The children were very proud of their story and even more proud that they could read such long words. An additional component to this story was the illustration project. They had to produce four drawings; one for the title page, one for the five Ws, one for the details, and one for the conclusion. When the drawings were done I took the students to the computer and helped them scan the illustrations into a graphics program, which allowed them to incorporate text into their drawings. Finally, we printed small four-page booklets.

As the booklets rolled off the press the students were delighted with their projects. To encourage them even more, Sue and I told them that they were producing Maliseet books when nobody else in the world was doing it. While, strictly speaking, this was not true, it had the positive effect of making the students very proud of their work.

Time was getting short and Sue wanted to review the "Tan Kahk" dialogue. The dialogue is identical to the third grade dialogue except that the last exchange asks what the respondent's mother's name is.

*Kewk liwisu kikuwoss?*
*Liwisu_____.*

Again the dialogue went around the room until everyone had a chance to practice both parts.

### GRADE TWO CLASS ROUTINE—NOVEMBER 4, 1996

Grade two is one of the larger classes when all students are present. On the day of these notes eleven students were present, seven of whom were boys. The second grade curriculum and instruction are similar to those for the third grade. For the following discussion I focus on the differences between activities.

Some differences worthy of note are the review of verb flashcards; use of the same animal flashcards but with emphasis placed on the plural forms of the nouns; and the first four pages of the *Ehem* book. First, the students review the verb cards. Sue has a set of cards illustrated with stick figures engaged in some kind of action or activity (not all very active: *lossin kohutik* means "lying in bed"). Second, plural forms of animal names are not written on the cards but are presented orally. The importance of this exercise is to get the students to recognize the pattern for plural forms for nouns. Third, the first four pages of the *Ehem* book are translated as the following: page one—chicken or hen, page two—a small chicken, page three—a large chicken, and page four—the chicken is moving in. There are two important reasons for the differences between classes: each class works at a different pace, and variations in class instruction help alleviate boredom for Sue.

Grade two shuffling out of the classroom indicates that the native language classes are over for the day. Typically, Sue and I debrief some of the events in the classroom that transpired during the day. Considerations of what should be done next or how well current practices are being absorbed are most often the focus. Additional topics of discussion drift into community news or news about other Maliseet endeavors in language preservation. Sometimes there are special projects requiring attention from one or both of us. By three-thirty it is time to go home, the day's teaching being done.

**Summary**

The key points that need to be emphasized are (1) higher grades engage more complex language exercises that focus on grammar, vocabulary, pronunciation, and reading; (2) lower grades focus on the rudiments of Maliseet language, such as sounds, single words or short phrases, the alphabet, and many coloring activities; (3) variations exist between programmatic projects in each grade (for example, grade one does not do the *Ehem* exercise whereas grades two and three do; grades five and six have the same "Toqaqwiw" exercise but created their own stories, which in turn created different vocabulary lists; (4) differing personalities of the classes prompted adjustments in the pacing of the presentation of material as well as in Sue's expectations.

In each of the classes Sue made adjustments from time to time based on the feedback from student performance or parents' and grandparents' comments. I too would offer comments on occasion. Regarding point (1), the experience with French and English enabled students in higher grades to work with more complex material. On point (2), teaching required adjustment as the first grade class was still being "socialized" into the school setting. The second and third grades had already been socialized and therefore knew what to expect in class. They also knew what was expected from them. The first grade students were still learning about the rules and expectations of the system. Their projects remained more rudimentary than those of grades two and three until they became habituated in the classroom setting. The third point addresses the variations between projects. As mentioned, the Toqaqwiw story, although the same exercise, differed in vocabulary but also in the subsequent vocabulary and illustration exercises.

By way of illustrating the fourth point, I remember one student who skipped class in grade three. That student's performance in Maliseet language class was exemplary. He outdistanced his peers by a wide margin. The dilemma Sue faced was between tailoring class instruction for the majority and running the risk of boring the exceptional student, or trying to push the class along to accommodate the student's language-learning capability. The decision went in favor of the majority. Sue was disappointed to have had to make that decision, but the other students would not have been able to keep up with the accelerated pace. In each of these examples Sue worked from her assessment of the attentiveness of the class, individual performance, and sometimes feedback from parents and grandparents (she received input from them only rarely).

There were some pedagogical practices that were used, suspended, and sometimes used again. The decision-making process for those practices was also based on feedback. For example, the use of flashcards to review vocabulary was often suspended for a while then reintroduced at a later time. In these cases the children either learned the vocabulary quickly and thereby did not need the drilling, or the students would make little effort in remembering the vocabulary, and on occasion Sue decided to change the pace to maintain some variation in pace and instruction. At one point we introduced personal flashcards that the students made themselves to try to provide more contexts for the vocabulary exercises. The idea was not only to provide additional contexts but also to allow the students to take the cards home to practice their vocabulary. Great idea! However, within a week we discovered that the project was unsustainable. The students would make the cards in class and lose them the same day. That great idea was suspended. Another great idea was to have the children make their own dictionaries. It was already a part of the daily class routine. At one point I suggested that we utilize the computers in the school to make the students' dictionaries on the computer and save them on diskettes. The exercise would fulfill the vocabulary and spelling requirement, but it also had the added advantage of familiarizing the students with making documents on the computer, saving the documents to their diskettes, and expanding their dictionaries as new words were introduced to them. The greatest problem with the diskette dictionaries was the competition for use of the computers. Although there were plenty of computers to choose from, the computers were used primarily as game platforms. While the Maliseet language students were working on their dictionaries they were constantly distracted by students from other classes playing games (in addition to their constant switching from terminal to terminal). It was obvious that the potential for that exercise would not be fulfilled, and that plan was therefore discontinued.

In short, each idea to enhance the potential for reinforcement was considered, practiced, evaluated, and then either continued as part of everyday practice or suspended; some were suspended until a later time when the situation would be more conducive for success, and other practices were completely discontinued. All the examples given reflect the kinds of adjustments Sue had made in the first two years of teaching Maliseet language. As noted earlier, Sue was working without the benefit of formal training in teaching language or putting together materials for language teaching, yet she managed to assemble a complex program that acknowledges the varying needs of each grade and the personalities of the classes. Perhaps the most significant aspect to her efforts was the decision to move from oral pedagogy to textual pedagogy. Most important, she accomplished all this largely through her own efforts and resourcefulness (see Perley 2006).

### Key Pedagogical Maliseet Language Projects

Summarized in this section are some of the key pedagogical projects already mentioned that seemed to present the greatest opportunities for the students to learn the language and maintain their knowledge.

#### *Interactive Projects*

It was recognized early in the first year of language classes that passive learning was not going to be an effective means of language transmission.[3] One solution to this was to create projects that were more interactive; projects that made the students engage the spoken and written aspects of the language in multiple and meaningful ways. Some projects were art oriented. Others were oral tradition oriented. Some others were natural science oriented.

An excellent example of an art-oriented activity is a leaf collage project. The idea came from one of the craft books Sue often used. The project entailed the collection of many leaves of different shapes, sizes, and colors. Once the gathering was done, all the students were to decide what they would create with various combinations of leaves. The objects were usually chosen based upon the possibilities the leaves suggested. One restriction was to pick something that allowed students to illustrate a Maliseet word. For example, a student can choose to collage the leaves into a form approximating *mokalip* (caribou). The students enjoyed going outside in the early morning and picking leaves, especially in the autumn, and then coming back inside to start their projects.

Another interactive project that stands out among the rest was a story describing the life cycle of salmon. The sixth grade class had taken a field trip to a salmon hatchery and brought back some eggs to put into an aquarium where they could watch them hatch and then watch them grow. During their science class they were getting all that information in English. Sue thought it would be great to do the same project in Maliseet. She had obtained a version of a story titled "Blum" (salmon) that was created and illustrated by Christine Saulis, a Maliseet language teacher at South Devon Middle School in Fredericton.[4] After making minor modifications to the story (in terms of some vocabulary and spelling conventions), Sue gave me the story so that I could enter the information into a computer program. I was then able to produce master copies of each page that allowed the students to practice spelling the text and that also provided space to create their own illustrations. It turned out to be a valuable exercise in illustrating the potential for Maliseet language exercises that went beyond arts and crafts as well as beyond the Maliseet language classroom walls.

These two preceding examples were important contributions to teaching and learning the language, but the examples to follow were the foundation of the interactive approaches toward teaching the Maliseet language to the Mah-Sos Elementary School children.

*Nolosweltom*

One of the recurring exercises is what I describe as the prayer, a collaborative project titled "Nolosweltom." A number of aspects of the exercise were designed to reinforce the Maliseet language in the minds of the children. It is difficult to assess which of the factors are most important because they are so closely tied together. The one common denominator in all the practices was that all the students (except grade one) had to read the prayer. A second common denominator was the inculcation of the prayer's message. It is a prayer of thanksgiving and respect for the earth. It was hoped that the thanksgiving message would be clear enough that it would not need explanation.

There are some noteworthy differences between grade levels. Grade six was engaged in a long-running project of illustrating each line of the prayer. The anticipated benefit was to produce an illustrated version of the prayer that would be personalized according to the students' appreciation of what each line of the prayer meant individually. In contrast with the lower grades, grades four, five, and six would practice reading the prayer individually.

In addition to Sue's expectations that they should be able to read the prayer individually, they were also given vocabulary exercises from the prayer. At first the students were intimidated by "all those words" on the printed page, but once it was clear to them that they were familiar with most of the words in one form or another, the exercise became less intimidating. The other benefit of the prayer was the formulaic quality of the text. It was a good example of grammatical patterning. The students were able to see how words could be substituted and why some words did not fit in particular positions. It was a grammar exercise without the technical terms. The prayer was successful as a pedagogical tool because of its multidimensional quality. The positive student responses were indicative of its pedagogical value.

### Booklets

The booklet project earlier described at length is the Toqawiw story. Other stories include titles like "Puniw Tokec" (It is now winter), "Mokalip" (Caribou), and "Siqoniw" (Springtime). These projects work best with grades four, five, and six because of the five Ws format for creating the stories. However, there is great potential for similar projects for the younger students. In all instances I was able to scan student illustrations into the computer and print them out into miniature four-page booklets. The students were extremely pleased with the results.

### Talking Animals Book

The title is meant to suggest that the exercise required student oral interaction rather than a book in which animals talk. The animals corresponded to the basic ten animals that were repeatedly presented on the flashcards. The big difference was that the animals were engaged in various activities like going home, digging, eating, walking, and so forth. Sue obtained the images from the book *Teaching an Algonkian Language as a Second Language* (DIAND 1978).

A number of exercises from that book were suitable for Maliseet language instruction. The talking animals book was just one example. This exercise was especially important for grades one, two, and three. The images were easy and large enough to color, and the texts were simple sentences. Not only did this provide entertainment in the form of coloring, but it also gave the children a chance to practice their printing skills while reinforcing Maliseet phonetic equivalents for the alphabet. By the end of the project the book would have twenty pages of images with corresponding text.

### *Traditional Stories and Student Illustrations*

Much like the prayer mentioned, the stories and illustrations were intended to serve multiple goals, among them to introduce the students to Maliseet oral tradition, to allow students to explore their creative abilities, and to instill pride and self-respect in aspects of identity to which they might not have been exposed before. As earlier described, Maliseet (and related Algonquin) story collecting by various scholars has occurred over at least one hundred years. But those stories are translations that reflect the attitudes of non-Indians toward Indians at each particular sociocultural period. However problematic those translations may be, they did find their way into the classroom. One of the most important goals for introducing these translations was to allow the students to interpret local significance from the stories. The resultant imagery and graphic meta-narrative was an intriguing blend of local and pan-Indian representation.

There were constraints in deciding which stories to read to the students. Time was one of the most inflexible. The stories had to be short enough to allow the students some time to illustrate their favorite parts of each. Sue also had to consider the appropriateness of the stories for the different grades, and we had to remember which stories we had presented before.

The illustrations varied across grades. The younger students typically drew their illustrations then colored them. The older students would participate in more involved projects, such as papier-mâché masks, sand paintings, and bas-relief paper illustrations.

Finally, the purpose of these projects was to create an interactive atmosphere to give Maliseet language instruction additional contexts in which the students can establish multiple cognitive links to spoken Maliseet. These interactive projects were subject to adjustments by Sue for each grade over three years. The adjustments were always in accordance with the feedback from the students and parents. Thus all projects accommodated immediate needs.

### Key Developments

The observations presented in this chapter were made during the third year of the Maliseet language program. Many of the rough edges had been smoothed out, and the methods that did not work had been eliminated. In addition to eliminating methods that did not work, there were important developments that contributed to stabilizing class instruction. I identify those key developments to be the introduction of the computer into the classroom, increasing class meetings, integrating arts and craft exercises into language and cultural projects, and the decision to go from oral-based instruction to text. The benefit of having a computer in the classroom is reflected in the ability to produce booklets, calendars, exam forms, review sheets, alphabet master copies, and numerous other teaching aids. As we have seen, class time was increased from the first year twice-a-week schedule to three times a week. It is not much, but at least the class meets more often. Third, art is used as a teaching medium more often than before, as indicated by the interactive projects described. Perhaps the most significant development was the decision to teach the language in a text-based method. Finally, all these developments are significant and find their way into the language curriculum from a variety of social entanglements. Entanglements, especially Maliseet language maintenance politics and text-oriented pedagogy, did stabilize classroom instruction, but they also raised a number of unexpected pedagogical challenges that neither Sue nor I anticipated. Some of these challenges were discussed in the preceding chapter under problematic orthographies.

While Sue's efforts to teach the children the Maliseet language were enhanced by her participation in continued education, visiting the Mohawk immersion school, and participating in conferences and workshops, she also needed support from the community and the band government. One teacher teaching for forty-five minutes twice a week will not maintain—much less revitalize—the language. I recall an early conversation I had with Sue and the principal regarding how best to approach Maliseet language immersion given our limited resources. We outlined the curriculum from Head Start to grade six. We knew it would take at least six years. We also knew that Maliseet had to be incorporated into other classrooms and other subjects such as science, math, and history. In short, we recognized that one teacher cannot do it alone. We also realized that without community support the program would not interest the children. Equally significant, without the support of chief and council in providing the necessary resources, the efforts at the school would fall short of the desired goal of Maliseet language maintenance and fall well short of the goal of language revitalization. This lack of support has profound implications for Maliseet language death.

# 6. Death by Suicide

The form of language death that best characterizes the Maliseet case for Tobique First Nation is death by suicide. I argue that the Maliseet language is undergoing a shift in ontological states from a living language to a language imminently to be dead. I do so for the following reasons. First, it recognizes the language experts' "problematic" use of affective metaphorical descriptors in calling attention to a serious linguistic problem. But as a native and anthropologist, I am more interested in the community of speakers and their relationship to their heritage language than I am in the language per se. By pushing the metaphor to extremes we shift the analysis from language to the circumstances prompting a community to cease transmitting their heritage language to their children (Denison 1977:21). Second, I do not make this claim for casual or flippant reasons. Language scholars suggest that the term *language suicide* blames the victim. My decision to use *language suicide* may seem to blame the community for Maliseet language death, but I use the phrase to make a case to community members that it is not a foregone conclusion the language will die due to outside pressures. Language death due to outside pressures may be called language murder (and has been by some scholars and activists). This framing of language death rightfully acknowledges the long colonial histories that forced minority and heritage language speakers to abandon their languages. But it also perpetuates ideologies of victimization. Those outside factors contribute to social and psychological traumas that lead to language abandonment and thus language suicide (Denison 1977: 22). I argue that if we change the terms of imminent language death to language suicide, then we acknowledge our own complicity in the erasure of the Maliseet language from our lives. This is important because it grants the community members the opportunity for linguistic self-determination. This chapter is an appeal to the community of Tobique First Nation to reestablish their relationship to the Maliseet language by approaching Maliseet language life as a vital component of the everyday lives of the Maliseet community.

The processes contributing to Maliseet language shift are also responsible for increasing the "disembodiment" of the Maliseet language from the speaking community. This ontological shift in the language reflects a shift in identity politics for the community. Identity was once expressed in Maliseet when Maliseet was the dominant mode of intersubjective (face-to-face) communication among members of the Tobique community. Today English is the dominant communicative mode of intersubjective identity expression among members of the community. This contemporary reality contributes to the increasing disembodiment of the Maliseet language and pushes the language toward the void of complete silence. It is in silence that the Maliseet language will take on a new ontological state; namely, extinct, dead, and disembodied. The process toward the projected total disembodiment (death) of the Maliseet language is often characterized as "dying" by scholars working on language death. The Maliseet case is not so simple. It is a case of "assisted suicide."

As Nancy Dorian and other scholars have pointed out, the term *death* to describe the silence of once vibrant languages is not a perfect label, but the metaphorical allusion is suggestive of the state of being for such languages. I too have difficulty with the metaphorical allusions, but I see the utility in characterizing the state of being of languages in anthropomorphized terms. Critics of such terms would point out that languages are not living things like plants and animals. How, then, can they die? The counterargument has been that living and breathing humans use language for communication. It is through human articulation that languages can participate in the living world. Similarly, I view the abstraction (Denison 1977:13; Harpham 2002) called "language" as incorporeally inert and as requiring speakers to activate all the potential tools that languages provide to facilitate intersubjective relationships. Arguing that languages are dependent upon humans for their "lives" makes the metaphors of life, living, dying, and dead all dependent upon the human language-speaking community. Can a language commit suicide? No, it cannot. But I argue that it requires the assistance of the language speaking community to either breathe life into the language by continuing to use it as a daily communicative tool or to assist in the death of the language by refusing to breathe life into it. It is not the language that commits suicide; it is the community that commits linguistic suicide. I suggest that the literature on language death, the utility of metaphorical allusions to life, and the complicity of the human speakers of languages have neglected to approach the issue of language death from the perspective of social and psychological traumas and the resultant disinterest or inattentiveness to the endangered state of many languages. This chapter explores these issues and the resultant disinterest of the community in the efforts of the language maintenance advocates.

To contextualize the following discussion I reexamine the material on factors contributing to language death by considering how such factors contribute to shifts in the ontological states of language and identity. The pathological effects of such factors are considered through personal accounts of how embodied experiences are related to changing notions of language and self. This phenomenological perspective shifts the focus of analytical attention from language (as presented in chapter 2) to the community members.[1] In doing so I retain the analytical observer perspective to establish a dialectical movement between detached observer and engaged subject, to illustrate the value of both perspectives in understanding the nature of Maliseet language death. As a note of personal reflection, I see the diagnostic analysis of the material in chapter 2 as akin to the "god-trick"[2] of seeing the material from nowhere. This chapter seeks to correct that oversight by attempting to see the material from somewhere—the perspective of the Tobique community members. Finally, I mentioned in the first chapter that my position as native and anthropologist presented some existential dilemmas that required some personal negotiation. Some of those dilemmas are presented in this and the following chapters to emphasize the community's intersubjective embodiments of Maliseet language politics and Maliseet identity politics.

### When Words Fail Us

I impressionistically remember the elementary school in Limestone, Maine. It was an old two-story brick building (white, maybe yellow). For a first grader it was imposing. For a first grader who did not speak English it was frightening. I seem to remember it from the road but not from the playground nor from inside. I just have the distanced view. The other memory I have of the school is a bus ride home. I do not remember how I got on the bus. I do not remember where the bus went. I do not remember where the bus ended up. But I do remember the bus driver. I also remember where I was sitting. I was sitting in the front seat by the door. I also remember sitting there on that afternoon with tears running down my cheeks. More important, I was mute! The bus driver, however, was not mute. He was sitting in his driver's seat and twisted around so he could see and talk to me. I vaguely remember a look of consternation and frustration on his face. But there is no question about my memory of his mouth moving and a stream of sounds coming out of it. We were both frustrated. Years later my mother recounted that day and said the bus driver took me back to the school. Once I was back at the school the principal had to call my mother and ask her to come to the school to pick me up. I do not remember any of that. I do remember that moment on the bus when both Maliseet and English words failed me. Maliseet was my first language, and I had not yet learned English. Suddenly, I was thrust into an English-only environment and Maliseet as an embodied communicative tool for me was condemned to die.

The bus ride prompted my mother to make the critical decision to begin an English immersion program for me. She reasoned, "If my son is to survive out there, he'll have to master English." Her reasoning was not unusual for many other parents at that time. There were a number of sociopolitical factors brought to bear on aboriginal language speakers pressuring them to discontinue Maliseet language transmission and communication to their children. My mother's generation was not the first generation to experience this and it certainly was not the last. The process of language decay has been in progress since aboriginal peoples had to negotiate with colonial governments. In the last several decades that process has increased to the point of seemingly inevitable extinction for many aboriginal languages. These social and psychological pressures are the result of colonial histories that promoted the forced disembodiment of aboriginal languages from aboriginal peoples.

## Forced Disembodiment

"I remember when I was in school the nuns made sure we didn't speak Indian in the classroom. When we did, we were punished. The nuns would tell us, 'It's the Devil's tongue.' So we would stop speaking Indian because we were ashamed of it. Nobody wanted to be embarrassed in front of the class." Karen shared her memory of how the nuns prevented the children from speaking the Maliseet language in school. Karen is in her late seventies. She was going to the reservation school operated by the church in the 1930s. At that time the church had great influence on the reservation. Karen's daughter does not speak Maliseet and neither do her grandchildren. Karen does speak the language, but she admits that she has forgotten much vocabulary. She had spent a considerable amount of time off the reservation. Her case is similar to many life stories of the elders. The reservation was home, but there were extended periods of time spent off the reservation. It recalls the urbanization factor in language endangerment. Both the schooling under the direction of the nuns and the residence off the reservation were social environments that curtailed opportunities for intersubjective Maliseet language maintenance.

Diane sends her children to the non-native elementary school. The irony is that she comes from a family who promote themselves as traditionalists. While one part of the family name their children with Maliseet names and assert native cultural values, Diane decides to send her child to the white school. When I asked her why she did not want to send her child to the reservation school her response was, "I want my child to learn French." I was startled! I asked, "Why?" She responded, "My son will be able to get a government job if he knows French." This account recalls the rationale my mother used when I was thrust into an English-speaking school. The children have no choice in the matter. In my case the opportunity for exercising Maliseet as the embodied communicative tool was absent because the educational system in which I was a student did not support Maliseet. These examples also show the aspect of changing economics and values. Both mothers had decided what they felt was best for their children. In effect, English and French were the languages of opportunity. Maliseet had no such prestige, nor did it have the symbolic capital that may be redeemed for real capital, as was perceived for English and French. The phenomenological stance of "being in the world" was a shifting category that required strategic action on the part of the subject. The perception that to survive in the "world out there" required skills in a language other than Maliseet is indicative of the shifting consciousness of whose world was deemed the most important for survival.

Today some of the bright children who took Maliseet language classes at Mah-Sos school have had to transfer downtown to attend middle school and high school. Cathy and her friends complained that there were no Maliseet classes offered at the schools. Mikey also left

Mah-Sos school to go to the neighboring middle school. Mah-Sos is an elementary school, requiring the students to transfer to the other schools. The children who have taken the Maliseet language classes at Mah-Sos Elementary School felt a sense of loss and disappointment. Some voiced their complaints to their parents, and the parents voiced complaints to the band government. The result was a dialogue between the schools and the band government to find a way to remedy the oversight. As the parties discussed plans to offer Maliseet language classes, they recognized the same problem that we recognized early in the native language class: simply put, the resources and the teachers are not available. The local schools are unable to give the children the opportunity to continue Maliseet language training. It becomes another example of continued disembodiment of the language from the potential speakers. Although there are good intentions, this particular example implicates the dominant culture's education system as one of the key factors that continue to undermine Maliseet language vitality.

I mentioned in chapter 3 the good news that the Native Language class meeting times were increased from two forty-five-minute sessions each week in the first year to three times a week for the subsequent years. That was a victory for Sue. But it was only a symbolic victory. French was still taught four or five times a week for forty-five-minute sessions. Even in the reservation school the Maliseet language was relegated to the tertiary position. The school, as decided by the principal and the band government, had the responsibility to prepare the children for the eventuality of going to middle school and high school off the reservation. Therefore the teaching philosophy was to adopt the provincial standards for classroom instruction. The consequence is that the time devoted to Maliseet language and culture has to be at the expense of other course requirements. The extra meeting time mentioned was begrudgingly granted. I was excited about the gains we had made by the end of the second grade as the children displayed greater literacy in Maliseet than they did in either French or English. But that was a short-lived victory. We lost the advantage as the children took more French classes. Through the Maliseet language class the children were given the opportunity to experience the Maliseet language as a form of communicating ideas, and they thereby developed a greater degree of Maliseet language embodiment. But they were also gaining much more embodied practice in French and almost incessant embodiment of English communicative practice. Comparatively speaking, their minimal Maliseet language embodiment was forced to the background through the coercive force of dominant language politics and ideologies.

These accounts serve to illustrate the various ways in which diagnostic factors contributing to language death have, in the Maliseet case, precipitated the ontological shift mentioned at the beginning of this chapter. In chapter 2 I stated that not all the factors discussed contributed to the moribund status of the Maliseet language at Tobique First Nation. Rather, it was a combination of factors. Each endangered language has its own particular constellation of detrimental pressures. Yet these pressures in the many varieties of combinations produce the same general effect—language shift. In some cases the shift is toward a synthesis and produces a pidgin or Creole language. In the Maliseet case, however, the shift is toward language death. As indicated, the smaller the number of speakers, the fewer the social contexts in which the language can be used communicatively, and the more likely the language is to become silenced, extinct, and dead. It will be in a state of communicative nonexistence; it will have become disembodied.

The last example from the native language instruction at Mah-Sos School introduces my critique of the approach that language advocates have taken toward analyzing processes of language death. The advocates emphasize external pressures in characterizing language death. In effect, external factors relegate the communities suffering language endangerment as victims. In contrast, I see the community as a decision-making participant in the process. In the preceding example, only half of the eligible students from the reservation attend the reservation school. This also introduces my argument that it is not enough to lament how the community is a victim of powerful hegemonic forces that exert an ideological and practical will over the powerless aboriginal community. That view may have been strongly supported in the past, but today the Canadian sociopolitical environment is more conciliatory regarding aboriginal language and culture. The Tobique community does have the option to maintain the language. In the next part of this chapter I discuss how "we fail words." That is, I discuss how we—members of Tobique First Nation—are committing linguistic suicide.

## When We Fail Words

It is important to take account of Emile Durkheim's distinguishing of the positive and negative acts that will knowingly result in self-destruction.

*Though suicide is commonly conceived as a positive, violent action involving some muscular energy, it may happen that a purely negative attitude or mere abstention will have the same consequence. Refusal to take food is as suicidal as self-destruction by dagger or fire-arm. The subject's act need not even have been directly antecedent to death for death to be regarded as its effect; the causal relation may be indirect without that changing the nature of the phenomenon. . . . We may then say conclusively:* the term suicide is applied to all cases of death resulting directly or indirectly from a positive or negative act of the victim himself, which he knows will produce this result. *(Durkheim 1951:42, 44; italics in the original)*

His argument that "mere abstention" may also be considered as evidence for a suicidal trajectory reflects the Maliseet community's benign neglect of the Maliseet language. Languages cannot obliterate themselves (contrary to Aitcheson 1991:198). Rather, the speakers of the language are the ones committing linguistic suicide by not speaking the language as a daily communicative practice. Does it work to call this benign neglect? Drawing from Durkheim as quoted, the negative act of not maintaining the communicative practice of the Maliseet language, especially with the knowledge that the language is in a serious state of decay, implicates the speakers as complicit participants in Maliseet language suicide.

Suicide has an expressive—albeit disturbing—quality about it when one is talking about human beings who have attempted or committed suicide. To use Durkheim's expression again, it often implies a "pathology" that is personally experienced. What are the clues that suicidologists use to detect suicidal behavior? In his review of suicide psychology Edwin S. Shneidman identifies "ten commonalities of suicide" as:

- The common purpose of suicide is to seek a solution.
- The common goal of suicide is cessation of consciousness.
- The common stimulus of suicide is unbearable psychological pain.
- The common stressor in suicide is frustrated psychological needs.
- The common emotion in suicide is hopelessness—helplessness.
- The common cognitive state in suicide is ambivalence.
- The common perceptual state in suicide is constriction.
- The common action in suicide is escape.
- The common interpersonal act in suicide is communication of intent.
- The common pattern in suicide is consistency of lifelong styles. (Shneidman 1996:131)

I include Shneidman's list to draw parallels to the affective aspect of language suicide. Language cannot commit suicide; the speakers of the language assist in this. Although the literature addresses individual acts of suicide, I see the commonalities as applicable to the community's response to the shift in the ontological state of being in the world and its direct effect on the Maliseet language. This is explored further later, but first I present the community's response to projected Maliseet language death as well as their responses to the efforts of the few individuals promoting Maliseet language maintenance.

## Voluntary Disembodiment

There were perhaps twelve people attending the language immersion meeting that raised the specter of Maliseet language death. The meeting did much to sound the alarm that the Maliseet language was dying. However, the hope was that this would mobilize the community to do something about language death; namely, that it would enlist their support for a Maliseet language immersion program.

As the meeting went on and those in attendance were voicing their support, the moment of truth came. The organizer suggested a follow-up meeting the following week to begin distributing the names of Tobique community parents with children in preschool. In the meantime, the organizer would get the list together. The following week arrived. As before, I was on time and everybody else was on Indian time. I was in the lobby of the school waiting for the others to arrive. Sue came in, one parent with her child came in, and the organizer arrived. We chatted for a while waiting for the arrival of the rest of the interested community members. Some time passed, and we finally had to assume that the full complement of interested participants was in attendance—Sue, the native language teacher; the organizer; Lucy, a concerned mother (a white woman); and I, the anthropologist.

So what was the anthropologist thinking at this point? I thought it was ironic that the only mother to show support for the immersion program was a white woman. I asked Lucy why she was attending the meeting. She responded by saying that she thought it was important for her child to learn the Maliseet language because the child's father is Maliseet. This is in contrast to the large numbers of Maliseet mothers whose children have either one Maliseet parent or two. None of them attended the second meeting. Attending the first meeting were the Head Start teachers. Not one of the four Head Start teachers attended the follow-up meeting. Only one of the parents, Lucy, returned. Sue was there, so was the anthropologist. My impression of the lack of attendance was that there simply was no community commitment to the proposed program.

As this small meeting broke up I talked with the organizer for a few moments. I asked her if she was discouraged with the turnout. She surprised me by saying, "No, not at all. At least somebody showed up." I asked why that was significant. She replied that she had tried to have a similar meeting a few years before and the response at that time had been worse. Not a single person showed interest in the idea. From her perspective the reservation had at least been responsive this time. Just having someone show up to the meetings was a symbolic victory. So how effective was the "shock" of extinction the organizer gave those attending that first meeting? From the subsequent interest shown by the community it appears that the shock was momentary. There were other pressing issues that needed their attention. This was just the first example of neglect that I witnessed during fieldwork. However, neglect in this case is not benign. In the terms defined by Durkheim, neglect is a negative act that the community knows will result in Maliseet language death.

Two years after the "specter" meeting, the Maliseet language class had been taught to the students attending Mah-Sos School. The children were producing little booklets of Maliseet texts illustrated with their own drawings. They were taking home quizzes, papers, and art projects that were related to topics of instruction in the classroom. Sue was getting feedback from parents and grandparents saying they were thrilled by their children's ability to read and speak the Maliseet language. One of the demographic peculiarities related to the Maliseet language is that the young parents who had children attending Maliseet language classes were overwhelmingly inarticulate in Maliseet. They were the second and third generations in which the language had not been transmitted to the children in the domestic sphere—the home. Today their children can read and speak a limited amount of Maliseet, while the parents are unable to take advantage of the opportunity for the intersubjective embodiment of the Maliseet language. Some of the parents decided to inquire about adult classes in Maliseet. When Sue learned about the interest on the part of some parents to learn the language, she and I were very excited! We felt we were seeing momentum building for language revitalization among the younger adults and their children in the community. Sue decided to allocate some classroom time for the purpose of teaching adult classes in Maliseet. She was the teacher and I was merely an assistant making photocopies or distributing handouts as required. I was also an observer—the anthropologist quietly sitting in the corner taking notes.

There was a general sense of excitement in the first class as everyone greeted one another, some muttering, "I didn't know you were going to take this class." The general buzz died down and Sue began to explain how she was going to teach the class. She was going to introduce them to the same instructions she gives the children so that the parents would know what the children were learning and could help the children with their homework. Everyone had a notebook we had distributed and the pencils were at the ready. I surveyed the room and counted fifteen adults. There were some familiar faces among the adult students. The Head Start teachers were present. They were there to try to coordinate Maliseet language teaching between the Head Start program and the Mah-Sos School program. That reduced the number of parents to eleven. There was one man among all the women, and he was the object of some playful teasing. Sue began by teaching them the alphabet and the corresponding sounds. The exercise was the same as the one the children did every class period (see chapter 5). The parents dutifully repeated after Sue, "ah, ah, ah; juh, juh, juh . . ." until the entire alphabet was done. The structure of the adult class was similar to that of the children's classes because the parents were at the same level as the children in language learning. This went on for several weeks, and one by one the parents began to drop out. Both Sue and I noticed the declining attendance. Sue made inquiries to the other adult students and the responses went from "I don't know where she is" to "They had something else to do." The Head Start teachers began to make excuses for not attending, like having to run errands or having to babysit. In the end the numbers dwindled down to one or two occasional students. Sue discontinued the classes.

What was behind the attrition rate for the adult classes? A number of possibilities were presented in the excuses given by the adults themselves. Their everyday worlds required their immediate attention in a number of other pressing problems such as babysitting or running errands. I often wonder if the parents, like the students (myself included), were impatient and wanted to become speakers overnight. In any case, the result was the cessation of the classes. The success would have been marginal had the classes continued. Not counting the Head Start teachers, the number of parents attending was only eleven. In a population of fifteen hundred people on the reservation, that number is insignificant. However, as mentioned, both Sue and I felt that any interest was a good sign full of potential for revitalization. But it was not going to happen with that group of parents. The adults attending the class had the will to engage the language as a communicative tool that they could use with their children and other adults. In the end, they ceased attending their Maliseet language classes and thereby chose to devote their attentions to other practical concerns at the expense of the Maliseet language. Is it benign neglect? Or is it about priorities? I suggest it is about priorities. The adults have made a decision not to take the Maliseet language classes. This corresponds with the list of factors as "change in values and economy." The Maliseet language was not valued enough for them to continue taking the class.

As the native language teacher, Sue was constantly working on enhancing her skills and repertoire for teaching the Maliseet language. To this end, she took language immersion training classes offered through St. Thomas University. The program consisted of practical classroom instruction projects and some linguistic studies. To complete the program successfully, students like Sue had to participate in a practicum. She and three other members of the Tobique community got together and decided to offer Maliseet language classes on Tuesday nights at the school. Just as the adult classes already discussed had generated some interest at the beginning, so did the practicum classes. The situation was ideal. There were four teachers so one-on-one instruction was possible, and the class could move forward more quickly. Unfortunately, I was unable to attend these classes because I had returned to the university by the time the new adult classes were offered. On my frequent visits to the reservation Sue and her husband Ben told me about the classes and how they were going. The experience of the adult classes was echoed in the practicum. On one of my visits I asked Ben how the classes were going. He responded by saying, "It started out great, but now we have four teachers for two students!" I asked why they kept the class going. "We have to complete the practicum to get credit for completing the immersion training courses." They witnessed the same attrition rate that I witnessed in the earlier adult class. I did not get any accounts of reasons given for the disinterest among the adults taking the classes, but the result was the same: at the beginning there was marginal interest and in the end there was minimal interest. Again the community decided not to take advantage of an opportunity to revitalize the Maliseet language.

Sue is persistent. She agreed to teach an adult class designed to teach adults how to read and write in Maliseet. Like the practicum, this class would meet in the evenings at the school. This time the class was on Monday nights. There was initial interest in the classes and the number of adults taking it was about eight. I was unable to attend the classes at the beginning. However, my brother Wendell and my mother were attending these new classes. From their accounts it seemed that the class attendance was declining, but there was a change in the students who did attend. At one point I returned from the university to enjoy a break in the semester at home and I was able to attend the class. It turned out to be a great experience.

We were late but so was everyone else. The Maliseet reading and writing class was about to start. The students consisted of Wendell, Ben, and me. I was a guest tonight. The teacher was the native language teacher, Sue. Her assistant was Henrietta Black, my mother. We sat at the little desks at the opposite end of the room while Sue approached the board.

The papers were shuffled around as the class was getting organized. They had started the story a couple of weeks earlier and since I was a guest, I had to dive into the middle of the text. As I was looking at the differences in the transcription of the story my mother said, "You had better pay attention because you'll have to participate in the exercises." The class was starting. Sue was writing the first sentence on the board as the regular students copied the text into their notebooks. I continued to peruse the bound notebook with the collected Maliseet texts gathered from sources going back over one hundred years. The teacher was ready. She began to read the sentence on the board. After reading it three times the class was automatically reading after her in the separate phrases of compound words or short noun and verb phrases. I also read along with the class. Once the teacher was satisfied that we had read the sentence adequately she erased the sentence. She called the first student to the board. Ben was first. He walked up to the board and took the chalk in his hand and held it up to the board. Sue then read the sentence to him word by word. Ben then wrote the sentence to the best of his understanding of the spelling. Once the sentence had been completed he was required to read the sentence out loud to the class. After the successful completion of the exercise we would all applaud. Next came Wendell's turn. He went to the front of the class after Ben erased the sentence from the board. With chalk in hand, Wendell waited for Sue to read the sentence to him. As with Ben, Wendell also had to spell the words to the best of his understanding. When finished he had to read the sentence aloud. Wendell successfully completed the task. It was my turn. "Okay professor, your turn!" said Sue. I went to the front of the class, took the chalk in my hand, and waited for the dictation of the sentence. I wrote the sentence to the best of my understanding of this latest iteration of Maliseet spelling and orthography. In the back of my mind I recalled the different orthographic standard used in the notebook I had been examining. Nonetheless I followed the spelling conventions that Sue was establishing. I did well. There were a couple of mistakes. I recalled the original convention of using the letter o (as in Passamaquoddy) in the place of a schwa as indicated by other orthographies, such as the one used by Szabó. The three of us took turns for the next two and a half hours. We finished transcribing one page of the story Sue was using for dictation. At one point Wendell was stumped by the word *wicewin* (come with me) and could not recall how it was spelled. As he stood at the board trying to recall the spelling, Ben decided to help. "It's 'wice win' Wend!" We all laughed because the English sounds made pronunciation sense but the words as clues were nonsense. However, the Maliseet compound *wicewin*, though spelled identically, was pronounced very differently. The class lasted three hours and we all had fun, but we were also exhausted. Our collective attention started to wane.

When these classes began there were eight students taking the class. In the ensuing weeks the students began to lose interest. Finally, there were only two students taking the class. It has been suggested by the remaining participants that the lack of interest may have been due to unfamiliarity with the language, the difficulty in recognizing the symbolic representations of a primarily oral language, other priorities and commitments, the slow rate of progress in the class, and finally a general lack of interest.

There was potential for training a generation of literate adults in Maliseet on the reservation, but unfortunately there was a general lack of interest in developing such literacy. This last project started after Ben recognized that there was a potential for enhancing the survivability of the language when the government decided to arrange a fishing agreement with the community. When Ben approached the tribal government about supporting a language reading and writing class, the response was that the funding was to be allocated to fisheries projects alone. Ben nevertheless pursued the matter and was able to find some funding from other sources for his literacy project. However, one serious drawback to the project was that it needed to be completed in a predetermined amount of time. In March of 2002 when I participated in the project, there was only one week left for the Maliseet language reading and writing class. That class has ended, and the potential for the reading and writing of Maliseet has been curtailed due to lack of funds. But more important perhaps, it ended due to lack of community interest.

At the beginning of the class there were a reported eight participants. The participants were varied in their speaking skills from minimal to fluent. There was also a good range of ages among people taking the classes. Yet when I visited the class it was down to two students. Those two students had been associated with the school program in the past and continue to have occasional tasks that bring them back into the Maliseet language classroom. When I asked why the others had quit attending classes the excuses ranged from "they have other priorities" to "they were confused by the materials." I could understand the disappointment that some of the nonspeakers might have felt. They were not getting the grammatical and rudimentary linguistic training that would help them learn and retain the material. The speakers, on the other hand, may have been frustrated at the orthographic representations of the Maliseet language. I also heard it expressed that some of them had other priorities such as "a life," bingo, or some other diversion. This later project mirrored what happened after the planning meeting for promoting a Maliseet immersion program, where numbers dropped from the initial ten to twelve to a single non-native mother. Disconcertingly, in that instance the organizer of the meeting was delighted that anyone was interested.

These accounts of language classes and the minimal participation suggest that the great majority of community members do not feel a need to participate in language maintenance and revitalization classes or programs. In addition, the classes are short term, and in the case of the language classes for the children at the school, they do not promote communicative competence. It may be a case of too little too late. The language shift may have gone to the point where the Maliseet language has tipped toward obsolescence. The Maliseet language may have lost all value for the great majority of the community. Is it fair, then, to characterize Maliseet language death as a case of suicide?

### Death by Assisted Suicide

It was a cold Sunday morning in January when my brother Wendell drove the forty miles from the reservation to the bus stop across the border in Presque Isle, Maine. We were early as usual. Winter driving conditions prompted us to allow extra time to get to the bus stop in case of unforeseen emergencies. No emergencies delayed our arrival at the bus station so we sat outside waiting for the bus. Every few minutes Wendell started the car to allow the heater to warm us up. We were chilled despite our heavy winter coats. While we waited Wendell asked, "What exactly are you writing about?" I gave him a synopsis of the language maintenance literature and the language death literature, describing how I saw the Maliseet case reflecting aspects of the literatures on maintenance and death. I explained that the indifference the great majority of the community has shown regarding the maintenance of the language indicated a form of linguistic suicide. The discussion included the outside factors, such as assimilation and missionization, and how they had catalyzed the demise of the Maliseet language. Wendell was quiet for a few moments. Finally he said, "So, we're practicing the Kevorkian School of language maintenance?" We both laughed. I replied, "Yeah, that about sums it up"—a bit of gallows humor at seven o'clock on a cold January Sunday morning. I promised to give him credit for the inspiration for "Kevorkian School" idea. His reaction indicated he thought that was a dubious honor.

It is with gratitude that I credit Wendell with positing the Kevorkian School of Language Maintenance. How is the language effort at Tobique First Nation indicative of the Kevorkian School? Just as Kevorkian was responsible for a number of assisted suicides, the Tobique community is also responsible for the metaphorical assisted language suicide by not actively participating in language maintenance programs. As a case of neglect it is not benign because, to paraphrase Durkheim's definition, even an indirect and negative act qualifies as suicide when the actor knows it will result in death—the Tobique community's indirect and negative actions will (with their knowledge) contribute to language death. Nettle and Romaine, in their discussion of the phenomenon of "vanishing voices" worldwide, suggest that it is "ill-founded" to use the term *suicide* to describe language death because it blames the victim (Nettle and Romaine 2000:5–6).

### Blaming the Victim?

In their 2000 work *Vanishing Voices* Daniel Nettle and Suzanne Romaine note that terms like *death, extinction, murder,* and *suicide,* are metaphors when applied to language.

*Are such metaphors useful? We will argue that the death and extinction (and even murder) perspective is useful because languages are intimately connected with humans, our cultures, and our environment. The notion of language suicide of course puts the blame squarely on the victim. This view is not constructive and in any case, ill-founded. People do not kill themselves on a whim. Suicide is indicative of mental and often physical illness brought about by undue stress. Likewise, people do not fling away their languages for no good reason. We will show throughout this book how many instances of language shift and death occur under duress and stressful social circumstances, where there is no realistic choice but to give in. Many people stop speaking their language out of self-defense as a survival strategy. (Nettle and Romaine 2000:5–6)*

I agree with Nettle and Romaine that "people do not kill themselves on a whim" and that "suicide is indicative of mental and often physical illness brought about by undue stress." I also agree with them on the point that people do not give up their languages "for no good reason." Their premise is that the cessation of speaking their languages is a survival strategy. Their work looks at ecological matrices for language: "A language is enmeshed in a social and geographical matrix just as a rare species is enmeshed in an ecosystem." They go on to add: "A small amount of environmental change can cause a cascade of extinction as the dependent species becomes stressed" (79). Their position makes me wonder if they are interested in the vanishing languages. Or are they using language as a lens through which they can discern the real focus of their attention? Nettle and Romaine state: "The first causes in language loss, then, are not themselves linguistic. As we indicated in Chapter 1, language use is more like a litmus test for what is happening in the wider society. Where language use changes, there is an underlying social upheaval that may have environmental, economic, or political causes. This litmus-test property of language is immensely significant. It means that the loss of a language—like the death of a miner's canary—is a good indicator of less visible stresses which might need investigating" (79). Their program is to explain language loss on a global scale through a punctuated equilibrium model that suggests there is no gradual loss of the world's language by attrition.[3] Rather, there are significant social, political, and economic changes that create large-scale shifts in states of equilibrium. That is to say, if an area has a stable economic, political, and social matrix of interdependence it can be described as being in a state of equilibrium. However, should there be a change in one of the factors—social, political, or economic—then the equilibrium is shifted and the "cascade of extinction" will proceed until a new stage of equilibrium is reached.[4] One of the examples Nettle and Romaine use to describe the process is the development of agriculture. They argue that language loss began on a massive scale "in the last thousand years," but they trace the causes to nine thousand years earlier! They argue that language disruption was precipitated by farmer communities overcoming hunter communities and continued until every corner of the globe was finally subjected to the expanding agricultural advantage. "When European farmers overcame Australian hunters and gatherers in the late eighteenth century, they were performing the final act of a drama which had begun nearly ten thousand years earlier in the Neolithic era" (98). The point they are attempting to present through millennia of social, political, and economic change is that the causes for language death have a deep history that have serious implications for the endangered languages today. I appreciate the deep history in language change, but that does not stop the continued disembodiment of the Maliseet language today. To argue that endangered languages are like endangered species that need protection from the "endangering" agents is the typical language advocate argument. My difficulty with this argument is that it perpetuates the victim status of all the communities with endangered languages.

Perhaps my greatest difficulty with the position that Nettle and Romaine take is their reticence to use "suicide" to describe language death. Yes, communities with endangered languages are victims of social, political, and economic forces greater than themselves, and those forces exert pressures to force them to assimilate into the dominant modes of relations. There are many case studies available showing that endangerment of languages can productively be compared and analyzed, as in chapter 2 of the present work. Yet I take the stance here that the Maliseet case is not as simple as linguistic victimization, as most advocates would suggest. It was the comparative analysis that alerted me to the possibility of articulating the "death by suicide" description as the process of Maliseet language change. I am, in a sense, blaming the victim, because there are members of the community working to preserve and revitalize the language and the community has the choice of either preserving the language or allowing the language to die and become totally disembodied from the potential speaking community of Tobique. Critics may argue that the community has been the victim of missionization, assimilation, education, and the other factors mentioned and that those forces continue to exert their coercive power on the community today. I agree with that argument, but I also point out that the language is not condemned to extinction; there are Maliseet language agents, and sociopolitical support exists in greater Canada, as does economic support for aboriginal language maintenance and revitalization from multiple governing entities from the tribal government to the provincial government and the federal government. The community members are exercising their collective will by choosing not to embody the language through the daily communicative use of it. They can also choose to re-embody the language. So, in contrast to Nettle and Romaine, I do use the term *suicide* to describe the Tobique school of language maintenance.

## Suicide as Disembodiment

"A pathologist is a doctor who knows everything—but it's too late" (Shneidman 2001:14). This quote from Edwin Shneidman suggests that the knowledge of the pathological states of the victim is comprehended only after the victim has died. Such is not the case with the Maliseet language. It has not died yet. There are community members actively attempting to re-embody the Maliseet language to other members who want to learn to speak, read, and write it. In the preceding discussion I presented several examples of the disinterest the community has shown regarding the language classes and programs. I have labeled the process as suicide because suicide best captures the affective quality of the accounts by members of the community who were denied the ability to speak the language in a number of social settings. Those settings were the settings where the coercive force of the dominant culture forced the disembodiment of the Maliseet language from the speaking community.

Shneidman, a suicidologist, classifies suicides into four clusters of frustrated psychological needs. In addition, the needs exhibit four kinds of pain:

1. Thwarted love, acceptance, or belonging—related primarily to the frustrated needs for succor and affiliation.
2. Fractured control, excessive helplessness, and frustration—related primarily to the frustrated needs for achievement, autonomy, counteraction, inviolacy, order, and understanding.
3. Assaulted self-image and avoidance of shame, defeat, humiliation, and disgrace—related primarily to the

frustrated needs for affiliation, autonomy, defence, shame avoidance, and succor.
4. Ruptured key relationships and attendant grief and bereftness—related primarily to the frustrated needs for affiliation and nurturance. (Shneidman 2001:202–3)

At the beginning of this chapter I shared my personal account of how words failed me as a first grader in an elementary school in Limestone, Maine. The event can easily be analyzed with the four needs and pains that Shneidman identifies as suicidal. I definitely felt a sense of "thwarted belonging," and the pain I felt was of "frustrated needs for succor and affiliation." I was completely alone, and it was an awful feeling. Sitting in the front seat of the bus was a moment of utter helplessness and frustration. The pain I felt was certainly commensurate with "frustrated needs for . . . order, and understanding." I do not remember with any certainty if my self-image was assaulted or if I felt the pains that Shneidman ascribes to such an assault. I have heard numerous accounts where the self-image was truly assaulted in the form of stigma. "That is the devil's tongue" or "embarrassment of public humiliation and punishment for speaking the language" were the typical responses to the language-related assaults to self-image. As the first grader unable to communicate in a world of strangers I certainly felt ruptures in relations. There was no opportunity to establish any relationships. There indeed was the pain of "frustrated needs for affiliation and nurturance." That moment when words failed me was the personal moment when the ontological shift for Maliseet moved toward increasing disembodiment. The accounts from Karen, Diane, Cathy and Mikey are examples of similar forced disembodiments that members of the Tobique community had to endure. The psychological needs and the related pains are echoed within each case.

The discussion of "voluntary disembodiment" presents more instances of suicidal tendencies. In all cases, the minimal interest in the language classes suggests that the great majority of the community decided not to participate in the structured embodiment of the Maliseet language through the various attempts to re-embody the language. In these cases, it is not the speakers who undergo the "thwarted belonging," or "fractured control, excessive helplessness," or "assaulted self-image, defeat, humiliation and disgrace," or most important, "ruptured key relationships." It is the Maliseet language. Although I stated earlier that the language cannot commit suicide and the speakers are the ones who commit language suicide, I do argue that the disembodiment of the Maliseet language as suicide is a useful metaphor for characterizing the current process of language change for the Maliseet language at Tobique.

At the beginning of this chapter I suggested that the Maliseet language and Maliseet identity were undergoing an ontological shift; a shift from living to dead. As Clifford Geertz cautioned in his essay "Thick Description," "The thing to ask about a burlesqued wink or a mock sheep raid is not what their ontological status is. It is the same as that of rocks on one hand and dreams on the other—they are things of this world. The thing to ask is what their import is: what it is, ridicule or challenge, irony or anger, snobbery or pride, that, in their occurrence and through their agency, is getting said" (Geertz 1973:10). I agree with Geertz that the import of the ontological state is what is getting said. The problem with language death as the ontological state for the Maliseet language is that nothing is getting said! That is important. However, as Geertz states in the same essay, anthropology is not a predictive science. The Maliseet language is not dead yet. The real import for the ontological status of the Maliseet language is the processual aspect of language shift. Neutral terms like *attrition*, *change*, or *shift* are thin descriptions of the phenomenon. Terms such as *death*, *obsolescence*, and *murder* are thicker descriptions that provide good interpretations of the events and their meanings. Again, as Geertz succinctly put it, "The essential vocation of interpretive anthropology is not to answer our deepest questions, but to make available to us answers that others, guarding other sheep in other valleys, have given, and thus to include them in the consultable record of what man has said" (30). Those thick descriptions, those "sheep in other valleys," those other cases of language death that I have consulted are the ones that compelled me to conclude that the process of language death at Tobique is a case of suicide. The irony in using Geertz to contemplate the ontological import of Maliseet language disembodiment is that the importance lies in the symbolic dimensions of social *inaction* rather than the symbolic dimensions of social action when interpreting the existential dilemmas of life for the language. It is about life and death, after all.

**Alternative Vitalities**
Having discussed at length the ontological states of language, I feel I should explain how ontology supports my project. This chapter is focused on the increasing disembodiment of the Maliseet language from the Maliseet community via general disinterest or inattentiveness on the part of the great majority of the community. In the course of the discussion I mentioned ontological states or status of the Maliseet language. I suggest that Maliseet language use is indicative of a "contingent ontology." I use the term *contingent* because the living, breathing, spoken vitality is dependent upon speakers. The contingent being of the Maliseet language is a processual ontology that fluctuates between live and dead. Simply put, as many of the language scholars and advocates argue, the potential ontological states for the Maliseet language in the next twenty years are death and extinction. However, I agree with Geertz's observation that anthropology is not a predictive science. I would not predict that the language will die in the next twenty years. As stated in chapter 2, the evidence for Maliseet suggests serious decay and endangerment. I do wish to put forward an argument that spoken language is not the only vital ontological state. I have described the various language programs, activities, and forms related to the Maliseet language, and I argue that texts, recordings, booklets, dictionaries, historical accounts, and documents are some of the various ways of being for the Maliseet language. Even

though these forms of the language are not experienced in the direct communicative ways that speaking is, they do constitute an equally vital relationship that I would characterize as subject to object. For example, active listening to tapes and other recordings, reading texts and using lexicons and dictionaries, producing booklets and language curricula, and researching old Maliseet documents are all active linguistic processes. In this way I posit the ontological state of alternative vitalities for the Maliseet language. I make this move deliberately to address the oversight in much of the language advocacy literature. The criterion for language vitality is based on speakers, a contingent ontology. From that perspective, when there are no speakers to speak the language, then the vitality of the language becomes nonexistent (just as the ontological state becomes nonexistent). I argue that this is not necessarily true. By ignoring the vitalities just mentioned, language advocates overlook some powerful tools in the revitalization of endangered languages. By recognizing the import of the meaningful actions of the few Maliseet language maintenance agents I recognize the continued vitality of the language despite the growing disembodiment. More important, the texts and records may be inert, but they also hold great potential for revitalization, or re-embodiment. These inert language entities can become intersubjective catalysts for individual subjects, or for a number of subjects, if the context of their animation will allow it.

Finally, one important aspect for positing alternative vitalities is directly related to the "alternative futures" Kay B. Warren (1997) articulated for the Maya in Guatemala. As indigenous peoples worldwide continue to fight to maintain their languages and cultures they do so in a world of possibilities. There are communities that continue to be victimized and are therefore powerless. But that is not true for all indigenous peoples and that is not true for all endangered languages, peoples, and cultures. To return to a theme presented in chapter 1, "We live in the flow of daily experience: we are intersubjective forms of memory and action. Our experiences are so completely integrated—narratized moments, transforming narratives—that the self is constituted out of visceral processes as much as expressed through them" (Kleinman and Kleinman 1995:117–18). I suggest that memory and action, narrative and transformation, self and visceral process all constitute the fertile grounds for Maliseet alternative futures.

## 7. Language and Being in Maliseet Worlds

The issue of identity has a vast literature in anthropology alone, and Native American articulations of identity have a rich history that goes back to time immemorial.[1] Time and space being limited for this project, I confine my discussion to three key components of Maliseet identity that I found to be particularly salient for this ethnography. They are language, blood, and aboriginality. I present "narratized moments" and "transforming narratives" (Kleinman and Kleinman 1995) that refer directly to the three aspects of identity as the embodied experiences of being Maliseet. In doing so, I present them from various generations of Tobique community members. As the Kleinmans so succinctly put it, "We live in the flow of daily experience: we are intersubjective forms of memory and action" (Kleinman and Kleinman 1995:117). As a member of the Tobique community I am part of that intersubjective community. Consequently, I am equally affected by the forms those memories and actions take.[2] It is with these considerations in mind—language, blood, and aboriginality; the various generations' narratives; continued embodiment discussions; and my native and anthropologist perspectives—that "being in Maliseet worlds" is explored.

Is it a case of drawing a bull's eye around the arrow, as Geertz (1973:27) wittily quipped when discussing anthropology theory? No. I am cognizant of the shifting, changing, and unstable grounds that are identity formation and lived experience. The question is: how best do I capture such a dynamic process with ethnographic and theoretical tools that can only record moments of experience collected at different times in different places? Victor Turner says of Dilthey's position on value: "It can show life as a series of choices between ends, but finds no utility in this sequence of choices. Ultimately, it is only the category of *meaning* that enables us to *conceive an intrinsic affinity between the successive events in life*, and all that the categories of value and end can tell us is caught up in this synthesis" (Turner 1987:96; italics in the original).[3] It is the thread of meaning that I use to conceive of the affinity between not only the successive events of individual lives but also the events between lives. Turner's focus on process and the discussion of successive events indicate a preoccupation with history and memory. He explicitly states: "Moreover, Dilthey tells us, since meaning is specifically based on the *cognitive attitude of memory*, and 'history is memory,' meaning is naturally 'the category most proper to historical thought'" (G. S., VII, 201–2, 236). I would add, to socio-processual thought also" (Turner 1987:96–97). Both Turner and the Kleinmans recognize the importance of the embodied memories of intersubjective agents in collective meaning (Turner) and collective memory and action (Kleinman and Kleinman). The task before me is, on the one hand, to make comprehensible the many embodiments (which can be complex and contradictory, as mentioned in chapter 1) of "being Maliseet" and, on the other hand, to articulate an open-ended processual aspect of Maliseet identity. This chapter approaches this emergent aspect of identity by (1) examining the changing temporal aspect of identity as memory, (2) considering the intersubjective dialogues as integral to Maliseet identity formation, and (3) suggesting that the subjects themselves also change through those memories and dialogues. These aspects are the moving targets of identity processes that make it difficult to draw a bull's-eye around my arrow. Instead, I trace the shifts in the ontological states of the Maliseet language, Maliseet blood, and aboriginality. I also argue that the distinctive Maliseet attributes that are still considered by many community members as essential—language and blood—are slowly being dissipated.[4] The phenomenon "aboriginality" is replacing them as a distinctive marker of a situational and complex Maliseet identity. Significantly, aboriginality as a process has important implications for understanding the interconnectedness of language and worldview (better known as the Sapir-Whorf hypothesis, or linguistic relativism) as well as the practical consequences of Bill C31, Canada's Aboriginal Reinstatement Act.

## Language

I argued in the last chapter that the Maliseet language was undergoing an ontological shift from living to dead. As Geertz (1973) cautioned, it is not the ontological status that is important, but it is what is meaningful about the status. It is my contention from the last chapter that the meaning behind the Maliseet language was based on embodiment on the part of the speaking community as communicative intersubjectivity and the disembodiment on the part of the nonspeakers (which precludes intersubjective communication). It is interesting to note that much of the advocacy surrounding the preservation of endangered languages has been diagnostic in the sense that the studies attempted to evaluate the contributing factors leading toward language death. The studies allude to the affective aspects of language loss on the speaking community and some provide brief testimonials from speakers who express the emotional sense of loss that language death elicited. Even so, the meaning for those analysts was suspiciously self-interested. For example, Hinton asks, "Why does it matter that the linguistic diversity of the world is diminishing? Why should anyone care if indigenous groups shift from their ancestral tongue to a world language?" (Hinton 2001:4) Her reply included: "Linguistic theory depends on linguistic diversity. It is one of the charges of linguistics to understand the range of possibilities within human language and cognitive models that would account for this" (5); "the loss of language is part of the loss of whole cultures and knowledge systems, including philosophical systems, oral literary and musical traditions, environmental knowledge systems, medical knowledge, and important cultural practices and artistic skills" (5). More recently, K. David Harrison (2007) argues that to lose a language is to lose important contributions to our human cultural heritage. His book makes an elaborate argument for recognizing that we stand to lose a "complex constellation of ideas" when "we" lose a language (Harrison 2007:vii). Benjamin Lee Whorf anticipated these arguments in his 1941 essay "Language and Logic" (Caroll 1970). Furthermore, he also anticipated the linguists' self-interest in the attention paid to other languages as other logics. For Hinton and Harrison (and there are many others), the loss of linguistic diversity is couched in terms that serve "our" common human heritage in the form of knowledge systems. For Whorf, the opportunity to solve "our" problems is enhanced by being able to see from the relative perspective of other logical systems. Linguistic relativism, the idea that language influences thought, has generated intense debates and arguments for and against the moderate version of the hypothesis (see Gumperz and Levinson 1996; Gentner and Goldin-Meadow 2003). The debate is not restricted to language experts. It is not uncommon to hear politicians proclaim that one language (usually theirs) is more logical than another. Nor is it uncommon to hear heritage language speakers say that something means more in their language than in the colonial language. Second languages learners often proclaim at some point that they can "think" in the target language. In this ethnography about Maliseet language death, the language-thought debate is complicated by the changing ontological state of the Maliseet language as well as the changing terms for Maliseet identity.

Hinton has been dedicated to working with communities on projects to revitalize their languages (see Hinton 2002). She writes: "Finally, as mentioned above, language retention is a human rights issue.... Indigenous efforts toward language maintenance or revitalization are generally a part of a larger effort to retain or regain their political autonomy, their land base, or at least their own sense of identity" (Hinton 2001:5). According to Hinton, identity is another important reason why "we" should care about endangered languages. Hinton approaches the revitalization issue from multiple perspectives because there are a great variety of approaches that respond to the variety of endangerments. The approach Hinton and Hale use in their 2001 study is to provide a variety of examples from various programs designed to combat language loss. The common denominator is expressed in Hinton's statement in the introduction: "Language and culture are closely intertwined. One important reason many people want to learn their ancestral language is that they want to regain access to traditional cultural practices and traditional values. It is often said that the language is the key to and the heart of culture" (Hinton and Hale 2001:9). This statement has an ironic resonance in the discussion that follows as applied to the various generations of Tobique community members. The irony is expressed in contentious claims across generations of what constitutes "authentic" Maliseet culture. Consequently, language has different identity values across generations of community members and, not surprisingly, in accordance with their Maliseet language skills. The language, culture, and identity entanglement across generations is further complicated by the varying assessments of Maliseet identity through blood.

**Blood**

At the 2001 American Anthropological Association meetings I was enjoying a round of beers with fellow anthropologists. The group represented anthropologists working with native groups and native anthropologists working in both Native American communities and other communities.[5] The conversation came to a round of telling jokes and riddles. In our little group one of the anthropologists is self-identified as Cherokee. Another member of group is non-native but works within a Native American community. It was his turn to tell a joke. He was smiling and shaking his head and we all convinced him it would be okay if he told an "Indian" joke. He finally said, "Okay! Okay!" We were all quiet and he asked, "Do you know what you get when you have sixteen Cherokee in the same room?" We all looked at the Cherokee anthropologist, who replied,

"Okay, I have to hear this." Our friend then quipped, "A full blood!" We were all laughing at the punch line, and the Cherokee anthropologist was laughing too. He said, "Oh! I have to tell that one when I get back to the Nation!" When I returned to campus I shared the riddle with a Cherokee friend of mine. She too enjoyed it. What is funny about the riddle is that it is not funny at all. As Basso discussed in his work on joking behavior among the Apache (1979), the key to jokes and riddles is the dangerous ground they occupy. All Apache imitations of white men run the risk of not being interpreted as a joke. The jokes are critiques, and if they are not received in the proper spirit, the result could be harmful or damaging to the joker or the audience. Similarly, the riddle of the blood quantum for Native Americans must be told to the right audience in the right context. That is why the non-native anthropologist who shared the riddle with us was reticent about telling it. I told the same riddle on the Tobique reservation and it was met with much laughter and appreciation. The joke perpetuates the myth that Cherokeeness is based on a portion of blood quantum that seems miniscule (see Sturm 2002 for a critical appraisal of race, blood, and identity among the Cherokee). The blood quantum issue is hotly debated and has a long literary tradition from the Native American writers in the nineteenth century to today.[6] The issues have not been resolved, and the existential crises of mixed-blood and blood quantum politics in contemporary Native American politics continue to inspire a burgeoning literature. Complicating blood quantum politics is the "Indian status" politics in Canada. Not only do the categories suggest different identity processes, but they are not mutually exclusive (Clatworthy 2003). Ethnographic examples in the following pages illustrate the complex and contentious deployments of blood quantum and language competence as markers of Maliseetness and how they are supplemented and/or supplanted by aboriginality.

## Aboriginality

When I first began the discussion on aboriginality I used the term *super-Indian* as the categorical rubric for the discussion on pan-Indian identity. The super-Indian is much like the "really Indian" that O'Nell (1996) describes as being a factor in Flathead identity politics (see chapter 1). Both are also a part of the phenomenon of the vanishing race discourse of the nineteenth century and its popular imaginings today (see chapter 2). All these forms of imagining Indians have been filtered, consumed, parodied, and co-opted by many Native American communities. The phenomenon is much like the "work of the imagination" that Appadurai posits in the following: "I show that the work of the imagination, viewed in this context, is neither purely emancipatory nor entirely disciplined but is a space of contestation in which individuals and groups seek to annex the global into their own practices of the modern" (Appadurai 1996:4). For this ethnography, regarding the particular case of the Maliseet of Tobique First Nation and more generally of aboriginal peoples worldwide, the "global" constitutes global communication between aboriginal and indigenous groups to share common frustrations and goals as they work to "annex the global into their own practices of the modern" (4). Furthermore, Appadurai states that ethnography "must redefine itself as that practice of representation that illuminates the power of large-scale, imagined life possibilities over specific life trajectories. This is thickness with a difference, and the difference lies in a new alertness to the fact that ordinary lives today are more often powered not by the givenness of things but by the possibilities that the media (either directly or indirectly) suggest are available" (55). Similarly, the idea of alternative futures and alternative vitalities are those emerging constellations of aboriginality that require ethnographers to recognize that "culture thus shifts from being some sort of inert, local substance to being a rather more volatile form of difference" (60). That volatility and imaginative potential play a significant part in determining what is at stake in the shifting ontological status of Maliseet language and identity. As the language and identity statuses shift, so too does the potential for an increased embodiment of aboriginality.

But what is aboriginality? Michael D. Levin defines aboriginality as "a more refined claim to distinctiveness based on historical experience. It emphasizes status as the original occupants of a place, adding depth to the idea of cultural differences. The use of aboriginality as a basis for ethnonational claims does not have the universalism of ethnic claims and is restricted to those places 'discovered' by Europeans after 1492 in both the Old and New Worlds. As well as a basis for ethnonational claims, it is also a claim against immigrant ethnic groups" (Levin 1993:4–5). Naomi Adelson is in agreement with his definition but she adds, "Aboriginality is thus a critical political tool: an essential 'space of otherness that is shifting, complex, and dynamic [yet] in which Aboriginal imagination can produce an identity.' . . . In this analysis I examine the contingency, fluidity, and vitality of aboriginality as it is shaped and expressed by the Cree people of northern Québec, Canada" (Adelson 2001:80).

I use "aboriginality" in the same sense that Adelson uses it to analyze aboriginal identity formation.[7] I would extend this identity self-making strategy to contemporary enactments by indigenous peoples that are discussed under the rubric "indigeneity." It must be noted that Vine Deloria Jr. (1988) and O'Nell (1996) remind us that there are always the expectations of popular imagination, be it the mythical super-Indian or the really "real" Indian, that serve as the backdrop for any enactment of aboriginality/indigeneity. I have referred to these popular expectations as the processual phenomenon "charismatic indigeneity"(Perley, unpublished). Understanding these processes is important in untangling what it means to be Maliseet.

### Generations of "Being" Maliseet

In this section I present conversations I have had with several members of the Tobique First Nation community across several generations. Roughly, the elders are in their mid-sixties and up, the adults are typically in their forties to the mid-sixties, the young adults are in their twenties and thirties, and finally the youngsters are the school-age children from elementary school to high school. I provide a brief commentary and analysis after each section.

*Elders*

"Auntie" speaks the language with the skill of one who uses the language on a constant communicative basis. Auntie is in her mid-eighties. She has spent some time off of the reservation for employment. Auntie has the gift of ready laughter. She enjoys a good story and enjoys telling good stories. Some of the stories are quite ribald and the more ribald, the more enjoyable. Auntie is perceptive and a sharp critic. She has been successful in transmitting the language to her daughter "Cuz," who is in her late sixties. Cuz speaks the language with the same proficiency her mother does. Cuz's children, on the other hand, are split into those who can speak with good skill and those who do not. Cuz has also spent time off of the reservation for employment. Both Cuz and Auntie do not question their Maliseetness and nobody else would dare do so. One day I asked Auntie what was left of Maliseet culture and her response was, "There is no Maliseet culture. The only thing left is the language but that's disappearing too. This sweat-lodge stuff isn't Maliseet. That came from somewhere else." Auntie is speaking about the pan-Indian influences that bear upon identity politics as discussed earlier as aboriginality. But her command of the language is excellent. When she talks about the "good old days when times were bad" in Maliseet, the Maliseet is the most fluid and confident I have ever heard it. Those conversations are around the dinner table with my mother. When I returned to the reservation for a Thanksgiving visit before I started my fieldwork, I was going to stay with my cousin, but my friends and I stopped at my brother's house first. Auntie and Cuz were there to greet me after many years. My friends entered the house first and I followed. It is customary to take your shoes off before entering the house. Everybody enters houses through the kitchen. Just at the entry to the kitchen, on either side of the door, are many pairs of shoes belonging to residents and guests. Introductions were taking place as I was taking my tennis shoes off. Of course I would have to wear the socks with the holes in them! As I entered the kitchen all eyes were on me. "Ipa! Harvard boy has holes in his socks!" I looked down and wiggled my toes as everyone laughed. Aside from the exclamation "Ipa!" (Look!), all the conversation was in English. In mixed company, not only out of politeness but also out of necessity, the conversation was all in English. The people at the my brother's house were a mixed group, native and non-native, Maliseet speakers, semi-speakers, and those who did not speak Maliseet. In this social setting on the reservation, in a household of mixed generations, despite my brother's skill in speaking the language and Auntie's, Sally's, Brenda's and Cuz's skill in speaking the language, it was clear that the language needed for effective communication was English, otherwise the children in the house and my friends and I would have been left out of the conversation. In this setting, half of the people had no embodied experience for communicative relations in the Maliseet language. It was the elder generations who had the command of the language, yet they shifted the conversation to English. For the elders, it was a temporary suspension of Maliseet while conversing in that context.

I mentioned in chapter 3 that an elder woman came into the native language classroom to discuss the possibility of working on oral traditional stories. Both Sue and I were excited about the prospect of having elders in the community come into the classroom and share stories with the children in Maliseet. Much to our surprise, however, the elder wanted us to share stories with her. The elder woman was a speaker of the language, but she did not know the stories. She had received some funding to do some story collecting. Disappointed, Sue told the elder she could not help and had thought the elder would share stories with the children. Similarly, we were assigned a teacher's aide to help the teacher produce teaching materials. Sue decided to take advantage of the opportunity of working with an elder with a good command of the language. Sue had visited the Mohawk Immersion School and was given a prayer book as a gift. The Mohawk prayer book was all in English, but it had wonderful color illustrations in the native genre.[8] Sue was hoping to develop a Maliseet prayer of thanksgiving. She asked the assisting elder to translate the text into Maliseet.[9] After about a week of work with no results to speak of, we inquired about the project. The elder was stuck: "We do not have a word for 'air.'" The three of us brainstormed, and Sue and I came up with a suggestion we thought would help. We asked the elder to forget about translating from English into Maliseet. Sue had noticed that the translation was word for word and seemed awkward in Maliseet. We asked the elder to think about how she would give thanks for the blessings of the earth if she were to do it in Maliseet. The elder kept going back to the English text to say "we don't have a word for . . ." Finally, we had to settle for the translation as an incomplete project until I was able to take the text home and consult my mother about the translation. Today there is a new translation for the prayer. My mother was hired as the teacher's consultant on the Maliseet language. The previously mentioned elder was upset that she did not get the job.[10]

One elder, Bob, has been working on the language over the years in various ways and continues to dabble a little. I suggested in chapter 4 that his orthography was a good attempt but ultimately confusing. The method was to use English phonetic syllabic clusters for Maliseet sounds. As an example, the word for eagle is *cipolakon* (transcribed using the classroom orthography). However, the way the Bob would transcribe the word is "jeep-a-log-in." I noted in chapter 4 that we had to label our school exercises in the weekly newsletter so that our work would not be confused with Bob's. Despite the problematic orthography, he was at least attempting to codify the Maliseet language to allow other members of the community to experience the language as a communicative practice. Some of his contributions were part of the classroom materials, but they were never used. This same elder had promoted other Maliseet language projects, such as attempting to bring the community elders together to produce a dictionary. I heard that the project was initiated but have not heard about any results.

The elders discussed in this section display varying degrees of language commitment and various forms of language use and competence. Auntie uses the language for communication. The elder woman at the school was collecting stories. Another elder was having difficulty translating the Mohawk prayer into Maliseet. Finally, Bob is active in producing and distributing texts. In a community where the language is at risk, Bob is one elder who has produced textual materials. Most community members may have ignored his efforts to codify the language, but at least he made the effort. (There may have been other elders producing texts, but I was not aware of them or their products.)

### *Adults*

As I talked to a number of adults I realized there was a wide range of Maliseet language embodiments. All the adults I talked to could speak the language but with varying degrees of proficiency. Some say they "speak a slang Maliseet." In making that statement they are displaying an objectification of the language, but they are also evaluating their competence in Maliseet in direct comparison to the elder speakers. It was often the case that many of the conversations between adults and elders to which I was privy would include queries by the adults to clarify a meaning or to identify a new word or phrase. This was the generation who were also involved, to varying degrees, in pan-Indian politics and economics. They are a generation who participate in sweat lodges, pow-wows, and pan-Indian conferences, committees, and meetings (most often as representatives of the community). They are also the generation who hold most of the political positions as well as directorships in the tribal government. Their duties require travel and dialogue with other aboriginal leaders. Other adults, who do not have such political responsibilities, also have extensive connections to other aboriginal communities in the United States as well as in Canada. In short, this is a mobile generation with extensive connections to other aboriginal communities. They are also members of the generation who have participated in the ethnic renewal or political resurgence that has characterized aboriginal politics since the sixties. The increased communication has given them an opportunity for comparative analyses for their common problems and goals. More important, it gives the aboriginal communities an opportunity to imagine alternative futures. It was their conception of Maliseetness that intrigued me. Thus when I got the chance to inquire about their vision of Maliseetness, I asked some questions that directly put language and blood in the conversation.

DECEMBER 25, 2000

Derek is in his fifties. He is a New York Yankees fan, but I do not hold that against him. He has three sons and a daughter. He and his wife speak Maliseet, but none of their children can speak the language. Derek is also a politician. He has served on the Band Council for years. He has done much traveling for political activities. He came by the house to wish my mother, my brother Wendell, and me a Merry Christmas. The visit always starts with coffee and casual conversation about family. After a few minutes the conversation went from Christmas to football, and then I introduced the subject of language and identity: "I have a question for you—Can a person be Maliseet without speaking the language?" He responded, "Yes." His point was that Maliseetness was in the blood. It was ancestral identity. My follow-up question was, "How much blood is necessary to be Maliseet? Half, quarter, one-eighth, one-sixteenth, one-thirty-second?" Derek answered affirmatively until I reached the sixteenth and thirty-second blood quantum level, when he wavered.

I then asked, "How important is it to keep the language alive?"

"Very important. That's why it should be part of the curriculum at the school." I followed up with, "Is a person less Maliseet if they don't speak the language?"

"No, but it helps."

I decided to press the issue by asking, "What things determine Maliseetness?" His response was, "Language, customs, culture and blood."

As we were chatting about these issues George came by. George is also in his fifties. He is not a politician. His work is most often earth moving and landscaping. He has grown up with traditional food, he speaks the language, and he is a levelheaded critic and observer. I asked George about language and Maliseetness. He agreed that blood is key.

I then asked, "What about language?" His comment struck me. He replied, "It's important but in twenty years it will be dead. The elders, Auntie, your mother, and a few others still speak the language and when they die much of the language will go with them." As mentioned in chapter 6, the community is fully aware of the precarious state of the Maliseet language.

I continued by asking a question of both Derek and George. "What about those who don't speak the language? For example, many people claim that the lack of speakers in the language creates a sense of sadness at the loss of the language that leads to depression. Do you guys find that to be the case?"

Derek responded first, "Well, there is a sadness in the realization that the language is dying but I don't get depressed over it. There's a guy in California that expresses the opposite. When he hears the language spoken and is able to speak in Maliseet he says that it makes him happy to be able to speak the language. But he doesn't get depressed over not being able to speak it."

I decided to ask a direct question about nonspeakers of Maliseet. "Well, what do you think of those Maliseet who can't speak the language and get depressed over it?"

George gruffly said, "It's their problem."

When I pressed on the issue of emotion and the use of the language, the comments (from Wendell, me, Derek, and George) were that those who make such emotional claims are overdoing it. Most communication is in English anyway. Derek talked about his kids and their use of English. They have to use it in the schools and everywhere else: "That's just the way it is." These comments about "It's their problem," "overdoing it," and "That's the way it is" are coming from adults whom I describe as practical minded. The answers reflect a disaffected recognition of the Maliseet language situation, as though there are other issues to worry about.

On the topic of the way things are, George spoke of the good old days. He said he was born at the right time. Ten years earlier he would have witnessed the Depression, and ten years later he might have been on alcohol and drugs. He considers himself fortunate.

Other comments about the language were equally illuminating. George commented that he could not make sense of the Maliseet writing that his sister Lily would occasionally show him.[11] That prompted him to add, "It is an oral language and it will die in twenty years." To this, Wendell commented that when the elders die, "we'll have only slang Maliseet." Derek and George were in agreement, and they commented that they learn from the elders.

A LAWYER'S VIEW

Michael came by and I pressed him about the language and identity issue. Michael is also in his fifties. His wife is identified as Maliseet, but she does not speak Maliseet. Their children do not speak the language either. Michael is a politician and a lawyer. He also claims that blood ancestry is the key to Maliseetness. Language is important but ancestry is key. There is no question that the language should be preserved, but in terms of Maliseetness, blood is key. Michael commented, "For example—if you were born on the reserve by Maliseet parents but raised for some reason by the queen of England and brought up as a prince, Bernie, you are still Maliseet. Because of blood." I then pressed the issue of blood quantum, and he tried to dodge the question by telling me, "You're the anthropologist. What's your answer?" I told him that I only ask questions. "You're the lawyer, you guys provide the definitions."

The criterion of blood for aboriginal status led to a conversation about a news report concerning a group of men who wanted to be recognized as native. They claimed that they could trace their aboriginal ancestry for proof of aboriginal status. But why was that important at that moment? Why didn't they pursue the claim before? Michael claims they only wanted to take advantage of the Marshall decision.[12] I then countered with the question of those students identifying as native to qualify for scholarships. They too found an opportunity and therefore claimed aboriginal status to improve their eligibility for scholarships.

Michael saw the dilemma, and I decided to inquire from him about the importance of language in Maliseetness.

ME: What about language?

MICHAEL: Language is about how a person views the world.

ME: So, to speak a particular language one thinks in a particular worldview?

MICHAEL: Yes.

ME: Can a Maliseet who doesn't speak the language be Maliseet?

MICHAEL: Yes.

ME: Can a non-native who speaks Maliseet become Maliseet?

MICHAEL: No. For example, there is one woman on this reserve who is French but learned Maliseet and has lived on the reserve for most of her life and has interacted with the community but she is not recognized as Maliseet. She is French.

ME: Okay. Do you then think that because her first language is French that makes her think in French?

MICHAEL: Yes.

ME: So learning another language like Maliseet will not make her less French?

MICHAEL: No.

ME: Can she think in Maliseet?

MICHAEL: That's a good question.

ME: Does Maliseet as a first language make a person cognitively Maliseet?

MICHAEL: Yes.

ME: What if a person, like myself, grew up speaking Maliseet as a first language but had to learn English and in the process lost the Maliseet, does that make me cognitively non-Maliseet?

MICHAEL: Good question.

ME: Okay. Now let's consider all the children on the reservation right now. They are learning English as a first language. Are they all cognitively non-Maliseet? If they are not cognitively non-Maliseet are they less Maliseet as a result?

MICHAEL: No, but it is part of Maliseetness.
ME: So language is just one of the factors that go into Maliseetness?
MICHAEL: Yes.
ME: So, it's blood, language, and culture?
MICHAEL: Yes. All of those.
ME: Okay, now what if the blood continues to thin, and nobody speaks the language and there are no cultural trappings. When a white person asks the Maliseet what makes them a distinct society will they be able to claim Maliseet ancestry? What will that do to rights, etc.?
MICHAEL: Gee, I don't know.

The conversation with Michael is especially important because Michael is a lawyer and was the chief for Tobique at the time. He is well aware of the legal stakes in Maliseetness and aboriginality in the Canadian context. Yet the conversation indicates the same kind of pragmatism that Derek and George had displayed. All three of them recognize the increasing disappearance of the language and the importance of blood in determining Maliseetness. However, by recognizing the ontological shift in the language, they also recognize the increasing importance of blood as a qualifier for Maliseetness. As I pressed the issue of the "thinning of the blood," the ratio of blood quantum became an uneasy criterion because of decreasing Maliseet blood quantum today. One of the keys in the conversations described was the lack of pan-Indian markers or ideologies. It could be reflective of the questions I asked rather than a conscious disregard of pan-Indian aboriginality. The adults who best display pan-Indianness are generally referred to as "traditionalist."

The traditionalists among the adult men are typically identified by long hair (in ponytails or braids); they are drummers and chanters, and the ones I knew spoke the Maliseet language. Among the adult women long hair is common, they engage in "native" arts and crafts, and again the ones I knew spoke the Maliseet language. Men also participate in arts and crafts production, but women do not drum or chant (or at least did not in any of the occasions I witnessed). A common feature among many of the traditionalists is participation in sweat-lodge ceremonies, vision quests, and intertribal activities such as pow-wows, visits, and ceremonies.[13] These members of the community share aboriginal experiences that bring them together as traditionalists. The activities add another layer of identity processes to their complex negotiations of being Maliseet. As Adelson indicates in the observations quoted, aboriginality can be used as a political tool as well as in identity formation.

Occasionally, various groups on the reservation would use the native language classroom for meetings and presentations. I came in from lunch one day to find the room filled with people. I noticed that the group was predominantly traditionalist. I quietly entered the room and went over to the computer to continue working on the language class materials. Sitting at the desk was the father of one of the students attending the school. He turned around, gave a brief nod of his head, and asked "Tan kahk?" (How are you?) I nodded back and replied, "Mec ote" (I'm fine). He smiled and then asked me what I was doing. I showed him the classroom materials on the computer. During the rest of the conversation we spoke in English. Graham speaks the language well, but I do not. Yet he did not press the point beyond the greeting. It was enough that I knew how to respond to a very basic greeting. Similarly, when I was at a language meeting in Fredericton, the attendees were lined up at the cafeteria for lunch. I was in line when an elder Maliseet woman approached me. She greeted me with "Tan kahk?" I replied "Mec ote." She pressed on, "Skicinuwato kil?" (Do you speak Maliseet?) I replied, "Uh-huh." She smirked, nodded, and repeated in a sarcastic manner "Uh-huh . . ." So I added, "Tapo kekesq" (Only a little). Then she genuinely smiled and we continued our conversation in English. On these two occasions, the language was a test of Maliseet language boundary maintenance. It was used to determine the respondent's fit in the identity matrix of Maliseet worlds. In both cases my rudimentary knowledge of the language allowed a continued conversation marked by conviviality, not antagonism.

## THE MEDICINE WHEEL

One of the benefits of doing my fieldwork at the school was that I was included in many of the events and responsibilities involving the other staff members. One such event was PD day, professional development day. The idea was to have workshops for the teachers to enhance their professional development. I was intrigued by one particular workshop: Teachings of the Medicine Wheel. The guest presenter was an acknowledged medicine wheel teacher and healer. She presented her credentials as having been trained by an Ojibwa medicine wheel medicine man. After her successful completion of his training she was told to go out and disseminate the message and knowledge about the medicine wheel.

Following the introduction the medicine wheel teacher presented the diagram and the philosophy behind the compass orientations, colors, wisdoms, and peoples represented by the wheel. She asserted that the philosophy was pre-European contact, so it was aboriginal from time immemorial. This statement puzzled me because the four colors on the wheel were white, yellow, black, and red. I asked, "If this philosophy was pre-contact then how did the aboriginal peoples know about the other races and their stereotypical attributes?" Oops! That was the anthropologist speaking. Her rebuttal was short and sharp: "You're just not a believer!" I bring up this example to indicate that the pan-Indian phenomenon has active agents who disseminate the material in community venues. This particular philosophy has prompted New Brunswick provincial programs to enhance the aboriginal history of the Maritime Provinces. An excellent case in point is the publication of *Maliseet and Micmac: First Nations of the Maritimes* (Leavitt 1995). The high school textbook uses the medicine wheel as the paradigm on which to weave the history and cultures of Micmac and Maliseet peoples. In addition, the Native Language Curriculum Committee had discussed adopting the medicine wheel for its development of language curricula.[14]

The problem is—I have not come across any historical evidence that the Maliseet have used the medicine wheel, nor the sweat lodge, nor the vision quest. Yet these elements are playing important roles in current aboriginal identity formation. I do not mean to suggest that they should not play important roles. Rather, I mean to redirect critical focus to the shifting emphases on the constituent elements of aboriginal and Maliseet identities. Interestingly, it was only this generation who made any comments (both solicited and spontaneous) concerning language and worldview and how they factor in Maliseet identity.

The adults' responses can be explained as a direct result of my queries but may also have to do with the fact that this generation experienced many of the factors contributing to language shift as discussed in chapter 2. All of the adults discussed in this section spoke Maliseet as their first language. Additionally, they are the generation of greater mobility and political activity. As children they witnessed Maliseet language use in all social domains. But as adults they witnessed fewer and fewer domains where Maliseet was the preferred language for communication. They may be the generation of language "tip" as English became the predominant language used in everyday interactions. The adults' configurations of language, worldview, blood, and identity were complicated by the tension between shifting practices of Maliseet and English language usage. Unfortunately, one consequence was that their children acquired English more often than not as their first language. The tip toward the obsolescence of the Maliseet language was occurring intergenerationally within their families. Significantly, despite acquiring English as a first language, their children experienced language and Maliseet identity in equally complex but experientially different ways.

### *Young Adults*
It was a summer afternoon, just before the black flies began biting, when Brad came into the back yard to chat. I was in the vegetable garden pulling weeds. As he approached I stood up, groaning as I straightened my back; I am getting old. Brad stopped in at the gate and we began a polite conversation with the customary niceties of "How are you?" "What are you up to?" and "What's new?" As we talked, the topic of being Maliseet came up. Brad is white and in his early twenties. He

is my brother's adopted son. He has spent time on the reservation but not all his life. I finally asked him if he identified as Maliseet. He responded that he thought he was. He attributed his Maliseetness to the lived experience of reservation life. There was some discussion about language and blood. I asked if blood and language were determining factors in Maliseetness, and Brad said yes, but they were not the only factors. The determining factor for Brad was his life experience on the reservation. In his words, "As long as I am Maliseet in my heart, then, I am Maliseet." On paper he is Maliseet due to formal adoption. Where is the source of Maliseetness? For Brad, it is neither language nor blood. It is the lived experience, the embodiment of intersubjective relations with other residents of the Tobique reservation. His half-brother is half Maliseet. They were raised together on the reservation as brothers and continue to think of themselves as brothers. There is a blood bond between them through their mother, but the mother and Brad do not have Maliseet blood. However, in the identity calculus for the non-native young man, blood has little to do with being Maliseet. Neither does language, for that matter.

Shirley is my cousin. She is in her mid-twenties. Her parents both speak Maliseet, but Shirley does not. Shirley is not a traditionalist. She often shares stories about her exciting evenings out enjoying the singles scene. One such evening found her and a friend of hers socializing at a pub in the neighboring French community. She told me that a conversation was going back and forth between them and a couple of young men. At one point she said to her friend, "Iyasis! N'kotowisk!" (a polite gloss would be Oh! I have to use the washroom!). Only then did the young men realize the women were aboriginal. The men asked Shirley and her friend if they speak the aboriginal language. Shirley said, "Of course!" The Frenchmen then wanted to know how they would greet a stranger. Shirley told me they told the Frenchmen, "Mocimahs n'tolasol." I exclaimed, "You didn't tell them that?!" She was smiling and said, "Sure." We were both laughing now. I commented, "So now, there are a couple of Frenchmen roaming around introducing themselves by telling strangers that their underwear stinks?" Shirley smiled and nodded. Shirley is familiar with phrases and some vocabulary, but she does not use the language for communicative purposes except in strategic situations like the one described. She and I did have a conversation once in which Shirley lamented the fact that she does not speak the language. But because of the shift in language through the social and political changes there are not many opportunities to learn or use the language for those who do wish to learn. Shirley is Maliseet. She has the blood, both her parents being Maliseet, and she has lived on the reservation all her life.

Maggie is the daughter of a traditionalist. How does her experience differ from Shirley's? Maggie participates in traditionalist activities. She attends pow-wows, participates in aboriginal youth programs, and occasionally dons native accoutrements such as beadwork, feathers, etc. Most important of all, she displays a traditionalist disposition or attitude. Although Maggie participates in the aboriginal experience, she does not speak the language. Her mother is an excellent speaker but did not transmit the language to her daughter. Maggie's grandmother was the native language teacher at the school during the first attempt to teach Maliseet in the school, sometime during the 1970s. Maggie's blood quantum is not an issue and neither is her aboriginality. However, the Maliseet language is not a factor in her identity. Like Shirley and Brad, she finds the reservation experience more important than knowledge and use of the language.

There are a number of other young adults I could use for this analysis, but the issue I want to highlight is the various ways in which Maliseetness was displayed, experienced, and articulated by this generation of young adults on the reservation. In each case the language was the common weakness in their Maliseet identity options. In Maggie's case, aboriginality filled the gap. In Brad's case, reservation experience accounted for his Maliseetness. In Shirley's case it was the experience and the selective use of language in some social contexts. For this generation language and its corresponding distinct worldview were not among their identity options.

## Youngsters

Chapter 5 presented a detailed description of the activities in the native language classroom. When I first arrived on the reservation to do my fieldwork I had long hair tied back into a ponytail. When I arrived in the classroom I was "adopted" by some children more readily than others. One such child was Mikey. His father is a drummer and chanter. His family is generally described as traditionalist. Mikey warmed up to me right away and would defend me when the other students would call me "Barney" instead of Bernie. "His name is Bernie!" Mikey would exclaim. The markers of aboriginality I exhibited were long hair, dark skin (comparatively speaking), and presence in the native language classroom. The children from traditionalist families and I established easy rapport. It took a little while longer for the other students to become familiar with me. My field observations are biased toward the Mah-Sos School children because that is where the tribal chief appointed me to work. I should point out that only half of the school-aged children attended the reservation school. As mentioned in chapter 2, some parents had decided to send their children "downtown" to learn French. I do not have firsthand observations or knowledge about their experiences. I rely on parental discussions, some conversations I have had with the children, and the education reports issued by the Micmac Maliseet Institute. One incident revealed the dynamics between the two different school experiences. A traditionalist mother, whose daughter attended Mah-Sos School, shared the event with me. The young girls were gathered at the woman's house when the mother overheard the girls' conversation. Apparently the downtown girls were bragging about their school and what they enjoyed about it. In response, the woman's daughter and her friends told the other girls about how much fun the Maliseet language class was. They then began to use the Maliseet they learned in class and left the other girls completely out of the conversation. The young girls from Mah-Sos School were using the Maliseet language as an identity marker that left the other girls unresponsive and excluded. The Mah-Sos School girls also became active in shawl dance lessons. The girls were eventually required to transfer to the downtown schools, where they do not have the opportunity to continue their Maliseet lessons with the same regularity. The student transfer to the downtown schools is another example of how the Maliseet language continues to suffer increasing disembodiment. However, pan-Indian activities or aboriginal culture (such as shawl dancing for the girls and drumming for the boys) is filling in the identity gaps for some of the children.

Among the exercises in the classroom were arts and crafts. Sometimes Sue would read a story to the children that came from either compilations of Maliseet myths or myths from some other aboriginal group. After the reading Sue and I would distribute blank paper so that the children could illustrate their favorite part of the story. One day Sue had finished reading the story and I distributed the blank paper. The children were diligently drawing their illustrations and were collecting the crayons from a large box of mixed crayons for the coloring. Suddenly one student matter-of-factly said, "I need peach." Sue asked, "What do you need peach for?" "I have to color the Indians." Sue said, "Indians aren't peach." Across the room, a light-complexioned boy exclaimed, "I'm peach!" Sue said, "No you're not!" Another child of darker complexion also exclaimed, "I'm peach too!" Sue replied, "No you're not! You're brown!" Another part of the room, another little voice quipped, "I'm peach!" Finally Sue said, "Nobody is peach! We don't have a peach crayon!"

There was another exercise in which Sue read a Kluskap story to the children. Instead of their drawing an illustration she decide to have the children make their own Kluskap puppet. She had a package of gingerbread-man-shaped cardboard cutouts arranged in different shades of colors ranging from dark brown to light peach. I distributed the cardboard shapes by presenting them in a fanlike spread so that the children could see all the options and choose the one they wanted to use. It was interesting to note that the students picked the shade that most closely resembled their own complexions. What might be the importance of this observation? There is a wide variation in complexion represented by the children attending the native language class that corresponds to a wide range of variation in the Maliseet phenotype. The children seemed to gravitate toward their own embodied physical characteristics. However, from my observations, physical characteristics do not factor in the level of accomplishment in the Maliseet language exercises. Neither did coming from a traditional household. In some cases it may have more to do with individual learning skills and discipline as well as reinforcement at home. In any case, the children illustrate the varying degrees of embodiment of Maliseet language and culture through the Maliseet language class as well as varying degrees of support at home. Also, the increasing presence of aboriginality as a viable identity process serves to augment their Indian identity in direct relation to the involvement of the parents in the various identity formulations. The children benefit from two social and cultural domains where aboriginality as identity process can be explored. The school setting provides some forms of aboriginality and the home setting provides additional forms of aboriginality. The children, with the help of parents, teachers, and friends, can creatively engage in intersubjective identity self-making.

## Disembodiments of Language and Blood

The preceding discussion prompts me to address a point that Nettle and Romaine make as a reason why "suicide" should not be used to describe the nature of type of language death and to reiterate the process of disembodiment of the language. Their claim is that the letting go of a language has much to do with survival strategies. As we have seen, they argue that it may have been necessary for a particular community to give up their language so as to survive, and therefore calling the process suicide is a case of blaming the victim. I do not blame the victim because I agree with Adelson when she states:

*Irrespective of its roots or effects, social suffering must not be viewed simply as a destructive or, for that matter, a creative force. The effects and processes of inequality can be dangerously romanticized simply by naming them. To be identified as "sufferer" or "victim" shackles individuals and groups to a particular history that was never theirs to decide. I cannot imagine that Indigenous Canadians want to be defined exclusively from within the narrow confines of "sufferer" or "victim." (Adelson 2001:78)*

The examples given in this chapter indicate the myriad of options that members of the Tobique community select from to enact aspects of self in varying kinds of social contexts. Embodiments of being are not static, nor are they necessarily consistent. They are fluid, contested, indeterminate, intersubjective, processual, and the result of action on the part of the subject. I have sketched a variety of embodiments and, by inscribing them to text, have frozen them into inert snapshots of experiences. As Dilthey and Turner suggest, "meaning" is the thread by which to "conceive an intrinsic affinity between the successive events in life" (Turner 1987:96). Yes, the options are partly the result of historical victimization, but the choices aboriginal peoples can enjoy today are rich in imaginative possibility. As the language continues the trajectory toward increasing disembodiment, it moves toward an alternative vitality based on text, recordings, artwork, and other forms of potential vitality (see chapter 8). As the blood continues to thin with increased intermarriage, it also takes on a particular kind of increasing disembodiment. The sketches indicate varying degrees of blood quantum that inevitably lead to contentious debates regarding recognition and evaluation.

### Bill C-31, Legislation for Extinction

Exacerbating the contentiousness of blood and Maliseetness debates are bureaucratic institutions that legislate definitions to determine who is and who is not "Indian." These institutional definitions of Indianness privilege formal political economies of identity management, often at the expense of the community informal and experiential management of identity. All nation-states have their own histories, politics, and interpretive frames of reference for managing the category Indian (or aborigine, indigenous person, minority, etc). Canada's attempt to manage Indians took the form of the Indian Act. In 1876 Canada institutionalized the Indian Act as a means "to 'civilize' the Native peoples by assimilating them into dominant life and culture, yet at the same time segregated them onto reserves" (Mackey 2002:36). Since 1876 the act has been amended numerous times, and each amendment reflected the sociopolitical ideologies for managing Indian affairs at that point in time. Of particular interest for this discussion are the amended Indian Acts of 1951 and 1985.

The 1951 amended Indian Act reinforced the "descent through the male line" ideology of earlier Indian acts by forcibly excluding Indian women who married non-Indian men and their descendants (Silman 1987:12; Clatworthy 2003:63). Furthermore, the Act also permitted Indian men to transmit their "entitlement to Indian registration" to their children and "provided for the non-Indian wives of Indian men to acquire Indian registration" (Clatworthy 2003:63–64). In short, the amended act ensured that "every Indian woman was dependent upon a man—first her father and then her husband—for her identity, rights and status under the Indian Act" (Silman 1987:12). The act perpetuated the disregard for Indian communities with traditional matrilineal descent in favor of the "the nineteenth century patrilineal European view of women as essentially the property of men" (12–13). Many Indian women who married non-Indian men returned to their reserves, only to find that they no longer had Indian status nor any of the rights of Indians, including housing, healthcare, and education for their children (Krotz 1992:178). During the 1970s at Tobique First Nation several women who returned to the reservation found themselves without housing rights and were forcibly evicted from their homes. Some of the women began to organize and protest the discriminatory practices against them (Silman 1987; Krotz 1992). These local acts of protest by the Tobique Women's Group grew to national prominence with the women's march to Ottawa in 1979 and then to international prominence with the 1981 condemnation of Canada by the International Covenant of Civil and Political Rights. Sandra Lovelace, one of the women from Tobique, "backed by the other women and the New Brunswick Human Rights Commission, had lodged a complaint at the international body about the loss of her Indian status. And the U.N., in response, slammed Canada" (Krotz 1992:178). Krotz quotes Sandra Lovelace as having explained, "We are Indians," she says. "It never occurred to us that we could lose our Indianness. And this community is our home" (in Krotz 1992:178).

The Tobique Women's Group efforts culminated in the form of an amendment to the 1985 Indian Act, better known as Bill C-31, the Reinstatement Act. It has important implications for Indian identity in Canada. "Bill C-31 introduced three main provisions. First, was the reinstatement of Registered Indian status to individuals who had been removed from the Indian Register by the rules of prior versions of the Indian Act. Second were new gender-neutral rules governing entitlement to Indian registration for all children born to a Registered Indian parent on or after 17 April 1985. Third, was the opportunity for individual First Nations to establish their own rules governing First Nations (band) membership" (Clatworthy 2003:64). While those were important amendments in eliminating gender discrimination against Indian woman, the 1985 act also established new rules ensuring that Indian registration is a birthright that cannot be "gained or lost through marriage or other events" (64). That is the good news. Now, the bad news. Under the heading "Definition and Registration of Indians" in the Indian Act, under section 6, "persons entitled to be registered," the act provides the new rules. When taken together "the inheritance rules in Section 6 imply that parenting patterns will greatly influence the future population entitled to Indian registration" (64). Among the members of the community, the common phrase is "the third generation rule": in effect, "Parenting between Indians and non-Indians (out-marriage) over two successive generations results in loss of entitlement to Indian registration among the offspring of the second generation" (64). The implications for such parenting patterns and the trends over the next one hundred years indicate that "within two generations, most of the children born to First Nations populations are not expected to qualify for registration under the new rules. Within four generations, only one of every six children . . . born to First Nations populations is expected to qualify for registration. Unlike the rules of the old Act, which guaranteed registration to nearly all of the descendants of Registered Indian males, Bill C-31's rules have the potential to result in the extinction of the Registered Indian population" (86–87). Beyond the Indian Act rules, the complexities of First Nations membership are also reflected in other more localized types of membership rules that include unlimited one-parent rules, blood quantum rules, two-parent rules, and any combination of the above. Despite the variety of membership rules, all the population projections indicate a demographic collapse of the Registered Indian population over the next one hundred years.

Today on Tobique First Nation, the third generation rule is not an abstraction, and it has become a common topic for conversation. Many young couples are grappling with the implications of the rules as they realize that Indian status will create a "status hierarchy" that will privilege some community members over others. Status inequalities have been a part of the identity conversations all along but the implications of Bill C-31 have intensified the debate. The demographic decline of registration-eligible children thanks to Bill C-31 is already becoming apparent, and the attendant inequalities are beginning to ripple through all the families on the reservation. Clatworthy warns, "These inequalities have the potential not only to produce or enhance internal conflicts within First Nations communities but also to lead to legal challenges and jurisdictional squabbles among governments (First Nations, federal, and provincial) over responsibilities for the provision and funding of services to the various classes of First Nations populations" (Clatworthy 2003:87).

The long project of "civilizing" the Indians through legislative processes such as the Indian Act, the White Paper of 1969, and now the amended Indian Act of 1985 may finally result in the extinction of the category "Indian" as a legal concept for the Canadian government. They need only to wait about one hundred years for legal disembodiment of the Indian population in Canada.

Disembodiment by blood and disembodiment by legislation are not just abstract concepts. Blood quantum and Indian status are embodied factors that the adults mentioned as an important criterion for Maliseetness. In the same breath they would mention "culture," but there was a range of responses to what constitutes Maliseet culture, with responses ranging from pan-Indian concepts such as the medicine wheel to one comment from an elder who told me there is no Maliseet culture left: "All that's left is the language." Despite the wide range of impressions regarding Maliseet culture, the discussions do suggest that the lived experience of Tobique life is a clear indication of Maliseetness.

**Complexities of Experiential Maliseetness**
The day ended with good deeds done. The Lone Ranger and Tonto were riding into the sunset. After they had ridden a while the Lone Ranger peered ahead and noticed silhouettes on the horizon. He turned to Tonto and said, "Tonto." Tonto replied, "Yes, Kimusabi?" (When you tell this joke you have to lower your voice and in speak in monotone when saying Tonto's lines.) The Lone Ranger continues, "Looks like hostile Indians ahead. Maybe we should change directions." So the two of them turn their horses and proceed in another direction. Some time goes by, and again the Lone Ranger peers ahead. He sees more silhouettes on the horizon. "Tonto." "Yes, Kimusabi?" "It looks like more hostile Indians ahead of us. Maybe we should go another direction." The two of them turn their horses 180 degrees and ride for a while. Once again, the Lone Ranger peers forward and again sees silhouettes on the horizon. Yet again, the Lone Ranger says "Tonto." "Yes, Kimusabi?" "It looks like more hostile Indians ahead. Maybe we should go back to the town." So they turn their horses to return

to town. After a few minutes the Lone Ranger looks ahead and sees figures on the horizon. He looks to the left and sees more figures. He looks to the right and sees more figures. He looks behind and sees even more figures. He stops and says, "Tonto." "Yes, Kimusabi?" "It looks like we're surrounded!" To which Tonto replies, "What do you mean 'we,' white man?"

I shared that joke with the native language teacher when we had become familiar with one another and were working well together in the classroom. She laughed at the joke, shook her head, and muttered, "Kah-rai, Bern!"[15] Little did I know at the time that the joke's punch line would come back to haunt me. The occasion was the fall of 1995, when the Royal Commission on Aboriginal Affairs had completed a five-year study (published in 1996 as the *Report of the Royal Commission on Aboriginal Peoples*, or RCAP report).[16] The published document reviewed the thousands of pages of testimonials collected from most (if not all) the First Nations communities in Canada over the five-year period. The report was an extensive five-volume synthesis of the findings of the commission, but more important, it was also a recommendation for policy development to address the needs and concerns of Canada's aboriginal peoples. The report and its recommendations were well received and supported by aboriginal peoples across the continent. Yet the federal government made no public statements regarding the commission's report. After the aboriginal leaders had pressed the government for a response and received no response, the aboriginal leaders, through the Assembly of First Nations, decided to mobilize aboriginal communities across Canada to force the government to make some kind of public statement. The force that was organized across Canada was the blockading of the Trans-Canada Highway. The Assembly of First Nations mobilized aboriginal communities to coordinate their efforts across the continent so that at the same time, from coast to coast, the highway was to be blockaded by aboriginal activists. On the appointed day and at the appointed hour, representatives from the Tobique community went to the designated spot on the Trans-Canada Highway. At the designated time the blockade was put into place. The Royal Canadian Mounted Police (RCMP) were there to oversee the event so that it would not escalate into a violent confrontation between aboriginal activists and non-aboriginal drivers. The blockade would close the highway for thirty minutes at a time. The traffic was not stopped as much as it was inconvenienced. There was fear that hostilities would break out. Fortunately, the demonstration was peaceful. The Tobique drummers were there and so were the singers. There were adults there and children of all ages. As the traffic was halted, members of the community would pass out pamphlets expressing support for the recommendations in the RCAP report. All in all, it was a peaceful event and the message was sent to the government that the aboriginal population wanted action taken in response to the report.[17]

Why go into all this detail about the demonstration? Sue, the native language teacher, was there. On the Monday morning following the demonstration, I asked her how it went. She described the event and some of the people she met during the afternoon. After she had finished her description of the events of that afternoon I asked her, "Do you think we accomplished what we wanted with the blockade?" She replied, "Whadda ya mean 'we,' white man? You weren't there."[18] Ouch! That stung. Her tone was half serious and half joking. Just as she challenged me in the first month of my field observations in the classroom, she was challenging me again by using a label that clearly suggested outsider status, and a dubious status at that. The example in chapter 1 was in the antagonistic refrain "Here come the anthros." This time it was the label "white man." In both cases I was clearly out of the aboriginal loop. From her perspective, I was not aboriginal, not Maliseet. Even if the comment was made in jest, it stung just the same. Why? I had always regarded myself as aboriginal, as Maliseet. Yet at that moment in the classroom, my Maliseetness and my aboriginality were challenged and undermined by a Maliseet aboriginal who was at the blockade. This highlights the importance of shared experience in the determination of who is and who is not a member of the group. I shared the classroom experience with Sue on a daily basis on weekdays. I was not there, however, during the blockade. In this last account the difference between "aboriginality" and "white man" was the embodiment of the blockade experience. My experience of being there was the disembodied observation from the news reports and after-the-fact accounts. Sue's experience was the embodied intersubjective collaboration of aboriginal protest. This was not the last time my failure to participate in the blockade would come back to haunt me.

The school principal asked me to represent Mah-Sos School at a meeting being held at the Bingo Hall. I agreed, and when I arrived I noticed many meeting participants were already there. The chairs had been arranged in a circle and everyone sat next to their respective constituencies. The New Brunswick provincial representatives sat along one segment of the circle, the community artists along another segment, and other interested parties filled out the circle. The chair called the meeting to order and apologized on behalf of one absent presenter. The meeting was an effort by the Province of New Brunswick to encourage aboriginal artists from the community to participate in the arts programs sponsored by the province. As the meeting progressed there were positive exchanges between provincial representatives and community members. Suddenly, entering the room in a hasty manner was the tardy presenter. She rushed to the vacant chair and apologized for being late. Then she exclaimed, "I'm mad! I'm mad! I just finished rereading an article I wrote on neocolonialism and I'm mad!" All of us were taken aback and braced ourselves for her next salvo. The angry woman continued by going around the room and charging everyone present with some kind of complicity in the continued subjugation of the native peoples of Canada. As she was going around the circle she arrived at me, looked at me, and said, "And those academics that don't stand at the blockades are equally guilty!" She continued around the circle until everyone, Indians and non-Indians alike, was charged with neocolonial crimes against Indians. She then stopped and slumped in her chair and said, "I'm exhausted." Everyone else was still dumbstruck by her charges and her rant. Finally, directly across from me, a traditionalist woman (in a wheelchair) who has the reputation of being a formidable person began to wheel herself toward me. I braced myself for more charges of Indian misconduct. The traditionalist stopped in the center of the circle and, looking directly at me, said, "Bernie, we just want you to know that we are very proud of the work you are doing at the school." She then turned away and left the circle. At that point the circle broke up and everyone got up to leave. I stayed in my chair, savoring the moment.

The moment illustrates several key points that were discussed earlier. Drawing from the discussion in chapter 6, I continued to follow the shifting ontological statuses of being for both Maliseet language and Maliseet identity. What makes Maliseet identity a challenging discussion topic is the variability of identity. I focused primarily on three variables: language, blood, and aboriginality. I described the shift that the Maliseet language is undergoing as a case of language death; more specifically, a case of language suicide. I also argued that blood as an additional marker for Maliseetness is undergoing a similar process of disembodiment that parallels the disembodiment of the Maliseet language, albeit more slowly. I argue that the key to Maliseet survival is in another form of embodiment that addresses the theme of alternative futures; namely, the phenomenon of aboriginality. Aboriginality is a process that promotes self-determination. It will become essential if Indians are going to survive Bill C-31. My brief discussion of Bill C-31 highlights some of the key implications of the 1985 amended Indian Act and how the new rules constitute legal disembodiment through the legislation of Indian extinction. These variables—language, blood, aboriginality, and Bill C-31—were important aspects of Maliseet and aboriginal identity politics as I have observed and experienced them. I have concluded with personal reflections and experiences to contextualize my discussion and analysis and to emphasize the importance placed on "being in Maliseet worlds" as the criterion for Maliseetness.

My loss of Maliseet language is also a loss of a Maliseet worldview that prompts me to work toward alternative Maliseet worldviews and futures for the Maliseet language. My failure to participate in the protest had been considered a failure to be a Maliseet subject among other Maliseet subjects in their intersubjective act of collective action and political defiance. My work at the school in the native language class redeemed my failure to participate in civil disobedience.

This ethnography is a focused study of language and identity politics particular to the Tobique Maliseet case. A larger discussion on language and identity politics in Canada would have drawn my attention away from what is at stake for the Tobique community and Maliseet language should the language die in the next twenty years. A broader discussion would have resulted in drawing a very large bull's-eye around my arrow! Besides, the target is moving. Although my own self-confidence about my Maliseetness was shaken with the charge of being a white man, I was granted a measure of reinstatement from the woman who expressed her appreciation for the work I was doing at the school. In this chapter I have presented parallel processes of disembodiment—language, blood, and legislation. I have also presented the complexity of Maliseetness and the ever-changing expectations within as well as outside the community. More important, I argue that aboriginality, as a process of self-determination, will provide Maliseet language and identity advocates the opening to create alternative vitalities to ensure that future generations of Maliseet children will survive as Maliseet.

## 8. Emergent Vitalities of Language, Culture, and Identity

Linguists, sociolinguists, and other language scholars have published numerous comparative studies of endangered languages detailing common causes for the decline of minority and indigenous languages. My analysis of the Maliseet case at Tobique indicates that the language is indeed in serious jeopardy. Even though the many factors contributing to language shift are individually unlikely to undermine languages, collectively they are serious threats to minority languages. Maliseet represents a case where a particular constellation of factors eroded the communicative health of the language and has propelled the Maliseet language toward extinction.

**Defying the Odds**
Working to reverse Maliseet language shift, a number of individuals from the Tobique community are engaged in various programs to preserve the Maliseet language and culture. The language and culture agents are all members of the Tobique community, but they are also serving a variety of constituents. Nonetheless, they are engaged in a common cause: language maintenance and revitalization as a vital part of Maliseet cultural identity. After assessing their programs and their institutional ideologies plus the efficacy of their attempts for the Maliseet community at Tobique, I came to the unsettling conclusion

that despite their efforts the language continues to be endangered. As a result, a key aspect of Maliseet cultural identity is undermined. Furthermore, the efforts were not coordinated, and each agent/program/institution had varying experiences and training in language maintenance and revitalization work. In effect, their efforts may be too little too late.

Equally unsettling was the community response to projected Maliseet language death. Despite the many programs initiated to maintain the language there was minimal interest, and that minimal interest waned. I was left with the impression that the community was generally indifferent to the communicative health of the language. This was evidenced by the lack of interest in the language classes and meetings. Furthermore, the attrition rate for those attending the classes and meetings was such that either the meetings and classes were canceled or there was a solitary student in attendance. These numbers must be regarded in the context of a community of fifteen hundred individuals. The only individuals attending language classes regularly are the students taking the native language class at the school. The good news from the school was that at the end of the second grade the students were equally skilled in reading Maliseet as they were in French and English. But that gain was quickly lost in the following year as English was a constant learning exercise, and French was taught four (sometimes five) times a week, while Maliseet was taught only three times a week. The limited success at the school and the lack of interest in maintaining the language prompted me to characterize the type of language death the Maliseet language is suffering as death by suicide. The community was committing linguistic suicide!

Although the general disinterest is an important factor in the potential extinction of the language, there are other important factors. The most critical factor is the death of Maliseet language speakers. Each year the community loses a number of elder speakers of the language. With the death of each speaker we lose examples of language use as well as vocabularies. Compounding the problem, the elders are not transmitting their linguistic knowledge. One adult community member told me he was saddened by the fact that the elders do not use the language among themselves. Thus even the social contexts that were once the one area where the language could be heard in its most fluid and poetic expressiveness is losing its daily practice.

The disappearance of the Maliseet language in daily usage from elder speakers is just one aspect of the disappearance of Maliseet from everyday lives. For example, everyday business transactions are done in English. No new efforts have been made to use Maliseet as the language for official business. Tobique First Nation has its own radio station, but the reservation radio station does not have Maliseet programming. The signs on the reservation are either in English, or, as in the case of the highway signs leading into the reservation, bilingual in French and English.

The odds seem to be overwhelmingly against revitalizing the Maliseet language. But that is no reason to give up. Opportunities exist for action that may not have direct results today for the effective revitalization of the language, but they may provide the foundation for Maliseet language revitalization in the future. There are a number of community members who are defying the odds and have initiated creative Maliseet language, culture, and identity projects that could collectively reverse language shift from endangerment to revitalization.

**Current and Projected Maliseet Language and Cultural Resources**
Every time I return to the reservation to visit friends and family I hear about new and exciting language and culture projects. The projects range from art exhibits and children's books to translation services. Many of these projects are informal local initiatives and can serve as potential catalysts for tipping Maliseet language shift toward revitalization. Three developments related to language and culture are the planned Cultural Resource Center, aboriginal self-determination, and new media practices.

### Cultural Resource Center

During a past conversation I had with a former chief regarding the state of the language and his programs for Maliseet language and culture, the chief voiced a commitment to do what he can to promote language and cultural survival. His stance regarding Maliseetness was anchored in language. Using this as a basis, he also wanted to follow through by establishing some kind of program that would encourage Maliseet language and cultural survival. His solution is to create a central location for collecting and archiving Maliseet language and cultural artifacts. Equally important is the subsequent dissemination of the knowledge that the resource center would facilitate. I see this development as an important step toward reversing the trajectory toward language morbidity. The idea is to preserve the memories of Maliseet pasts so that the community may have access to those shared memories. In effect, it would enhance the chances for intersubjective embodiments of Maliseet pasts. Displaying and collecting such memories would "codify" Maliseet pasts for the benefit of the whole community, not just for a few families (or generations) who remember the Maliseet past. As I mentioned earlier, the linguistic shift is away from the domestic economy of Maliseet language and culture to a political economy of language and culture. The resource center will still signify a move from the homes to a central institution for redistribution. I believe this to be an important move that recalls the argument O'Nell makes of "the empty center" as the locus of the "really Indian." If the Maliseet resource center does become a reality, it can serve as that important symbolic center determining the discourse of Maliseet cultural identity. The empty center could be filled with memories and artifacts of the varieties of ways of being Maliseet. The present and future generations will have models from which they can imagine their own constellations of Maliseet cultural diacritics. Even though these are my personal projections of the potential language and cultural revitalization projects the proposed center could promote, the important point to remember is that the current sociopolitical climate makes feasible the planning for language and cultural revitalization projects as the chief proposed. The center could be an important investment in the survival of Maliseet language and Maliseet cultural identity.

It has been a few years since I had that conversation. Over those years the chief did establish the Maliseet Language Curriculum Committee and provided supplies and office space. Sue, the native language teacher, and her assistant moved to the new office to begin work on the curriculum. They were assisted in the project by various clerical and research partners. The result of their efforts was a Maliseet language course curriculum from kindergarten to grade six. However, it remains to be seen whether Maliseet or non-Maliseet schools will adopt the course curriculum. Meanwhile, the committee members continue to develop Maliseet language projects. Unfortunately, budgetary shortfalls have forced them to spend some of their time applying for grants.

The budgetary shortfall has also postponed any action on developing and building a Maliseet language and cultural resource center. I am unaware of any concrete plans for the center. Despite the positive sociopolitical climate in contemporary Canada, the economic climate has forced community members to focus on more pressing needs.

## *A Sense of Aboriginality*

The growing discourse of aboriginality in Canada has been an important intertribal dialogue in sharing aboriginal values and goals. The shared knowledge of surviving their collective colonial past and their individual efforts to "survive as Indians" (Boldt 1993) has established a nationwide network of political and cultural awareness. Such awareness led to collective actions such as the peace protests during the Oka crisis in 1990 and the highway blockades in 1995.[1] The continued conversations have led to the organization of new political affiliations like the Atlantic Policy Congress in the Maritime Provinces and the Mawiw Council in New Brunswick. Both organizations are aboriginal and intertribal. Through such intertribal dialogues and community visits, aboriginal cultural modes and practices are also exchanged and disseminated. This is not new. The Maliseet have been members of the Wabanaki Confederacy and the Union of New Brunswick Indians. Some tribal members continue to maintain those intertribal associations. What is new is the renewed sense of aboriginality. The new sense of aboriginality is not founded on victim status. The claims to self-determination and the tactics toward achieving self-determination have taken new directions. This historical moment recalls Kay B. Warren's description of the success of the Maya intellectual activists in Guatemala. Simply put, Warren identifies a political opening she describes as "a democratic opening" that allowed a political space for the Maya activists to articulate their vision of self-determination.[2] Their vision was described as Maya cultural "revindication." I see similar processes taking place with the pan-Indian discourse on aboriginality. It is language and cultural revindication that initiates projects such as a Maliseet language and cultural resource center to promote a discourse of survival as Maliseet. The chief was attempting to make his vision of Maliseet language and cultural revitalization a reality by taking advantage of the opening in the sociopolitical climate in Canada.

The concept of aboriginality is "essentially" anchored in the aboriginal origins of the various indigenous peoples of Canada.[3] I see the larger discourse of aboriginality as similar to the distinct cultures stance that the Québecois used for their claims to autonomy. Yet, as a pan-Indian political tool, aboriginality is of limited use locally. In local contexts the discourse uses more locally specific rhetoric. For example, members of Tobique First Nation speak of traditional foods as well as the places where such foods were gathered and hunted. I have heard and participated in conversations discussing Maliseet place names that were subsumed by English names. I have observed historical reenactments of the "founding of Tobique" and heard pronouncements of revitalizing the Wabanaki Confederacy by establishing a constitution.[4] There have been discussions of not letting what happened in the past happen again, such as the institution of an Indian agent, governmental receivership, and the disregard of aboriginal voices. In all these examples the memories of the past are local and the actions taken today are also local; yet they are national as well (international, in some cases). Further, the actions indicate the imaginative formulations of what Maliseetness means today. In short, aboriginal identity assertions across Canada are creating more opportunities for local language and cultural survival programs (Perley 2006).

I was told that one of the native teachers in the school has started a project to translate the Beatles' song "Yellow Submarine" into Maliseet. This is yet another development that may tip the language toward revitalization. Other songs that have been translated are "Silent Night" and "O Canada." Other projects include translating a Mohawk thanksgiving prayer into Maliseet ("Nolosweltom") as well as the Catholic Mass. In the local newsletter cartoons like "Peanuts" and "The Wizard of Id" are sometimes translated into Maliseet. The newsletter also provides crossword puzzles and word searches in Maliseet along with English translations for the Maliseet words. These examples illustrate the increasing reach of intercultural exchange and that it is happening more often. These are critical examples of local community efforts to re-embody the Maliseet language into everyday Maliseet lives. The examples also illustrate the variety of ways the Maliseet language finds its way into more venues. These moves are significant because they take cultural forms from the dominant culture and translate them into Maliseet. It is a healthy recognition of popular media and a way of enhancing them with distinctive Maliseetness. The effect will be to bring prestige to the Maliseet language, but it is also indicative of the resourcefulness of members of the community in finding alternative vitalities for the language. All these projects indicate a continued life in the Maliseet language and that the pressures brought to bear on the language toward death, formidable as they are, do not necessarily mean that the language is condemned to extinction. Rather, the speakers and advocates of the Maliseet language are finding alternative venues for the ongoing life of the language. Imagining alternative vitalities is a fundamental aspect of aboriginality.

### New Media

The prospects for the survival of the Maliseet language are not exclusively contingent upon Maliseet community members using the language in daily communicative events. There are a number of factors involved in undermining the viability of Maliseet as the primary communicative medium at Tobique First Nation, among them media. Despite the claims by many community members that media are responsible for the cessation of Maliseet language use, we are faced with the irony that two important forms of media may actually provide the community with viable options for promoting Maliseet language revitalization and cultural identity. The Internet and television, as media of instant access, are poised to convert mediated representations into daily speaking opportunities. Although the representations are texts and are removed from immediate social interactions, their importance is their availability as models for alternative Maliseet language vitalities. The Internet and television make Maliseet discourses available to anyone who decides to access those discourses. The potential for these alternative forms of Maliseet language is that these media may become instrumental in revitalizing the Maliseet language. Ironically, they can do so through the virtual disembodiment of the Maliseet language via mechanical reproduction. That disembodiment may benefit the Maliseet community as the Internet and television become a factor in promoting the revitalization of the Maliseet language.

While doing research for this chapter I typed the word *Koluhskap* into an Internet search engine and was given the link to a Virtual Museum.Ca website. To my surprise the link took me to a site that gives the viewer the option to view the site in Maliseet! The other language options were English (apparently the default page for English-centric web browsers) and French. I decided to explore the Maliseet version and I moved the curser to *Wolastoqiyik*. I was linked to a completely Maliseet text. Unfortunately, my paltry language skills in Maliseet necessitated my return to the English version of the site. I was and am delighted to see Maliseet alongside French and English as options for viewing the site.

The Maliseet language has found virtual equality on the worldwide web. This virtual disembodiment of the Maliseet language gives the viewer the option at the top of the homepage to listen to Maliseet stories told in Maliseet by several different Maliseet storytellers. In the "Stories" section of the site you are presented with a list headed by the category "stories" and followed by a series of .wav files. In the stories section you are offered an index of stories presented in Maliseet. This alternative form of language and cultural dissemination provides community members with access to Maliseet storytellers telling Maliseet stories in the Maliseet language. The materials on this website are good examples of alternative vitalities for Maliseet language and culture. However, the ideal solution would entail Maliseet storytellers telling Maliseet stories in Maliseet in Maliseet homes, so that the stories are not displaced or disembodied (Perley 2012b). Despite the fact that the stories are displaced and disembodied, their ontological status as virtual alternatives give members of Tobique First Nation an opportunity to hear the stories in Maliseet in their own homes.

Another example of potentially beneficial mediated representations of the Maliseet language is a television programming project currently under way at Tobique First Nation. I describe the following ethnographic account as "Clip 17."

Clip 17 was the designation given to the script by the director of the Maliseet language recording session. The recording session required that clip 17 be translated from English into Maliseet. The event took place in December 2006, in the home of Kris. Three speakers of Maliseet were seated at a table; John, a middle-aged Maliseet man from Tobique and the director of the project, was seated at one end of the rectangular table in front of his laptop computer. Kris, John's elder sister, also from Tobique, was seated on one side of the table with a hard copy of the script on the table in front of her. My mother was seated at the other end of the table opposite John, and she had a copy of the script in front of her. I was a last-minute invitee who had no contribution to make to the project. I sat in a chair against the wall out of the way of the production team. The sound studio was a small room in Kris's basement and it was fitted with audio equipment, a small sound booth, a table with chairs, and video equipment on tripods positioned along the wall where I was sitting. Pat, the videographer, was sitting in the chair next to me. Pat and I watched and listened as the audio team went about their work.

The process was simple. The script, taken from an earlier recording, was distributed among the three Maliseet speakers. All three would read through the script and translate from English into Maliseet. All three would stop at particularly difficult words and discuss what the proper translations were for those words. Once the three speakers were in agreement my mother would disappear into the recording booth and read/speak the Maliseet translation. While my mother performed the translation, the other two speakers would follow along and at various points they would look at each other and smile broadly while nodding to indicate their delight at my mother's skill at translation on-the-fly as well as at the beauty of the Maliseet language.

A number of things stood out as significant from this event. In my fieldnotes I had written down the following observation: "Three speakers working together—'decolonization' came up. A discussion of how to translate the word resulted in an agreement by all three. I interpreted this event as 'coming up with new words.' My mother corrected me and asserted that they didn't make up a new word. They were just finding the right translation." My mistake was to consider *decolonization* a word; that is, text. The three Maliseet speakers were thinking process; that is, discourse. The lesson for me was that this project was not about translation. It was about representing discursive processes into Maliseet experiential terms. My impression was rooted in text, not discourse. Ironically, the three speakers were giving Maliseet voices to a transcribed English text that was drawn from an interview of an aboriginal woman activist who used terms such as *truth, honesty, newspaper, storytelling,* and *journalism ethics* as well as *decolonization* during the interview. The three speakers negotiated the proper representation for the problematic elements. They were also voicing their aboriginal experiential representations of those processes as coded in English terms. At the close of the recording session John mentioned that the project would be broadcast on the Aboriginal Peoples Television Network (APTN) and everyone across Canada would be able to hear the Maliseet language. At this point Kris interjected, "Yes, but nobody'll understand." The program did air across Canada, and I have since heard that the feedback from the community was expressed as pride and excitement that the Maliseet language was being broadcast across Canada. The non-natives in the neighboring community also expressed their delight in the Maliseet voice-overs.

Those television programs have the potential to help revitalize the language and promote Maliseet cultural identity. For members of the community who understand the Maliseet language they can enjoy another venue where the language is being used. For those who do not understand the language, the programs provide additional examples of language use in practice. The television and Internet offerings, both mediated forms of Maliseet, are easily accessible to the community for further listening and viewing pleasure. Media have been identified as a key factor in Maliseet language contraction. Now it seems that new media may be important in reintegrating the Maliseet language into Maliseet cultural and social worlds and thereby providing alternative vitalities for the Maliseet language, culture, and identity.

Nettle and Romaine (2000) argue that the speakers of endangered languages had to "let their languages go" because of the greater need to survive. That case may be argued for the Maliseet community of Tobique sixty years ago. It may have been necessary to let the language go in order for the people to live, but in the subsequent decades the situation has changed in Canada. It may be the case that the reverse may be true today and tomorrow; namely, that the Maliseet language needs to live for the people to live. More reports are being published that argue for language as essential for identity, and I hear similar claims being made by members of the Tobique community. The chief can be that pivotal figure who articulates ideologically a community commitment to revitalize the language through the establishment of the language and cultural resource center. I argue that the efficacy of the projected language and cultural resource center will be in the way it fills the "empty center" of aboriginal identity with a specifically Maliseet cultural identity, by consolidating the various forms of the Maliseet language such as recordings, texts, lexicons, stories, and expressive media yet to be imagined. The physical center may become the center of action and innovation where emergent vitalities for the Maliseet language are developed and subsequently transmitted.

### Reflections on Maliseet Emergent Vitalities

This ethnography is still in progress. My critical assessment of the communicative health of the Maliseet language is an analysis from a perspective that looked at a number of outside factors and the probable causes and effects of those various factors. Although the cause-and-effect projections are not decisive, they categorically suggest probable causes for observed effects. Yet, important as this analysis is, I regard this ethnography as one piece of a much larger ethnographic project. Just as we need to rethink language and language communities, we also need to rethink ethnographies. The analytical tools of linguistics and anthropology have contributed greatly to the understanding of the global phenomenon language endangerment. But personally, I find that the analysis of language shift has come to a point where the next steps must be considered and taken.

My professional development as an anthropologist has been a long series of engaging conversations with remarkable colleagues from many fields of research. It has become clear to me that there are always more articles to read, more conferences to attend, more conversations to have, and new friends to make. My professional development has been challenging, exciting, and ongoing. Early in my career I was asked a critical question that changed my perspective on language death:

"How do you feel about the loss of the language?" The context of the question was in the midst of a discussion regarding my description of the shift of research interest in language away from "communication" and toward language as "object." To summarize, the language advocates were ostensibly involved with language for communicative purposes, but their involvement in language programs was contingent upon adequate funding to keep their respective programs operating. Consequently, language commitment was based on outside funding and not on a sacrifice of personal time to promote language maintenance and revitalization. These considerations prompted me to infer that the language was largely used for its symbolic capital (Bourdieu 1977, 1990, 1991). Even though the Maliseet language was not used communicatively on a daily basis, either politically or domestically, it was continually argued that it was the "official language" of Tobique First Nation. This sentiment runs parallel to the "distinct culture, distinct language" argument used by many ethnonationalist ideologues. My explanation of this situation to a reader was what prompted him to ask me the question about how I felt. As I left that meeting I was immersed in self-reflexive contemplations of my commitment to the Maliseet language. At that time, my answer was not a direct response because I had not forced myself to answer the question. I remember my answer being vague and hesitant—to paraphrase, "I recognize that my thesis is another example of academic profiteering from an endangered language, an objectification of an endangered language, and another instance of 'cashing in' on the symbolic capital of language advocacy. But is there anything emotionally at stake for me should the language die? That's hard to say."

Since that moment of question and reflection I have changed the terms of my study and changed the direction of my work. An early conceptualization of this research was framed in quasi-religious undertones. Most notably, I used expressions such as "death and resurrection." I decided to change my stance to death by suicide because it reflects my decision to take a more active role in politicizing the precarious state of the language vis-à-vis the Tobique community and larger Canadian language politics as well. I changed the direction of the work to support the politicization of aboriginal languages but also to confront my ambivalence toward anthropology practice. I have been admonished to distance myself from the research on one occasion with the advice, "Remember, Bernie, this is social analysis." I do believe that advice steered me away from making a commitment to the language; my stance was still undetermined at the time I received that admonishment. However, as a result of a later discussion when I was asked how I felt about Maliseet language death, I decided to take an active role as an advocate as well as an analyst in my capacities as native and anthropologist.

My role as native in the context of this ethnography brings to consideration the multiple responsibilities as well as the multiple possibilities I can bring to the work. I have outlined and complicated my articulation of being Maliseet and Native American in the preceding chapter. It is a form of identity politics that posits multiplicity of self-consciousness finding opportunities for action and planning. In addition, it promotes vitalities in the present as they unfold in the intersubjective unfolding of being in the world. But more important, it also promotes vitalities of the self in their potential becomings. It coincides with Appadurai's salient concept of "imaginings" in contemporaneous worlds. It is a conception of the self that can be imagined from a variety of possibilities and strategically deployed in the intersubjective becomings in the world.

Similarly, my role as anthropologist is equally multiple and complicated. During my early training as an anthropologist, I naively thought the demarcation between anthropologist and subject was neatly defined. Even after fieldwork and the admonition about social analysis, I thought the roles could be disentangled. Yet after my reflexive moment I realized that the complications of being both native and anthropologist gave me opportunities to situate my dual identity in ways that would allow effective advocacy as well as effective analysis. By taking for granted the divide between the received categories of native and anthropologist I allowed the suppression of agency for both personas. As long as I saw the duality as producing irreconcilable differences, I could not see the potential in my situation. Happily, the reflexive moment allowed me to rethink the duality not as a separation of the self but as the articulation of an intra-subjective self that can work intersubjectively in a field of potential projections into the world at large. The anthropologist was equally contaminated and contaminating, just as the native was equally contaminated and contaminating. In this formulation of self as native and anthropologist I can deploy an agent active in advocacy and analysis where both the native and the anthropologist can constructively advocate and analyze. It is about alternatives. One such alternative is my program for reintegrating the Maliseet language into Maliseet lives. The program is also an expansion of ethnographic representation. Ethnographies need not be restricted to textual representations of fieldwork years after the fact. As a native and an anthropologist I advocate engaged ethnographies that support emergent constellations of language, culture, and identity. One such project I call Wəlastəkwi Cosmogenesis (Maliseet Cosmogonical Beginnings).

Wəlastəkwi Cosmogenesis is my deliberate attempt to initiate a new Maliseet cosmogony that incorporates the Maliseet language, Maliseet oral traditions, Maliseet prayer, and the Maliseet landscape. The project is an arrangement of twelve three-foot by seven-foot paintings. The center of the arrangement of paintings is my axis mundi, the Tobique Rock located at the confluence of the Tobique and Saint John rivers. The background landscape is a reconstructed 360-degree primordial landscape as seen from the Tobique Rock. The twelve panels correspond to twelve lines of the Maliseet prayer of thanksgiving. Four of the twelve panels are oriented to the four cardinal directions where East represents the first light of dawn, the first line of prayer, and the direction for new beginnings. On each of the twelve large paintings there are five smaller panels (suspended just above the surface of the painting) that pay homage to the five Wabanaki Nations. A large birch bark panel represents my adaptation of a traditional Maliseet art form and graphically illustrates a single line of the Maliseet prayer. A smaller hand print panel is my signature as well as a marker indicating the viewer's location in the prayer. The smaller text panels provide the text for each line of prayer in Maliseet and English. An even smaller panel depicts the traditional food mahsosiol (fiddleheads) as a symbol for Tobique First Nation. The smallest panel is a reinterpretation and revitalization of a tradition birch bark pattern. Together, arranged in a circle, the twelve panels create a sacred space for prayer and meditation.[5] The process of designing, constructing, and experiencing Wəlastəkwi Cosmogenesis was itself (and continues to be) an act of prayer. The goal for this reintegration project is to instill prestige in Maliseet language, culture, and identity. It is designed to inspire Maliseet community members to reintegrate the Maliseet language into their everyday lives.

The planned Cultural Resource Center promises to be an important place to celebrate Maliseet culture in all its complexity. Aboriginality, as a strategy for aboriginal self-making, allows Maliseet people to imagine possible futures for Maliseet identity. The creative use of new media presents alternative and emergent vitalities for Maliseet language, culture, and identity. These recent developments are important contributions to providing alternatives to Maliseet language suicide. Wəlastəkwi Cosmogenesis is also an alternative to language suicide. However, it is not enough to provide alternatives to language suicide. Most important, Wəlastəkwi Cosmogenesis is about beginnings. It is my hope that Wəlastəkwi Cosmogenesis will be a catalyst for reintegrating spoken Maliseet into the everyday lives of the community members of Tobique First Nation. In the end, this ethnography is less about language death and more about language life. The life of the Maliseet language depends upon its reintegration into the lives of the Maliseet people. If the Maliseet language is reinstated in its role as the mediator for Maliseet culture, Maliseet identity, and everyday conversations, then we can celebrate the life of the Maliseet language and the survival of Maliseet cultural identity for generations to come.

Let us give thanks for life.
 Wəlasweltəmohtine ciw pəmawhsowakən.[6]

# Notes

### 1. The Specter of Language Death

1. I have received permission from Chief Stewart Paul of Tobique First Nation to use the actual name of the community for my publications. He has also given me permission to use the research data from my fieldwork for teaching and publication purposes.

2. See http://www.unesco.org/culture/ich/index.php?pg=00206.

3. See http://www.nationalgeographic.com/mission/enduringvoices/.

4. In the years since my initial fieldwork the sign has since come down and been replaced by a more distinguished looking sign. After the earlier sign came down one of the eagles was salvaged and mounted on one of the remaining steel pipes.

5. I was coming out of the band office one morning and a woman was walking toward the office entrance and we were both noticing the number of headstones in the immediately adjacent cemetery. The woman looked at me with a mischievous smile and shook her head, saying, "Ever since they opened the new cemetery people have been dying to get in!" I could only smile back and shake my head in agreement.

6. The band office has moved since my fieldwork. The band government decided to move into a newly completed complex that was originally designed to be a "Lodge" for tourists as part of an economic development program. For reasons unknown to me, the band government decided to use the Lodge as the new band office. This may be the only band office that has jacuzzis in each office!

7. The Tiger's Den no longer exists. It burned to the ground after a kitchen accident set the building ablaze.

8. At the time of writing Mah-Sos School has been vacated while serious mold problems were addressed.

9. It was fortunate for the Tobique community that the neighboring non-native communities sent their volunteer fire fighters to put out the blaze because the Tobique fire engine was absent, undergoing repairs.

10. I was born in the Convent on Main Street, across from the church. The Convent no longer exists; it was demolished during the time I was doing fieldwork.

11. Maliseet community members also use the term because of the dominant cultural pressures for effective communication. This issue is developed later in the book.

12. This spelling is on the official letterhead. I discuss orthographic ideologies in chapter 4.

13. This was true at the time of fieldwork but the intervening years have seen changes in tribal government as well as in the fortunes of the families on Rodeo Drive. The term is seldom used today.

14. American Friends Service Committee (1989:D-8).

15. American Friends Service Committee (1989:D-8).

16. There is no consensus on either the use of this term or the spelling. For example, I have heard it said by a "fluent" speaker of Maliseet that the term should be Wolastokukwiyik, and yet many others cannot agree on the spelling of either term.

17. On vocabulary see Barratt (1851), Alger (1885), Jack (1895), and especially Chamberlain (1899). For grammar see Teeter (1967, 1971). For story collections see Charles Godfrey Leland (1992, originally published in 1884 and reprinted in 1902) for his two collections and respective translation attempts as a professional response to Henry Rowe Schoolcraft's *Algic Researches* (1839). See also John Dyneley Prince for his collaborative work with Leland (Leland and Prince 1902) and his "correction" to Leland's "poetic" impulse in his representation of *Passamaquoddy Texts* (1921). Prince published additional Passamaquoddy papers (1897, 1899, 1901, 1916, 1917). For Maliseet-specific tales, see Frank Speck (1917) and W. H. Mechling (1913, 1914). On prayers see Vetromile (1857), a small prayer book with some "Maliseet prayers."

18. See *Kolusuwakonol: Philip S. LeSourd's Passamaquoddy-Maliseet and English Dictionary* as edited by Robert M. Leavitt and David A. Francis (1984). For grammar see Leavitt and Francis, *Passamaquoddy-Maliseet Verb Paradigms* (1986). The resource book is Leavitt, *Maliseet and Micmac: First Nations of the Maritimes* (1995).

19. There were several books from WBEP in the classroom but the two that

were adjusted for classroom instruction were *Amucalu* (The Fly) and *Espons* (The Racoon). *Amucalu* was used as a simple and interactive text while *Espons* is a nicely illustrated reading and vocabulary text that required some adjustments in terms of dialect and local expressive idioms.

20. See Ganong (1899), Prince (1921), Erickson (1978), Sherwood (1986), and LeSourd (2007).

21. Although Michael Herzfeld is referring to three vignettes of Greek "cosmologies" I see similar cosmological imaginings among ethnographers.

22. Kay Warren is discussing a Pan-Mayan movement designed to consolidate Mayan cultural and political efforts in the face of state oppression. The Maliseet case is similar but is neither as dramatic nor as large scale. Yet I argue the goals are the same; namely, cultural, linguistic, and personal survival.

23. I draw from Donna Haraway's (1991) discussion of "situated knowledge" as she asserts her interpretive observational stance as a woman and a scientist. Similarly, I assert a situatedness that observes from the different epistemic positions of native and anthropologist.

24. Anthropologists sometimes claim to understand the "native" mind, as exemplified by Lévi-Strauss in *The Savage Mind* (1966), Marshall Sahlins in *How Natives Think* (1995), and Leland in *Algonquin Legends* (1992); also see the following note). I find it amusing to think that members of the Tobique community (or other native/aboriginal communities) may react to my studying anthropology with "Oh my! He's gone anthropologist!" If so, can I make the claim—"I understand how anthropologists think"? I explore this as "epistemic slippage" in an unpublished essay (Perley 2012a).

25. One of the most striking examples of "going native" is in the person of Frank Hamilton Cushing during his five-year stay with the Zuni (Cushing 1970). I am also struck by Evans-Pritchard's comment in *Witchcraft, Oracles, and Magic among the Azande* that he "was thinking black" (Evans-Pritchard 1976:45) when he too saw "witchcraft on its path" (11). I, on the other hand, while going native, saw "rationality" at work!

26. The term *reflexivity* can be quite slippery and can have multiple uses for various disciplines. For theoretical consideration I draw from George E. Marcus (1998) as he presents his analysis of varieties of reflexivity in his 1994 essay "On Ideologies of Reflexivity in Contemporary Efforts to Remake the Human Sciences." Michael Herzfeld (2001) also presents an extended discussion on reflexivity. Additional works that inform my engagement in reflexivity include Vine Deloria Jr.'s *Anthropologists and Other Friends* (1988), for reasons why anthropologists became reflexive; Biolsi and Zimmerman's (1997) edited

volume, including essays by Grobsmith, Wax, and Whitely, for reactions from the anthropology community; Deloria's reaction to anthropologists' reactions, in the same 1997 volume; Peter M. Whiteley's *Rethinking Hopi Ethnography* (1998); Kay B. Warren's *Indigenous Movements and Their Critics: Pan-Maya Activism in Guatemala* (1998), for assessing the practice of reflexivity; and especially Paul Kroskrity's (2000) account of Edward P. Dozier's experiences in the Arizona Tewa community. There are others that I have read and considered with interest but the authors mentioned are the ones who have contributed most to my deliberations on reflexivity theory, reaction, and practice.

27. This is not to suggest that such doubts did not exist before, but the field experience presented additional frames of reference from which my doubts began to crystallize into differing critical perspectives that lead to my conception of aboriginality.

28. Rather than use the term *intrasubjective*, I use *intersubjective* in this passage to indicate that the subject, myself, as both native and anthropologist, undergoes the dialectical/dialogical negotiations of both epistemic worlds. Hence the intersubjective is also negotiated within an individual. However, the intersubjective negotiations that I discuss more often occur between subjects, such as between the anthropologist and his or her subject.

29. The literature encompasses fields of inquiry such as philosophy of science, social sciences, cultural studies, epistemology, feminist theory, etc. For purposes of this argument I reference only those sources that directly inform my argument.

30. Such ideas continue to draw on popular science periodicals, films, newspaper accounts, and television documentaries. Often the topics are archaeological or about "primitive" peoples doing strange things.

31. *Interobjective* is a term I use to describe the moment when I realized that the agents in the field had already formed notions of what anthropologists are and do. Equally important, they were also watching me to see if I matched their impressions of who anthropologists are and what they do.

32. This episode is akin to the kinds of social dramas that fascinated Victor Turner (1987) as he posited his postmodern turn toward using social tensions and processual resolutions as his ethnographic and theoretical foci. In this particular drama the process from the moment of initial enactment of public tension to the acceptable resolution took several months. More important, I mention process to indicate that the negotiations between the teacher and me were intersubjective dialogues that changed as we became familiar with each other.

33. Dennis Tedlock and Bruce Mannheim's argument of dialogics in the field suggests that the ethnographer and the subjects are both changed through the dialogue established between them (Tedlock and Mannheim 1995:15). The point I emphasize here is that the subject's objectification of the anthropologist is determined by observation and based on past knowledge and impressions of what anthropologists are and what they do. On the reservation most people who gave it any thought would comment on dinosaurs and archaeological projects. Others, who are familiar with Vine Deloria Jr.'s critique, are suspicious of anthropologists and their research.

34. Bauman states that intertexuality is the "relational orientation of a text to other texts" (2004:4). Allen offers the following: "The text becomes the intertext" (2000:1). While I agree with both statements I would add Agha's statement, "the social relevance of inter-event semiosis, its capacity to formulate and maintain social formations, depends on a complex interplay between language and non-language" (2005:4). Maliseet language is inherently intertextual in all its creative complexity, as this ethnography shows.

35. See Perley (unpublished) for a critical discussion on performances as related to expectations of indigeneity.

## 2. "Tipping" toward Maliseet Language Death

1. The vanishing race is a deeply rooted modern social imaginary that continues to resonate in popular culture today as part of the "moral order of society" (Taylor 2004:2).

2. It should be noted that Edward Curtis manipulated some of the images to give the subjects an authentic Indian appearance (see, for example, Makepeace 2001). It would seem O'Nell's "really Indian" existed in Curtis's imagination and subsequently in his photographs. Other images were staged to preserve romantic impressions of Indians in their natural elements. The Indians in the photos were sometimes dressed in buckskins and feathers provided by Curtis. The accoutrements were often of a very different culture group.

3. Quote taken from a ten-page compilation of quotations titled "Selected Quotes from Aboriginal Language Literature" distributed by the chair of native studies, St. Thomas University, New Brunswick, Canada.

4. From "Selected Quotes from Aboriginal Language Literature."

5. The accompanying footnote reads: "A biography of Roger Hart, describing consequences of his dormitory experience, is provided by Haviland (nd): 'I got my own word': Languages, Identity and Autobiography in North Queensland." John Beard Haviland presented this paper at the American Anthropological Association's annual meeting in Washington DC in 1985.

6. Notes for an address by the Honourable Jane Stewart, Minister of Indian Affairs and Northern Development, on the occasion of the unveiling of "Gathering Strength—Canada's Aboriginal Action Plan," Ottawa, Ontario, January 7, 1998.

## 3. Programming Language Maintenance

1. Telephone interview by the author, March 1997.

2. Although this book focuses on the efforts of Maliseet language agents, the Micmac-Maliseet Institute has great potential for influencing the way native studies may be taught in the province. For example, my comment about the limited application of the medicine wheel is not completely correct. New Ireland Press published the high school textbook *Maliseet and Micmac: First Nations of the Maritimes* (1995) authored by Robert M. Leavitt. Throughout the textbook the medicine wheel is a generative paradigm for much of the discussion concerning aboriginal culture in the Maritime Provinces; specifically Micmac and Maliseet. The author asserts that the textbook "emphasizes the Native point of view. The hope is that this text will provide insights for those who would not otherwise be able to 'walk a mile in another person's moccasins'" (Leavitt 1995:viii). He asserts further that "the circle is powerful symbol of the way of life of the Native peoples of North America" (xvii). This is not simply a circle. It is a medicine wheel. On the previous page the author quotes from the popular book *The Sacred Tree* (Bopp et. al. 1984), which makes the claim that "almost all Native people in North and South America" use the medicine wheel (Leavitt 1995:xvi). No author is cited for *The Sacred Tree*, but its intended audience is broad and it is intended to be a spiritual handbook; in other words, the implication is of a pan-Indian medicine wheel. More important, the textbook author states: "The circle offers a balanced way of thinking about what it means to be Maliseet or Micmac in a time of rapid change—with new values, new technology, and a new sense of community, in an increasingly global society" (Leavitt 1995:xvii). As a collaborative project the author and his aboriginal advisors certainly look to the circle for cultural, social, and spiritual stability—so much so that the aboriginal education consultant for the New Brunswick Department of Education has endorsed the textbook with the following: "The Department of Education is proud to sponsor the publication of this book" (David Perley 1995:vi). I have some personal concerns regarding that paradigm (Bernard C. Perley 2000).

## 4. From Spoken Maliseet to Text

1. Recent developments in functional MRI scanning and cognitive and linguistic studies have collaborated across disciplines to address the brain's

function in language-related issues such as language acquisition, reading and brain plasticity, language and perception, etc. The effect of developing an orthographic system for an oral language in cognitive shift is a fascinating research topic, but the constraints of time and space prevent further exploration here.

2. J. Nicholas and D. Francis, *Nitawi Skicinuw* (I know how to speak Indian), book 1: *Passamaquoddy/Maliseet* (Pleasant Point, Perry, Maine: Waponahki Museum and Resource Center, n.d.), no page number.

## 5. Elementary Language Curriculum and Practice

1. In the latest dictionary the spelling is *mahsus*, plural *mahsusiyil* (Leavitt and Francis 2008:248). As more Maliseet use this reference and as more students attending the University of New Brunswick are trained in this orthography this spelling may soon become the standard.

2. Mah-Sos School is richly intertextual in the broad semiotic sense as Agha (2005) explains intertextuality (see chapter 1, note 39).

3. The Micmac-Maliseet language instruction book *Nihtawewest: I Know How to Speak* (Leavitt 1986:xxi) makes a similar argument for "activities" as part of classroom procedures to enhance learning of the language.

4. In the current dictionary the orthographic representation is *polam* (Leavitt and Francis 2008:434).

## 6. Death by Suicide

1. The phenomenological approach has a variety of meanings and implications for ethnography and analysis. Arthur and Joan Kleinman (1995) as well as Michael Jackson (1998) provide excellent commentary on phenomenological approaches in anthropology. The key concepts are *experience, intersubjectivity, being in the world,* and *embodiment*. I use these terms throughout the text to indicate embodiments of intersubjective experience similar to those described by these authors.

2. See my comments on Donna Harraway in chapter 1.

3. They are not the first to posit a punctuated equilibrium model for language change. R. M. W. Dixon used this model to describe *The Rise and Fall of Languages* in 1997. Dixon states: "In this book I put forward a hypothesis. Inspired by the punctuated equilibrium model in biology (first expressed by Eldredge and Gould 1972), a punctuated equilibrium model is suggested for development (and origin) of language" (Dixon 1997:3).

4. Their point is well taken. In the case of Eastern Algonquian languages, a 1970 report listed twenty-nine languages and dialects. Of those twenty-nine,

twenty-one are listed as "extinct" and the remaining languages had number of speakers listed as Micmac, 6,000; Maliseet, 600; Passamaquoddy, 200; Penobscot, 10 (I have heard from one member of the Penobscot Nation that the last speaker passed away in 1993); Western Abenaki, 22; Moraviantown, 30; Muncey, 3; Unami-Southern, 25 (Goddard 1978:71).

### 7. Language and Being in Maliseet Worlds

1. I use "time immemorial" to indicate the temporal expansiveness and Native American cultural inclusiveness in my use of "identity" for this particular discussion. I have included accounts of the "Tobique Rocks" earlier in this book and could have pushed back farther into mythic time by sharing the creation story of how the Maliseet people came to be denizens of the Wolastokuk (St. John River) Valley. Ideally, I would have liked to include the generations of Native American writers who have shared their existential dilemmas over the centuries, such as Aztec chroniclers, Native American orators, nineteenth-century novelists, and contemporary theorists and novelists. But an adequate discussion of these important contributions to Native American identity meditations must be reserved for another publication.

2. As discussed in chapter 1, even if I were not a member of the Tobique community I would be unable to avoid intersubjective dialogues that would contribute to their impressions of me as well as my impressions of them.

3. Turner, in his essay *The Anthropology of Performance*, has used the work of Sally Falk-Moore to support his "postmodern" approach to examining social processes (Turner 1987:77). In the same paragraph in which he discusses Falk-Moore he adds, "Like Heraclitus she is insisting that the elements (in her case, the sociocultural elements) are in continual flux and transformation, and so are people" (77).

4. I do not make an essentialist argument here, nor do I suggest that community members do so. However, there is a tendency by some members of the community to make arguments that can be interpreted as essentialist. These "essential" tendencies are highlighted where appropriate.

5. It is interesting to reflect that in this context the native communities were not labeled with the same "otherness."

6. Zitkala-Ša (1985), Mourning Dove (1981), Leslie Marmon Silko (1990), Gerald Vizenor (1990), and many more Native American writers have explored the existential dilemmas of "mixed-blood" politics as well as "two worlds" negotiations.

7. Much literature is devoted to what has been labeled *Native American Political*

*Resurgence* (Cornell 1988) and *American Indian Ethnic Renewal* (Nagel 1996); topical surveys on politics, history, and identity (Johnson 1999; Hoxie, Mancall, and Merrell 2001; Wilkins 2002); *Surviving in Two Worlds* (Leibold 1997, with foreword by Sarris); and "mixed-blood essays" (Penn 1997). For in-depth discussions I refer the reader to these authors and texts.

8. The native genre usually fulfills the expectations of the popular imagination of what is deemed Native American. It usually features the same symbolic references, such as Indian phenotypical figures in natural landscapes populated by animals corresponding to clan totems. The style is clean and simple, almost silkscreenlike.

9. The irony here is that the prayer is a Mohawk prayer in English. This calls into question the anticipated audience for whom was the prayer written and published. To be fair, there is a Mohawk version accessible on the Internet.

10. The job of native language teacher's assistant was never an advertised job. Rather, it was based on consultant status, and a temporary one at that. However, critics perceived it to be a political appointment and it therefore elicited some disaffection from some individuals who wanted the job.

11. Lily is a woman in her fifties. She assisted in the native language class for a short time. She had shown George some of the texts with which we were working.

12. The Marshall decision is a 1999 Supreme Court of Canada decision in the case of *Marshall vs. the Crown*, where the right to hunt, fish, and gather for the purpose of sustaining a "moderate living" was recognized. This led to bitter animosities between natives and non-natives over access to natural resources for economic gain. This in turn led to instances where a non-aboriginal group made claims to aboriginal status because they saw economic opportunities they could take advantage of if they were recognized as aboriginal. Another intriguing example is the hiring of an aboriginal person to pose as the owner of a logging operation that is really operated and owned by whites, for the purpose of gaining access to logging resources otherwise denied to them. This issue has led to bitter politics in subsequent years.

13. The vision quest is typically described as a three-day fasting exercise and sweat ceremony. At the end of the fast and the third-day sweat it is expected that the vision quest participant will have a "vision" that will help resolve a problem or quandary that prompted the quest.

14. I was shown an early version of the curriculum but never shown the final copy. To this day, I do not know if the curriculum was ever completed.

15. "Kah-rai!" is a common expression to indicate disbelief, appreciation, or exasperation. It depends on context and how it is expressed.

16. The five-volume *Report of the Royal Commission on Aboriginal Peoples* is available on the Canadian government website at http://www.collections canada.gc.ca/webarchives/20071115053257/http://www.ainc-inac.gc.ca/ch/rcap/sg/sgmm_e.html.

17. The Department of Indian Affairs did make a statement soon afterward indicating their serious consideration of the RCAP report, but it took time to digest all the recommendations and determine how best to implement them.

18. That is true. My memory of the events was based on the television reports later that evening. I could see the drummers and chanters, I could hear the drums and the chanting, I saw teenagers I knew from the schools ambling about, and I heard the responses of people I knew as they answered the reporter's questions. I also drew from Sue's account of the events. I knew the location of the barricade from the landscape in the background of the television report. Why wasn't I there? My first defensive explanation was that my fear of losing my "objective" distance in such a charged event kept me from the scene. I did not see the possibility of running from the police (as Clifford Geertz had to do in a police raid on a Balinese cockfight) as a constructive episode for my fieldwork. I had decided to work on language to avoid the highly contentious domain of politics. However, many years later, I have to be honest and confess that I really do not remember the circumstances that prevented my participation at the blockade.

## 8. Emergent Vitalities of Language, Culture, and Identity

1. In 1990 the municipality of Oka planned to expand their nine-hole golf course into an eighteen-hole golf course. To do so, they sent earth-moving equipment into a sacred Mohawk burial ground. The Mohawk were waiting and refused to allow access to the burial ground. The "Oka crisis" was a highly and internationally publicized confrontation between thirty Mohawk warriors and the Sûreté de Québec. During the confrontation one officer was killed. Following the death of the officer the confrontation escalated into a standoff between the Mohawk warriors and over two thousand of Canada's armed forces; see Perley 2006:191, 2009:260.

2. Kay B. Warren credits political scientist Deborah Yashar (1997) for formulating the concept through her comparative work on several Central American countries. I have been unable to find the exact source for Warren's use of the phrase.

3. I mention the double entendre of *essential* here also to indicate that aboriginality and Maliseetness do entail the complex negotiations of essentialist argumentation.

4. The Tobique community celebrated its two-hundred-year anniversary in 2001 with a staged reenactment of the original families landing on the shores of what is now the Tobique First Nation Reservation. The event was sparsely attended and was rife with ironies and humor. I was recruited to be a "founder" but opted out of the drama so that I could observe the event in the role of anthropologist.

5. See https://pantherfile.uwm.edu/bcperley/trickstercosmos/Visual_Anthropology/Pages/Wolastokwi_Cosmogenesis.html.

6. This is the second line of Wəlasweltəmwakən, the Maliseet prayer of thanksgiving, as developed and orthographically represented by the native language teacher and her elder consultant at Mah-Sos School, Tobique First Nation.

# References

Abu-Luhod, Lila. 1991. "Writing Against Culture." In *Recapturing Anthropology: Working in the Present*, ed. Richard G. Fox, 137–62. Santa Fe: School of American Research Press.
Adelson, Naomi. 2001. "Reimagining Aboriginality: An Indigenous People's Response to Social Suffering." In *Remaking a World: Violence, Social Suffering, and Recovery*, ed. Veena Das, Arthur Kleinman, Margaret Lock, Mamphela Ramphele, and Pamela Roberts, 96–101. Berkeley: University of California Press.
Agha, Asif. 2005. "Introduction: Semiosis across Encounters." *Journal of Linguistic Anthropology* 15(1):1–5.
Aitcheson, Jean. 1991. *Language Change: Progress or Decay?* 2nd ed. Cambridge, UK: Cambridge University Press.
Alger, Abby Langdon. 1885. "A Collection of Words and Phrases Taken from the Passamaquoddy Tongue." In *Proceedings of the American Philosophical Society* 22:240–55.
Allen, Graham. 2000. *Intertextuality*. New York: Routledge.
American Friends Service Committee. 1989. *The Wabanakis of Maine and the Maritimes: A Resource Book about Penobscot, Passamaquoddy, Maliseet, Micmac, and Abenaki Indians*. Bath: Maine Indian Program of New England.
Appadurai, Arjun. 1996. *Modernity at Large: Cultural Dimensions of Globalization*. Minneapolis: University of Minnesota Press.
Augustine, Stephen J. 2005. *Mi'kmaq and Maliseet Cultural and Ancestral Material: National Collections from the Canadian Museum of Civilization*. Gatineau: Canadian Museum of Civilization Corporation.
Baldwin, Daryl, and Julie Olds. 2007. "Miami Indian Language and Cultural

Research at Miami University." In *Beyond Red Power: American Indian Politics and Activism since 1900*, ed. Daniel M. Cobb and Loretta Fowler, 280–90. Santa Fe: School for Advanced Research Press.

Barratt, Joseph. 1851. *Key to the Indian Language of New England in the Etchemin, or Passamaquoddy Language, Spoken in Maine and St. John, New Brunswick*. Middletown: C. H. Pelton, Printer.

Basso, Keith. 1979. *Portraits of "The Whiteman": Linguistic Play and Cultural Symbols among the Western Apache*. Cambridge, UK: Cambridge University Press.

Bauman, Richard. 2004. *A World of Others' Words: Cross-Cultural Perspectives on Intertextuality*. Malden: Blackwell.

Biggs, Bruce. 1972. "The Maori Language Past and Present." In *The Maori People in the Nineteen Sixties*, ed. Erik Schwimmer, 65–84. Auckland: Longman Paul.

Biolsi, Thomas, and Larry J. Zimmerman. 1997. "Introduction: What's Changed, What Hasn't?" In *Indians and Anthropologists: Vine Deloria Jr. and the Critique of Anthropology*, ed. Thomas Biolsi and Larry J. Zimmerman, 3–24. Tucson: University of Arizona Press.

Boas, Franz. 1940. "Introduction: International Journal of American Linguistics." In *Race, Language, and Culture*. New York: Free Press.

Boldt, Menno. 1993. *Surviving as Indians: The Challenge of Self-Government*. Toronto: University of Toronto Press.

Bopp, Judie, Michael Bopp, Lee Brown, and Phil Lane Jr., collaborators. 1984. *The Sacred Tree: Reflections on Native American Spirituality*. Lethbridge AB: Four Worlds International Institute for Human and Community Development.

Bourdieu, Pierre. 1977. *Outline of a Theory of Practice*. Cambridge, UK: Cambridge University Press.

———. 1990. *The Logic of Practice*. Stanford: Stanford University Press.

———. 1991. *Language and Symbolic Power*. Cambridge MA: Harvard University Press.

Brenzinger, Matthias, ed. 1992. *Language Death: Factual and Theoretical Explorations with Special Reference to East Africa*. Berlin: Mouton de Gruyter.

Caroll, John B., ed. 1970. *Language, Thought, and Reality: Selected Writings of Benjamin Lee Whorf*. Cambridge MA: MIT Press.

Chamberlain, Montague. 1899. *Maliseet Vocabulary*. Cambridge MA: Harvard Cooperative Society.

Clatworthy, Stewart. 2003. "Impacts of the 1985 Amendments to the Indian Act on First Nations Populations." In *Aboriginal Conditions: Research as a Foundation for Public Policy*, ed. Jerry P. Shite, Paul S. Maxim, and Dan Beavon, 63–90. Vancouver: UBC Press.

Cobb, Daniel M., and Loretta Fowler, eds. 2007. *Beyond Red Power: American Indian Politics and Activism since 1900*. Santa Fe: School for Advanced Research Press.
Cornell, Stephen. 1988. *The Return of the Native: American Indian Political Resurgence*. New York: Oxford University Press.
Cowan, Susan, ed. 1976. *We Don't Live in Snow Houses Now: Reflections of Arctic Bay*. Ottawa: Canadian Arctic Producers.
Crystal, David. 2000. *Language Death*. Cambridge, UK: Cambridge University Press.
Cushing, Frank Hamilton. 1970. *My Adventures in Zuñi*. Palo Alto: American West Publishing Company.
Deloria, Vine Jr. 1988. "Anthropologists and Other Friends." In *Custer Died for Your Sins: An Indian Manifesto*, 78–100. Norman: University of Oklahoma Press.
———. 1997. "Conclusion: Anthros, Indians, and Planetary Reality." In *Indians and Anthropologists: Vine Deloria Jr. and the Critique of Anthropology*, ed. Thomas Biolsi and Larry J. Zimmerman, 209–222. Tucson: University of Arizona Press.
Denison, Norman. 1977. "Language Death or Language Suicide?" In *Linguistics: An International Review* 191:13–22.
DIAND. 1978. *Teaching an Algonkian Language as a Second Language: A Core Program for Kindergarten*. Ottawa: Department of Indian Affairs and Northern Development.
Dixon, R. M. W. 1997. *The Rise and Fall of Languages*. Cambridge, UK: Cambridge University Press.
Dorian, Nancy C. 1981. *Language Death: The Life Cycle of a Scottish Gaelic Dialect*. Philadelphia: University of Pennsylvania Press.
———. 1989. "Introduction." In *Investigating Obsolescence: Studies in Language Contraction and Death*, ed. Nancy C. Dorian. Cambridge, UK: Cambridge University Press.
Dove, Mourning (Hum-Ishi-Ma). 1981. *Cogewea, the Half-Blood: A Depiction of the Great Montana Cattle Range*. Lincoln: University of Nebraska Press.
Durkheim, Emile. 1951. *Suicide: A Study in Sociology*. New York: Free Press.
Erickson, Vincent O. 1978. "Maliseet-Passamquoddy." In *Handbook of North American Indians*, vol. 15: *Northeast*, ed. Bruce Trigger, 123–36. Washington DC: Smithsonian Institution.
Errington, J. Joseph. 1998. *Shifting Languages: Interaction and Identity in Javanese Indonesia*. Cambridge, UK: Cambridge University Press.
———. 2008. *Linguistics in a Colonial World: A Story of Language, Meaning, and Power*. Malden: Blackwell.

Evans-Pritchard, E. E. 1976. *Witchcraft, Oracles, and Magic among the Azande.* Oxford: Clarendon Press.

Fabian, Johannes. 1986. *Language and Colonial Power: The Appropriation of Swahili in the Former Belgian Congo 1880–1938.* Berkeley: University of California Press.

Fishman, Joshua A. 1991. *Reversing Language Shift.* Clavendon, UK: Multilingual Matters.

Fishman, Joshua A., ed. 2001. *Can Threatened Languages Be Saved?* Clavendon, UK: Multilingual Matters.

Fleras, Augie. 1991. "Preschooling with a Cultural Difference: A Maori Language Education Program in New Zealand." In *Aboriginal Languages and Education: The Canadian Experience,* ed. Sonia Morris, Keith McLeod, and Marcel Danesi. Oakville, Ontario: Mosaic Press.

Ganong, William F. 1899. "Introduction." In *Maliseet Vocabulary,* ed. Montague Chamberlain. Cambridge MA: Harvard Cooperative Society.

Geertz, Clifford. 1973. "Thick Description: Toward an Interpretive Theory of Culture." In *The Interpretation of Cultures,* 3–30. New York: Basic Books.

Gentner, Dedre, and Susan Goldin-Meadow, eds. 2003. *Language in Mind: Advances in the Study of Language and Thought.* Cambridge MA: MIT Press.

Goddard, Ives. 1978. "Eastern Algonquian Languages." In *Handbook of North American Indians,* vol. 15: *Northeast,* ed. Bruce Trigger, 70–77. Washington DC: Smithsonian Institution.

Goody, Jack. 1977. *The Domestication of the Savage Mind.* Cambridge, UK: Cambridge University Press.

Greenblatt, Steven J. 1992. "Learning to Curse: Aspects of Linguistic Colonialism in the Sixteenth Century." In *Learning to Curse: Essays in Early Modern Culture,* 16–39. New York: Routledge.

Grenoble, Lenore A., and Lindsay J. Whaley. 2006. *Saving Languages: An Introduction to Language Revitalization.* Cambridge UK: Cambridge University Press.

Grenoble, Lenore A., and Lindsay J. Whaley, eds. 1998. *Endangered Languages: Current Issues and Future Prospects.* Cambridge, UK: Cambridge University Press.

Grobsmith, Elizabeth S. 1997. "Growing up on Deloria: The Impact of His Work on a New Generation of Anthropologists." In *Indians and Anthropologists: Vine Deloria Jr. and the Critique of Anthropology,* ed. Thomas Biolsi and Larry J. Zimmerman, 35–49. Tucson: University of Arizona Press.

Gumperz, John J., and Stephen C. Levinson, eds. 1996. *Rethinking Linguistic Relativity.* Cambridge UK: Cambridge University Press.

Haraway, Donna J. 1991. *Simians, Cyborgs, and Women: The Reinvention of Nature.* New York: Routledge.

Harpham, Geoffrey Galt. 2002. *Language Alone: The Critical Fetish of Modernity*. New York: Routledge.

Harris, Randy Allen. 1993. *The Linguistics Wars*. New York: Oxford University Press.

Harrison, K. David. 2007. *When Languages Die: The Extinction of the World's Languages and the Erosion of Human Knowledge*. Oxford: Oxford University Press.

Herzfeld, Michael. 1997. "The Taming of the Revolution: Intense Paradoxes of the Self." In *Auto/Ethnography: Rewriting the Self and the Social*, ed. Deborah E. Reed-Danahay, 169–94. Oxford: Berg.

———. 2001. *Anthropology: Theoretical Practice in Culture and Society*. UNESCO 2001. Malden: Blackwell.

Hinsley, Curtis M. 1981. *The Smithsonian and the American Indian: Making a Moral Anthropology in Victorian America*. Washington DC: Smithsonian Institution Press.

Hinton, Leanne. 2001. "Language Revitalization: An Overview." In *The Green Book of Language Revitalization in Practice*, ed. Leanne Hinton and Ken Hale, 3–16. San Diego: Academic Press.

———. 2002. *How to Keep Your Language Alive: A Commonsense Approach to One-on-One Language Learning*. Berkeley: Heyday Books.

Hinton, Leanne, and Ken Hale, eds. 2001. *The Green Book of Language Revitalization in Practice*. San Diego: Academic Press.

Hoxie, Frederick E., Peter C. Mancall, and James H. Merrell, eds. 2001. *American Nations: Encounters in Indian Country, 1850 to the Present*. New York: Routledge.

Irvine, Judith T., and Susan Gal. 2000. "Language Ideology and Linguistic Differentiation." In *Regimes of Language: Ideology, Politics, and Identities*, ed. Paul V. Kroskrity, 35–83. Santa Fe: School of American Research Press.

Ives, Edward D. 1965. *Northeast Folklore VI: 1964, Malecite and Passamaquoddy Tales*. Orono: Northeast Folklore Society, University of Maine.

Jack, Edward. 1895. "Maliseet Legends." *Journal of American Folk-Lore* (Washington DC: American Folklore Society) 8(30):193–208.

Jackson, Michael. 1998. *Minima Ethnographica: Intersubjectivity and the Anthropological Project*. Chicago: University of Chicago Press.

Johnson, Troy R. 1999. *Contemporary Native American Political Issues*. Walnut Creek CA: Rowman and Littlefield Publishers, AltaMira Press.

Kideckel, David A. 1997. "Autoethnography as Political Resistance: A Case of Socialist Romania." In *Auto/Ethnography: Rewriting the Self and the Social*, ed. Deborah E. Reed-Danahay, 47–70. Oxford: Berg.

Kleinman, Arthur, and Joan Kleinman. 1995. "Suffering and Its Professional

Transformation: Toward an Ethnography of Interpersonal Experience." In *Writing at the Margin: Discourse between Anthropology and Medicine*, 95–119. Berkeley: University of California Press.

Knockwood, Isabelle. 1992. *Out of the Depths: The Experience of Mi'kmaw Children at the Indian Residential School at Shubenacadie, Nova Scotia.* Lockeport, Nova Scotia: Roseway Publishing.

Kroskrity, Paul V. 2000. "Language Ideologies in the Expression and Representation of Arizona Tewa Ethnic Identity." In *Regimes of Language: Ideologies, Politics, and Identities*, ed. Paul V. Kroskrity, 329–59. Santa Fe: School of American Research Press.

Kroskrity, Paul V., and Margaret C. Field, eds. 2009. *Native American Language Ideologies: Beliefs, Practices, and Struggles in Indian Country.* Tucson: University of Arizona Press.

Krotz, Larry. 1992. *Indian Country: Inside Another Canada.* Toronto: McClelland and Stewart.

Kulick, Don. 1992. *Language Shift and Cultural Reproduction: Socialization, Self, and Syncretism in a Papua New Guinean Village.* Cambridge, UK: Cambridge University Press.

Leavitt, Robert M. 1985. "Confronting Language Ambivalence and Language Death: The Role of the University in Native Communities." *Canadian Journal of Native Studies* (Brandon: Brandon University) 2:262–67.

———. 1986. *Nihtawewest: I Know How to Speak.* Fredericton: Micmac-Maliseet Institute, University of New Brunswick.

———. 1995. *Maliseet and Micmac: First Nations of the Maritimes.* Fredericton, New Brunswick: New Ireland Press.

Leavitt, Robert M., and David A. Francis, eds. 1984. *Kolusuwakonol: Philip LeSourd's Passamaquoddy-Maliseet and English Dictionary.* Pleasant Point, Perry: Passamaquoddy/Maliseet Bilingual Program, ESEA Title VII.

———. 1986. *Passamaquoddy-Maliseet Verb Paradigms*, 2nd ed. Fredericton: Micmac-Maliseet Institute, University of New Brunswick.

———. 2008. *Peskotomuhkati Wolastoqewi Latuwewakon: A Passamaquoddy-Maliseet Dictionary.* Orono: University of Maine Press.

Leibold, Jay, ed. 1997. *Surviving in Two Worlds: Contemporary Native American Voices.* Austin: University of Texas Press.

Leland, Charles Godfrey. 1992. *Algonquin Legends.* New York: Dover Publications. Originally *The Algonquin Legends of New England; or, Myths and Folk Lore of the Micmac, Passamaquoddy, and Penobscot Tribes.* 1884. Boston: Houghton, Mifflin, and Company.

Leland, Charles Godfrey, and John Dyneley Prince. 1902. *Kuloskap the Master and Other Algonkin Poems*. New York: Funk and Wagnalls Company.

LeSourd, Philip S. 2003. "The Noun Substitute in Maliseet-Passamaquoddy." In *Essays in Algonquian, Catawban, and Siouan Linguistics in Memory of Frank T. Siebert, Jr.*, ed. Blair A. Rudes and David J. Costa, 141–63. Winnipeg: University of Manitoba Press.

———. 2004 "The Internal Structure of the Noun Phrase in Maliseet-Passamaquoddy." In *Papers of the Thirty-Fifth Algonquian Conference*, 35:239–263.

LeSourd, Philip S., ed. 2007. *Tales From Maliseet Country: The Maliseet Texts of Karl V. Teeter*. Lincoln: University of Nebraska Press.

Levin, Michael D. 1993. "Introduction." In *Ethnicity and Aboriginality: Case Studies in Ethnonationalism*. Toronto: University of Toronto Press.

Lévi-Strauss, Claude. 1966. *The Savage Mind*. Chicago: University of Chicago Press.

Limón, José E. 1991. "Representations, Ethnicity, and the Precursory Ethnography: Notes of a Native Anthropologist." In *Recapturing Anthropology: Working in the Present*, ed. Richard G. Fox, 115–36. Santa Fe: School of American Research Press.

Mackey, Eva. 2002. *The House of Difference: Cultural Politics and National Identity in Canada*. Toronto: University of Toronto Press.

Mandelbaum, David G., ed. 1985. *Edward Sapir: Selected Writings in Language, Culture, and Personality*. Berkeley: University of California Press.

Marcus, George E. 1998. *Ethnography through Thick and Thin*. Princeton NJ: Princeton University Press.

Makepeace, Anne. 2001. *Edward S. Curtis: Coming to Light*. Washington DC: National Geographic.

McRoberts, Kenneth. 1997. *Misconceiving Canada: The Struggle for National Unity*. Oxford: Oxford University Press.

Mechling, W. H. 1913. "Maliseet Tales." *Journal of American Folk-Lore* (Washington DC: American Folklore Society) 26(101):219–58.

———. 1914. "Malecite Tales." In *Geological Survey*, Memoir 49, no. 4. Anthropological Series. Ottawa: Government Printing Bureau.

Morrison, Alvin H. 1995. "Anglo-Wabanaki Relation: 1605–1630." In *Papers of the 26th Algonquian Conference*, ed. David H. Pentland, 26: 291–305. Winnipeg: University of Manitoba.

Motzafi-Haller, Pnina. 1997. "Writing Birthright: On Native Anthropologists and the Politics of Representation." In *Auto/Ethnography: Rewriting the Self and the Social*, ed. Deborah E. Reed-Danahay. Oxford: Berg.

Nagel, Joane. 1996. *American Indian Ethnic Renewal: Red Power and the Resurgence of Identity and Culture.* New York: Oxford University Press.

Nettle, Daniel, and Suzanne Romaine. 2000. *Vanishing Voices: The Extinction of the World's Languages.* Oxford: Oxford University Press.

O'Nell, Theresa DeLeane. 1996. *Disciplined Hearts: History, Identity, and Depression in an American Indian Community.* Berkeley: University of California Press.

Pagden, Anthony. 1993. *European Encounters with the New World.* New Haven: Yale University Press.

Penn, William S., ed. 1997. *As We Are Now: Mixblood Essays on Race and Identity.* Berkeley: University of California Press.

Perley, Bernard C. 2002a. "Medicine Wheelers and Dealers." In *Spirit Wars: Native North American Religions in the Age of Nation Building*, ed. Ronald Niezen, 217–19. Berkeley: University of California Press.

———. 2002b. "Language, Culture, and Landscape: Preserving Aboriginal 'Deep Time' for Tomorrow." Paper given at the UNESCO Conference Protecting the Cultural and Natural Heritage in the Western Hemisphere: Lessons from the Past; Looking to the Future, Harvard University, December 5–7, 2002. www.gsd.harvard.edu/heritageintheamericas.

———. 2006. "Aboriginality at Large: Varieties of Resistance in Maliseet Language Instruction." *Identities: Global Studies in Culture and Power*, 13:187–208.

———. 2009. "Contingencies of Emergence: Planning Maliseet Language Ideologies." In *Native American Language Ideologies: Beliefs, Practices, and Struggles in Indian Country*, ed. Paul V. Kroskrity and Margaret C. Field, 255–70. Tucson: University of Arizona Press.

———. 2012a. "'Gone Anthropologist': Epistemic Slippage, Native Anthropology, and the Dilemmas of Representation." In *Anthropology and the Politics of Representation*, ed. Gabriela Vargas-Cetina. Tuscaloosa: University of Alabama Press.

———. 2012b. "Silence before the Void: Language Extinction, Storytelling, and the Semiotics of Survival." In *Telling Stories in the Face of Danger*, ed. Paul V. Kroskrity. Norman: University of Oklahoma Press.

———. Unpublished. "Identity, Embodiment, and the Intermedialities of Self-Determination: A Manifesto for Critical Indigeneity." In *Performing Indigeneity: Historic and Contemporary Displays of Indigeneity*, ed. Laura Graham and Glen Penny.

Perley, David. 1995. "Foreword." In *Maliseet and Micmac: The First Nations of the Maritimes*, ed. Robert M. Leavitt, v–vi. Fredericton: Micmac-Maliseet Institute, University of New Brunswick.

Prince, John Dyneley. 1897. "The Passamaquoddy Wampum Records." *Proceedings of the American Philosophical Society* (Philadelphia) 36:479–95.

———. 1899. "Some Passamaquoddy Witchcraft Tales." *Proceedings of the American Philosophical Society* (Philadelphia) 38:181–89.

———. 1901. "Notes on Passamaquoddy Literature." *Annals of the New York Academy of Sciences* 13:381–86.

———. 1916. "The Passamaquoddy Wampum Records." *New York State Museum Bulletin* 184:119–25.

———. 1917. "A Passamaquoddy Tobacco Famine." *International Journal of American Linguistics* (Chicago: University of Chicago Press) 1:58–63.

———. 1921. *Passamaquoddy Texts*. Publications of the American Ethnological Society, vol. 10. New York: G. E. Stechert and Company.

Ramos, Alcida. 1994. "The Hyperreal Indian." *Critique of Anthropology* 14:153–71.

Reed-Danahay, Deborah E. 1997. "Introduction." In *Auto/Ethnography: Rewriting the Self in the Social*, ed. Deborah E. Reed-Danahay. New York: Berg.

Sahlins, Marshall. 1995. *How Natives Think: About Captain Cook, for Example*. Chicago: University of Chicago Press.

Schmidt, Annette. 1990. *The Loss of Australia's Aboriginal Language Heritage*. Institute Report Series. Canberra: Aboriginal Studies Press.

Schoolcraft, Henry Rowe. 1839. *Algic Researches, Comprising Inquiries Respecting the Mental Characteristics of the North American Indians. Indian Tales and Legends*. New York: Harper and Brothers.

Sherwood, David Fairchild. 1986. *Maliseet-Passamaquoddy Verb Morphology*. Ottawa: Canadian Museum of Civilization.

Shneidman, Edwin S. 1996. *The Suicidal Mind*. New York: Oxford University Press.

———. 2001. *Comprehending Suicide: Landmarks in 20th-Century Suicidology*. Washington DC: American Psychological Society.

Silko, Leslie Marmon. 1990. "Interview." In *Winged Words: American Indian Writers Speak*, ed. Laura Coltelli, 135–54. Lincoln: University of Nebraska Press.

Silman, Janet, ed. 1987. *Enough Is Enough: Aboriginal Women Speak Out*. Toronto: Women's Press.

Speck, Frank G. 1917. "Malecite Tales." *Journal of American Folk-Lore* (Washington DC: American Folklore Society) 30(118): 479–85.

Sturm, Circe. 2002. *Blood Politics: Race, Culture, and Identity in the Cherokee Nation of Oklahoma*. Berkeley: University of California Press.

Szabó, László. 1981. *Indianisches Wörterbuch: Malecite-Deutsch-English*. Wiesbaden: Harrassowitz.

Taylor, Allan R. 1989. "Problems in Obsolescence Research: The Gros Ventres of Montana." In *Investigating Obsolescence: Studies in Language Contraction and Death*, ed. Nancy C. Dorian, 167–80. Cambridge, UK: Cambridge University Press.

Taylor, Charles. 2004. *Modern Social Imaginaries*. Durham NC: Duke University Press.

Tedlock, Dennis, and Bruce Mannheim. 1995. "Introduction." In *The Dialogic Emergence of Culture*, ed. Dennis Tedlock and Bruce Mannheim, 1–39. Urbana: University of Illinois Press.

Teeter, Karl V. 1971. "The Main Features of Malecite-Passamaquoddy Grammar." In *Studies in American Indian Languages*, ed. Jesse Sawyer, 191–249. University of California Publications in Linguistics 65. Berkeley: University of California Press.

———. 1967. "Preliminary Report on Malecite-Passamaquoddy." In *Contributions to Anthropology: Linguistics I (Algonquian)*, ed. A. D. Deblois, 157–62. Anthropological Series 78, National Museum of Canada Bulletin 214. Ottawa: National Museum of Canada.

Turner, Victor. 1987. *The Anthropology of Performance*. New York: PAJ Publications.

Vetromile, Eugin. 1857. *Alnambay Uli Awikhigan*. New York: Manhattan Udenek, Edward Dunigan Hatchi Awidjal (Sak B. Kirker).

Vizenor, Gerald. 1990. "Interview." In *Winged Words: American Indian Writers Speak*, ed. Laura Coltelli, 155–84. Lincoln: University of Nebraska Press.

Wallis, Wilson D., and Ruth Sawtell Wallis. 1957. *The Malecite Indians of New Brunswick*. Bulletin no. 148, Anthropological Series no. 40, Department of Northern Affairs and National Resources. Ottawa: National Museum of Canada.

Warren, Kay B. 1997. "Narrating Cultural Resurgence: Genre and Self-Representation for Pan-Mayan Writers." In *Auto/Ethnography: Rewriting the Self and the Social*, ed. Deborah E. Reed-Danahay, 21–45. Oxford: Berg.

———. 1998. *Indigenous Movements and Their Critics: Pan-Maya Activism in Guatemala*. Princeton NJ: Princeton University Press.

Wax, Murray L. 1997. "Educating an Anthro: The Influence of Vine Deloria Jr." In *Indians and Anthropologists: Vine Deloria Jr. and the Critique of Anthropology*, ed. Thomas Biolsi and Larry J. Zimmerman, 50–59. Tucson: University of Arizona Press.

*Merriam Webster's Collegiate Dictionary*. 1977. 10th ed. Springfield: Merriam Webster.

Whiteley, Peter M. 1997. "The End of Anthropology (at Hopi)?" In *Indians and Anthropologists: Vine Deloria Jr. and the Critique of Anthropology*, ed. Thomas Biolsi and Larry J. Zimmerman, 177–208. Tucson: University of Arizona Press.

———. 1998. *Rethinking Hopi Ethnography*. Washington DC: Smithsonian Institution Press.

Wilkins, David E. 2002. *American Indian Politics and the American Political System.* Lanham MD: Rowman and Littlefield Publishers.

Whorf, Benjamin Lee. 1970. "Languages and Logic." In *Language, Thought and Reality: Selected Writings of Benjamin Lee Whorf,* ed. John B. Carroll, 233–45. Cambridge: MIT Press.

Wilson, Angela Waziyatawin, and Michael Yellow Bird, eds. 2005. *For Indigenous Eyes Only: A Decolonization Handbook.* Santa Fe: School for American Research Press.

Woolard, Kathryn, and Bambi B. Schieffelin. 1994. "Language Ideology." *Annual Review of Anthropology* 23:55–82.

Yashar, Deborah. 1997. *Demanding Democracy: Reform and Reaction in Costa Rica and Guatemala 1870s–1950s.* Stanford: Stanford University Press.

Zitkala-Ša. 1985. *Old Indian Legends.* Lincoln: University of Nebraska Press.

# Index

*Page numbers in italic refer to illustrations.*

aboriginal communities demonstration, 179–81, 210n18
aboriginality, 9, 149–51, 154–56, 165–66, 170–71, 173, 180–83, 188–90, 199, 208n4, 210nn1–3
aboriginal literature, 54–55
Aboriginal Peoples Television Network (APTN), 194
academic context of language maintenance, 68, 81–92
Adelson, Naomi, 156, 166, 173–74
adult classes in Maliseet, 132–39
adults, identity and being of, 19, 160–68
agents of language maintenance, 69–77
alphabet, Maliseet-Passamaquoddy, 95–96
alphabet books, 75, 83
alphabet exercises, 91, 95–96, 98, 108, 110, 118, 133

alternative vitalities, 146–48. *See also* future of Maliseet language, culture, and identity
amended Indian Act of 1951, 175–76
amended Indian Act of 1985, 176, 178, 182
anthropologist, author as native, 20–24, 29–30, 203nn24–30
Appadurai, Arjun, 10, 155, 197
arts and crafts in classroom, 158–59
arts program meeting at Mah-Sos School, 181–82
Assembly of First Nations, 179–80
assimilatory pressure, 48–52, 78
assisted suicide, language, 139–40
Atlantic Policy Congress, 188
Auntie (Maliseet elder), 157
Australian Aboriginal languages, 43–45, 47, 50–51, 53–54, 56
autoethnography. *See* anthropologist, author as native

Baldwin, Daryl, 35

Bantu, 38–39
Barb (chair of Native Studies, St. Thomas University), 66, 68, 72, 81–83
basket making, 71
Ben (adult Maliseet student), 135–37
benign neglect, 129, 132, 134, 139–40
bilingual signs on reservation, 186
Bill c-31, 9, 174–78, 182
Black, Henrietta, 59, 135–37, 192–94
blaming the victim, 140–43
blood quantum issue, 9, 153–54, 161, 163, 165, 173–74, 177–78, 208nn5–6
boarding schools, 44–46, 49, 78
Boas, Franz, 32–33
Bob (Tobique community elder), 97–100, 159–60
booklet project, 117
boundary maintenance, language, 166
Brad (Maliseet young adult), 168–69
breakdown in isolation, 46–47
Brenzinger, Matthias, 33

"cascade of extinction," 140–41, 207n4 (chap. 6)
Champlain, Samuel de, 16
charismatic indigeneity, 156
classroom language practice, 102–3
classroom setup, 103
classroom time, lack, 87–89
Clatworthy, Stewart, 177
"Clip 17," 192
clusters of suicide, Shneidman's, 143–44
codification of Maliseet language. *See* Maliseet language codification
cognitive shifts in Maliseet language instruction, 7–8, 89–92
colonialism, 38, 78
color vocabulary, 105–6
commonalities of suicide, Shneidman's, 130
community context of language maintenance, 67, 79
constituent-directed ideology, 77–79
contextual constraints of language maintenance, 68–69
contingent ontology, 146–47
continuity of language and culture, 58–62
Crystal, David, 5, 10, 35, 39–41
cultural diacritics, 10, 187
cultural hegemony, 50–52
cultural identity, 15, 22, 30. *See also* future of Maliseet language, culture, and identity
Cultural Resource Center (proposed), 187–88, 195, 199
culture: and identity, 173, 178; and language ties, 136–39, 151–53, 161, 165. *See also* future of Maliseet language, culture, and identity
curriculum and practice. *See* Maliseet elementary curriculum and practice
Curtis, Edward S., 32
Cushing, Frank Hamilton, 32
Cuz (Maliseet adult), 157

Dan (aboriginal education consultant), 66–68, 78, 79–83

death of Maliseet speakers, 185–86
Deloria, Vine, Jr., 28, 156
depression: among Flatheads, 27–28; at loss of language, 161
diacritics, 10, 187
*The Dialogic Emergence of Culture* (Tedlock and Mannheim), 26
dialogue exercises, 106–7
Diane (Maliseet speaker), 126
dictionaries: elder's, 159; Passamaquoddy-Maliseet, 18, 93–94, 96, 100; student's, 108
directional signs on reservation, 186
disembodiment, language. *See* language disembodiment
domains of language maintenance, 65–68
domestication of language, 6–7, 38, 64, 89
Dorian, Nancy, 33, 39–41, 57–58, 61, 122
dormitory schools, 44, 78
drumming, 165, 171–72, 180
Durkheim, Emily, 129–30

East African languages, 33
East Sutherland Gaelic, 33, 39, 58, 61
economy, changes in, 52–57, 134
education as assimilatory pressure, 49
elders: classified by age, 19; as classroom resources, 70, 77, 158–59; death of, 185–86; identity and being of, 157–60, 209nn8–10
elementary curriculum and practice. *See* Maliseet elementary curriculum and practice
emotion and use of language, 162
empty-center Indians, 28
English: as language of children and youths, 37, 39; as language of economy and education, 53–54; as language of elders, 56–57; as language of everyday communication, 55–57; as language of instruction, 49; as language of media, 50; as language of politicians, 40; pressure to speak, 47; as prestigious viable code, 54
equilibrium model for language change, 141, 207n3 (chap. 6)
erasure, language. *See* language erasure, causes of
erasure of place names, 46
Errington, J. Joseph, 42–43
Etchemin, 16
ethics, 73
evolutionists, 31
experiential Maliseetness, 178–83
extinction: of aboriginal languages, 125, 140–41; and Bill C-31, 174–78, 182; of Maliseet language, 2, 19, 34, 36, 57, 132, 142, 146, 184–85, 190; of Native American languages, 32–33, 39

Fabian, Johannes, 38
"The Far Side," 24
fiddlehead ferns, 71, 101–2, 199, 207n1 (chap. 5)
Field, Margaret C., 7, 35
First Nations: aboriginal vs. indigenous as valid descriptor of, 9; membership in, 174–78

fisheries projects, 137
Fishman, Joshua, 33, 35
flashcards, 86, 90–92, 107, 111–14, 118
Flatheads, 27–28
Fleras, Augie, 47
flipcharts, 86, 91–92, 105–6
food vocabulary, 106
forced language disembodiment, 125–29, 144
forced relocation, 46
Francis, David A., 93, 100
French language: classroom hours devoted to, 87–89, 102–3, 185–86; and cognitive shifts, 91–92; importance of learning, 126–28; as language of economics, 53; in the Maliseet classroom, community, and politics, 85; pressure to speak in Francophone Canada, 47; as second language, 20
future of Maliseet language, culture, and identity, 184–200; and aboriginal self-determination, 186–90, 210nn1–3; and Cultural Resource Center (proposed), 187–88, 195, 199; defying the odds, 184–86; and new media, 186, 191–95; reflections on, 195–200; resources for, 186–95

Gaelic, East Sutherland, 33, 39, 58, 61
*Ga-kee-ma-neh* (native language interest group), 77
Geertz, Clifford, 145–46, 149, 151
gender discrimination against Indian women, 175–76
George (Maliseet elder), 161–63
George (Maliseet politician), 40–41
*Gig-na-moa-ne* (native language interest group), 77
Goody, Jack, 64, 85
government context of language maintenance, 67–68, 79–81
grade four class routine, 108–11
grade three class routine, 105–8
grade two class routine, 111–12
Grenoble, Lenore A., 35
Gros Ventre language obsolescence, 41

Hale, Ken, 35, 153
Haraway, Donna, 23–24, 203n23
Harrison, K. David, 35, 152
Hawaiian immersion program, 82
Head Start, 1, 120, 131, 133–34
Herzfeld, Michael, 203n21
Hinton, Leanne, 35, 151–53
hyperreal Indians, 28

identity and being, Maliseet. *See* Maliseet identity and being
identity politics: aboriginal, 9–10, 83, 157, 182–83; Flathead, 27–28, 155; Maliseet, 122, 124, 182–83, 197; Maliseet and Passamaquoddy, 17–18, 54
imaginings, 197
immersion programs: for adults, 77, 134–35; competing systems of, 100; English, author's participation in, 125; Hawaiian, 2, 82; Head Start to grade six curriculum, 120; ideology of, 81–82; importance of, 1–2; Maori, 2, 81;

Mohawk, 2, 81; organizational meeting for, 1–3, 34–36, 131, 138; promotion of, 64; at St. Thomas University, 96
imperialism, 38
Indian Act of 1876, 9, 174–78
Indian Act (amended) of 1951, 175–76
Indian Act (amended) of 1985, 176, 178, 182
*Indianisches Wörterbuch: Malecite-Deutsch-English* (Szabó), 18
Indianness, 27–28, 51, 174, 176
Indian registration rules, 176–77
"Indian time," 1
indigeneity, 9, 28, 156
institutional ideologies, 79
institutionalization of language maintenance, 64–69
interactive classroom projects, 115–16
intermarriage, 48
International Covenant of Civil and Political Rights, 176
"International Journal of American Linguistics," 33
Internet, 191–92
interobjectivity, 26, 204n31
intersubjectivity, 20, 27, 82–84, 151, 207n1 (chap. 6)
intertextuality, 27, 205n34, 207n2
*Investigating Obsolescence* (Dorian), 40–41
isolation, breakdown in, 46–47

John (Maliseet speaker), 192–94
jokes and riddles, 153–54

kah-rai, 179, 209n15

Karen (Maliseet speaker), 125–26
Kevorkian School of Language Maintenance, 139–40
*Kikahan* community health newsletter, 98
Kleinman, Arthur, 29–30, 149–50
Kleinman, Joan, 29–30, 149–50
Kluskap and Gwabid story, 58–60
Knockwood, Isabelle, 44–45
*Kolusuwakonol: Philip LeSourd's Passamaquoddy-Maliseet and English Dictionary*, 93–94
Kris (Maliseet speaker), 192–94
Kroskrity, Paul V., 7, 35
Kulick, Don, 42–43

language: and culture ties, 136–39, 151–53, 161, 165; as identity and being, 151–53; litmus-test property of, 141; as survival strategy, 126, 140, 173, 182
language ambivalence, 36
"Language and Logic" (Whorf), 151
language assisted suicide, 139–40
language boundary maintenance, 166
language death: as immediate and emotional community problem, 1–2; and language endangerment, 35–39; as language suicide, 8–10, 22. *See also* Maliseet language endangerment and death
language disembodiment: by blood, 173–74, 178; forced, 125–29, 144; by legislation, 178; suicide as, 143–46; voluntary, 131–39, 144

language domestication, 6–7, 38, 64, 89
language endangerment, 3–5, 15, 20, 33, 35, 84, 126, 128, 195
language equilibrium, 141, 207n3 (chap. 6)
language erasure, causes of, 43–57; aboriginal literature, lack of, 54–55; assimilatory pressure, 48–52; breakdown in isolation, 46–47; changes in economy and values, 52–57; education, 49; increased intermarriage, 48; media, 49–50; reduced language use and loss, 55–56; reduced number of speakers, 56–57; resettlement patterns, 46; social upheaval, 43–48; speaker attitudes, 57; stigma and cultural hegemony, 50–52; urbanization, 47–48
language hotspots, 4
language ideology, 6–7
language immersion meeting (1993), 1–3, 36, 131
language life, 10
language maintenance, 6–7, 63–84; academic context of, 68, 81–92; agents of, 69–77; community context of, 67, 79; constituent-directed ideology, 77–79; contextual constraints of, 68–69; government context of, 67–68, 79–81; institutional ideologies, 79–82, 206n2; institutionalization of, 64–69; overlapping domains of, 65–68; overview, 63–64. See also future of Maliseet language, culture, and identity
language murder, 121
language neglect, 129, 132, 134, 139–40
language nests, 80
language obsolescence, 39–42
language practice in classroom, 102–3
language prestige, 61
language retention as human rights issue, 152
language revitalization: among younger adults and children, 132–34; blaming the victim, 142; Hinton on, 152–53; by home-based learning, 10; tools for, 147; unifying standard for, 18. See also future of Maliseet language, culture, and identity; Maliseet language endangerment and death
language shift, 33, 42–43, 122
language suicide. See Maliseet language suicide
language use and loss, 55–56
Larson, Gary, 24
lawyer's view of identity and being, 163–65
Leavitt, Robert, 36–37, 72–73, 93, 100
LeSourd, Philip, 17
Levin, Michael D., 155–56
Lévi-Strauss, Claude, 85
"linguicide," 78
linguistic chauvinism, 32
linguistic colonialism, 32
linguistic recording and analyses, 32–33
linguistic relativism, 151
literacy, lack of, 54–55

INDEX | 231

literature, aboriginal, 54–55
litmus-test property of language, 141
Living Tongues Institute, 20
Lone Ranger joke, 178–79
Lovelace, Sandra, 176
Lucy (white woman, Maliseet speaker), 131

Maggie (Maliseet young adult), 170
mahsosiol (fiddlehead ferns), 71, 101–2, 199, 207n1 (chap. 5)
Mah-Sos School: arts program meeting at, 181–82; and community ideology, 79; and language domestication, 64; Sue as Maliseet language teacher, 66–72; symbolism of name, 101–2, 207n2. See also Maliseet elementary curriculum and practice; Maliseet language codification
Maliseet and Micmac: First Nations of the Maritimes (Leavitt), 167
Maliseet Cosmological Beginnings, 198–99
Maliseet elementary curriculum and practice, 101–20; booklets, 117; classroom setup, 103; curriculum and practice, 104–15; grade four class routine, 108–11; grade three class routine, 105–8; grade two class routine, 111–12; interactive projects, 115–16, 207nn3–4 (chap. 5); key developments in, 119–20; language practice, 102–3; Nolosweltom project, 116–17; pedagogical language projects, 115–19; symbolism of school

name, 101–2; talking animal books, 117–18; traditional stories and student illustrations, 118–19
Maliseet identity and being, 9–10, 149–83; and aboriginality, 149–51, 154–56, 165–66, 170–71, 173, 180–83, 188–90, 199, 208n4; adults, 160–68, 209n11; and Bill c-31, 174–78; and blood quantum, 153–54, 208nn5–6; complexity of, 15–20; and disembodiment of language and blood, 173–74; elders, 157–60, 209nn8–10; and language, 151–53; lawyer's view of, 163–65; and medicine wheel, 167–68; overview of, 149–51, 208nn1–4; shared experiences of, 178–83; young adults, 168–69; youngsters, 171–73
Maliseet language: adult classes in, 132–39; classification of speakers by age and proficiency, 19; disappearance of, from daily use, 186; extinction of, 2, 19, 34, 36, 57, 132, 142, 146, 184–85, 190; number of speakers, 4; as severely endangered, 4; as third language, 87; UNESCO online atlas assessment of, 4. See also future of Maliseet language, culture, and identity
Maliseet language codification, 7, 85–100; for adults, 132–39; classroom time, lack of, 87–89; cognitive shifts in, 89–92, 206n1; language domestication and, 6–7, 38, 64, 89; memories and, 187; orthographic models

Maliseet language codification (cont.) for, 93–95; orthographic representations of, 89–92; and orthographies, problematic, 95–100; overview of, 85–86; and unfamiliar sounds, 87; using English phonetic syllabic clusters, 159–60

Maliseet Language Curriculum Committee, 188

Maliseet language endangerment and death, 5–6, 31–62; and aboriginal literature, 54–55; and assimilatory pressure, 48–52; and breakdown in isolation, 46–47; and changes in economy and values, 52–57, 134; continuity submerged, 58–62; criteria for, 4; and cultural hegemony, 50–52; and education, 49; and intermarriage, 48; and language death, 35–39; and language obsolescence, 39–42; and language shift, 42–43; as language suicide, 8–10, 22; and media, 49–50; overview of, 31–34; and patterns of resettlement, 46; and reduced language use and loss, 55–56; and reduced number of speakers, 56–57; and social upheaval, 43–48; sounding the alarm, 35–39; and speaker attitudes, 57; and stigma, 50–52; tipping point for, 37, 57–62; and urbanization, 47–48. See also language erasure, causes of

Maliseet language suicide, 121–48; alternative vitalities, 146–48; assisted suicide, 139–40; author's role in politicizing, 196–97; blaming the victim, 140–43; as disembodiment, 143–46; disembodiment, forced, 125–29, 144; disembodiment, voluntary, 131–39, 144; language death as, 8–10, 22; and language disembodiment, 173–74; overview of, 121–24; phenomenological approach to, 123–24, 207n1 (chap. 6); when we fail words, 129–30; when words fail us, 124–25

Maliseet-Passamaquoddy dictionary (Leavitt and Francis), 18, 100

Maliseet-Passamaquoddy language, 17–18, 37, 54, 72, 93–94

Maliseet vs. Passamaquoddy, 16–18

manifest destiny, 31

Mannheim, Bruce, 26, 205n33

Maori, 47, 80, 81

Marshall decision, 163, 209n12

matrilineal descent, 175

Mawiw Council, 188

Maya, 21, 147, 189, 203n22

media: and emergent vitalities, 186, 191–95; and ethnography, 155; and language endangerment, 49–50

medicine man, 72–73

medicine wheel, 167–68, 209n14

memories, display and collection of, 187

Micmac Alliance, 16

Micmac-Maliseet Institute, 18, 36, 65, 72, 74, 100, 171

Mikey (Maliseet youngster), 171

INDEX | 233

murder, language, 121

native anthropologist, author as, 20–24, 29–30
Native Language Curriculum Committee, 167, 209n14
neglect, language. *See* language neglect
Nettle, Daniel, 35, 140–43, 173, 194
New Brunswick Department of Education, 79–81
New Brunswick Human Rights Commission, 176
newsletter, 190
*Nihtawewest: I Know How to Speak* (MMI), 93–94
"Nolosweltom" project, 116–17
nostalgia for simpler times, 52

obsolescence, language, 39–42
Oka crisis of 1990, 188, 210n1
Olds, Julie, 35
O'Nell, Theresa DeLeane, 27–28, 155–56, 187
one-parent rules, 176
ontology, contingent, 146–47
oral-based language instruction. *See* Maliseet language codification
oral traditions, 55, 60, 64, 70, 74, 90, 115, 118, 158, 198
orthographic models of Maliseet language instruction, 7–8, 93–95
orthographic representations of Maliseet language instruction, 89–92
orthographies, problematic, 95–100
orthography, politics of, 38

*Out of the Depths* (Knockwood), 45
overlapping cosmologies, 21, 203n21

pan-Indian identity influences, 157
pan-Indianness, 165
pan-Mayan movement, 21, 203n22
Papua New Guinea, language shift in, 42–43
Passamaquoddy, 16–18, 54
passing for white, 52
pedagogical language projects, 115–19
pencils, 85–86, 89, 100
phonemes, 90, 99
phonemic misrepresentation, 99
place-names erasure, 46
place signs on reservation, 186
posters, vocabulary, 75, 83, 86, 92, 97, 106
post–World War II social life and movement, 47
practicum classes, 134–35
professional development, 167–68

radio station on reservation, 186
Ramos, Alcida, 28
"really Indians," 27, 155, 187
reflexivity, 20–23, 203n26
Reinstatement Act. *See* Bill c-31
*Report of the Royal Commission on Aboriginal Peoples* (RCAP report), 179–80, 210nn16–17
reservation experience, 169–70
reservation schools, 49, 74, 102, 125–28, 171
resettlement patterns, 46
residential schooling, 44–46, 49, 78

riddles and jokes, 153–54
Romaine, Suzanne, 35, 140–43, 173, 194

sadness at loss of language, 161
Sam (Maliseet high school student), 42–43
Sapir, Edward, 33
Schieffelin, Bambi B., 6–7
Schmidt, Annette, 43–44, 46–48, 50–51, 53–54, 56
scholarship eligibility, 163
scientific objectivity, 23–24
self-determination, aboriginal, 186–90, 210n2
shawl dancing, 171–72
Shirley (Maliseet young adult), 169–70
Shneidman, Edwin S., 130, 143–44
Shubenacadie Residential School, 44, 46
signs on reservation, 186
situated knowledge, 23, 203n23
slang Maliseet, 160, 163
social Darwinists, 31
social upheaval and language endangerment, 43–48
Solomon, Viola, 59–60
song translations into Maliseet, 190
sounds, unfamiliar, 87
sovereignty issues, 17
speaker attitudes and language endangerment, 57
speakers, reduced number of, 56–57
spelling of Maliseet words, 16, 75, 93, 97, 99, 104, 108, 136–37
"Statement of Reconciliation," 45
status, women's loss of, 175–76

stigmatization, 50–52, 61
St. Mary's Reserve, 73–74
stories in Maliseet: on Internet, 192; on television, 192–94
storytelling, 58–60. *See also* oral traditions
St. Thomas University, 64–65, 81–82
student illustrations, 118–19
Sue (Maliseet language teacher): at aboriginal communities demonstration, 180–81; as arts and crafts instructor, 172; in community context, 66–72, 77; Cultural Resource Center and, 188; elders in the classroom, 158–59; and language maintenance, 83; and Maliseet Language Curriculum Committee, 188. *See also* Maliseet elementary curriculum and practice; Maliseet language codification
suicide: Shneidman's four clusters of, 143–44; Shneidman's ten commonalities of, 130. *See also* Maliseet language suicide
super-Indians, 28, 154–56
survival in conflict with language preservation, 194–95
survival strategy, language as, 126, 140, 173, 182
Swahili, 38
sweetgrass, 71
symbolism of Mah-Sos School name, 101–2, 207n2 (chap. 5)
Symposium on Native Languages, 72–76, 78
Szabó, László, 18–19, 82, 94, 96, 137

talking animal books, 117–18

Taylor, Alan, 41
Teaching an Algonkian Language as a Second Language (DIAND), 118
technology, 53–54
Tedlock, Dennis, 26, 205n33
Teeter, Karl V., 100
television, 49, 191–92
text-based teaching methods, 89–92
"Thick Description" (Geertz), 145
"third generation rule," 176–77
tipping point of language endangerment, 37, 57–62
Tobique First Nation: landscape of and access to, 11–14, 13, 201nn4–7, 202nn8–13; residential development of, 14–15
Tobique Narrows Dam, 47
Tobique Rock, 58–59, 198
Tobique Women's Group, 175–76
Toqawiw story, 117
traditionalists, 165–66
traditional stories and student illustrations, 118–19
Trans-Canada Highway blockade, 179–80
translation of songs into Maliseet, 190
Turner, Victor, 150, 174, 204n32
two-parent rules, 177

unfamiliar sounds, 87
Union of New Brunswick Indians, 189
University of New Brunswick, 64–65
urbanization, 47–48

values, changes in, 52–57, 134

vanishing race, 32, 205nn1–2
vernacular orthography, 97–100
victim, blaming of, 140–43
victimization, historical, 174
vision quest, 166–67, 209n13
vocabulary charts, 86, 91–92, 105–6
vocabulary exercises, 86–87, 90–93, 105–8
vocabulary posters, 75, 83, 86, 92, 97, 106
voluntary language disembodiment, 131–39, 144

Wabanaki Bilingual Education Program (WBEP) of Indian Township ME, 18
Wabanaki Confederacy, 16, 189, 211n4
Wallis, Ruth Sawtell, 17, 37
Wallis, Wilson D., 17, 37
Warren, Kay B., 21, 147, 189, 203n22
weather vocabulary, 105
Wəlastəkwi Cosmogenesis, 198–99
Wendell (adult Maliseet student), 135–37, 139
Whaley, Lindsay J., 35
White Paper of 1969, 9, 51, 178
Whorf, Benjamin Lee, 33, 152
Wolastoqiyik, 16, 202n16
women's loss of Indian status, 175–76
Woolard, Kathryn, 6
worldwide web, 191–92

young adults, identity and being, 19, 168–69
youngsters, identity and being of, 171–73

www.ingramcontent.com/pod-product-compliance
Lightning Source LLC
Chambersburg PA
CBHW030341240426
43661CB00052B/1704